THE SO-CALLED DEUTERONOMISTIC HISTORY

THE SO-CALLED DEUTERONOMISTIC HISTORY

A Sociological, Historical and Literary Introduction

Thomas C. Römer

t&t clark

Published by T&T Clark
A Continuum imprint
The Tower Building, 11 York Road, London SE1 7NX
80 Maiden Lane, Suite 704, New York, NY 10038

www.tandtclark.com

First published in hardback, 2005
Paperback edition published, 2007

Thomas C. Römer has asserted his right under the Copyright, Designs
and Patents Act, 1988, to be identified as the Author of this work.

British Library Cataloguing-in-Publication Data
A catalogue record for this book is available from the British Library

Typeset by Free Range Book Design & Production Ltd
Printed on acid-free paper in Great Britain by MPG Books Ltd, Bodmin,
Cornwall

ISBN-10: PB: 0-567-03212-4
ISBN-13: PB: 978-0-567-03212-6

CONTENTS

LIST OF ABBREVIATIONS

AB	Anchor Bible
ABD	David Noel Freedman (ed.), *The Anchor Bible Dictionary* (New York: Doubleday, 1992)
ABRL	Anchor Bible Reference Library
ATANT	Abhandlungen zur Theologie des Alten und Neuen Testaments
BAR	*Biblical Archaeology Review*
BATAJ	Beiträge zur Erforschung des Alten Testaments und des antiken Judentums
BBB	Bonner biblische Beiträge
BETL	Bibliotheca ephemeridum theologicarum lovaniensium
BN	*Biblische Notizen*
BWANT	Beiträge zur Wissenschaft vom Alten und Neuen Testament
BZAW	Beihefte zur *ZAW*
CBET	Contributions to Biblical Exegesis and Theology
CBQ	*Catholic Biblical Quarterly*
ConBOT	Coniectanea biblica, Old Testament
CRBS	*Currents in Research: Biblical Studies*
DBAT	*Dielheimer Blätter zum Alten Testament*
DH	Deuteronomistic History
FAT	Forschungen zum Alten Testament
FRLANT	Forschungen zur Religion und Literatur des Alten und Neuen Testaments
HAT	Handbuch zum Alten Testament
HDR	History of David's Rise
HSM	Harvard Semitic Monographs
ICC	International Critical Commentary
JBL	*Journal of Biblical Literature*
JNES	*Journal of Near Eastern Studies*
JNSL	*Journal of Northwest Semitic Languages*
JSNTSup	*Journal for the Study of the New Testament*, Supplement Series

JSOT	*Journal for the Study of the Old Testament*
JSOTSup	*Journal for the Study of the Old Testament,* Supplement Series
KHAT	Kurzer Hand-Kommentar zum Alten Testament
LCL	Loeb Classical Library
NCB	New Century Bible
OBO	Orbis biblicus et orientalis
OLA	Orientalia lovaniensia analecta
Or	*Orientalia*
OTS	Oudtestamentische Studien
SAA	State Archives of Assyria
SBA.AT	Stuttgarter Biblische Aufsatzbände: Altes Testament
SBL	Society of Biblical Literature
SBLDS	SBL Dissertation Series
SBLMS	SBL Monograph Series
SBLRBS	SBL Resources for Biblical Study
SBS	Stuttgarter Bibelstudien
SBTS	Sources for Biblical and Theological Study
SJOT	*Scandinavian Journal of the Old Testament*
SOTSM	Society for Old Testament Study Monographs
SN	Succession Narrative
SVT	Supplements to *Vetus Testamentum*
ThB.AT	Theologische Bücherei: Altes Testament
VT	*Vetus Testamentum*
VTE	Vassal Treaty of Esahaddon
WBC	Word Biblical Commentary
WMANT	Wissenschaftliche Monographien zum Alten und Neuen Testament
ZAW	*Zeitschrift für die alttestamentliche Wissenschaft*

INTRODUCTION

In the Hebrew Bible, the book of Deuteronomy is the last book of the Torah, the Pentateuch, which closes with the death of Moses (Deut. 34). This story is indeed a fitting end for the first part of the Hebrew Bible, since the Pentateuch can be understood as a 'biography of Moses', the books from Exodus to Deuteronomy covering his life from his birth (Exod. 2) to his death, whereas the book of Genesis forms a prologue of a sort to the Moses- and Exodus-story. But Deuteronomy is not only a testament that brings the former stories and law collections to an end. Deuteronomy is also an opening for the following 'historical' books Joshua, Judges, Samuel and Kings, which form in the Hebrew Bible the first part of the Prophets (the 'Former Prophets'). Even reading these books in an English translation, one easily recognizes therein the same style and vocabulary as in the book of Deuteronomy. But there are also other connections between the last book of the Pentateuch and the Former Prophets. In Deuteronomy Moses constantly alludes to the crossing of the Jordan and the coming conquest of the land (Deut. 4.1, 14; 7.1; 9.1 etc.). These events are related in the book of Joshua who is introduced as Moses' successor in Deut. 31. Because of these strong links between Deuteronomy and Joshua, scholars were often tempted to replace the Pentateuch by a Hexateuch, which would include the book of Joshua as the appropriate ending of a plot that starts with the divine promises to the Patriarchs in the book of Genesis. But Deuteronomy does not only prepare the reader for the conquest stories in Joshua, it alludes also to the following books. Deut. 6.12–15 contains an exhortation against the worship of other deities:

> Take care that you do not forget Yahweh, who brought you out of the land of Egypt, out of the house of bondage ... Do not follow other gods, any of the gods of the peoples who are around you, because Yahweh, your God, who is among you is a jealous God. The anger of Yahweh your God would be kindled against you and he would destroy you from the face of the earth.

1

The book of Judges opens with the statement that this exhortation had not been respected. In doing so, the author of Judg. 2.12–14 clearly refers to Deut 6.12–15:

> They abandoned Yahweh, the God of their fathers, who had brought them out of the land of Egypt; they followed other gods from among the gods of the peoples who were all around them ... So the anger of Yahweh was kindled against Israel ... and he sold them into the power of their enemies all around, so that they could no longer withstand their enemies.

The anarchic time of the Judges appears here as predicted by Moses in his final speech in Deuteronomy. But also the very end of the Former Prophets, the destruction of Jerusalem and the deportation of the people are already alluded to in Deuteronomy (see already Deut. 6.15). In the curses of Deut. 28 this catastrophe is envisaged: 'And just as Yahweh took delight in making you prosperous and numerous, so Yahweh will take delight in bringing you to ruin and destruction; you shall be plucked off the land that you are entering to possess.' (v. 63) And that is exactly what happens at the end of the second book of Kings: 'So Judah went into exile out of its land' (2 Kgs 25.21).

The close relation in style, vocabulary and content that links together the books of Deuteronomy, Joshua, Judges, Samuel and Kings has led to the idea that these books once constituted a 'Deuteronomistic History', and every student of the Hebrew Bible or of the history of Palestine in the first millennium BCE will be confronted from the very beginning of his or her studies by this enigmatic expression. Before presenting this thesis it will be useful to shed a glance on the content of the books which compose the so-called Deuteronomistic History.

Chapter 1

THE CONTENT OF THE SO-CALLED DETERONOMISTIC HISTORY (DEUTERONOMY–2 KINGS)

1. Deuteronomy

The book of Deuteronomy is conceived as a long speech of Moses – his testament of a sort (Deut. 1–30) – followed by his last actions and the report of his death (Deut. 31–34). The core of the speech is to be found in chs 12–26, which contain a collection of laws. The first part of this collection (Deut. 12–18) includes laws which are mostly concerned with the ideology of *centralization*, as expressed in the opening chapter (Deut. 12). According to this perspective, there is only *one* legitimate sanctuary in 'Israel',[1] which, as the reader will understand later, corresponds to the Jerusalem temple, although the name of the city is never mentioned either in Deuteronomy or in the whole Pentateuch.[2] Cultic centralization also implies centralization of *economics* and *politics*, as shown by the laws collected in Deut. 13–18. Chapters 19–25 contain a mix of private and public laws and do not have, at first glance, a clear structure.

Deut. 12–26 is preceded by two introductions (Deut. 1–4; 5–11; cf. the interruption of the Mosaic speech in 4.41–48 and the new introduction in 5.1). The first introduction is a 'recapitulation' of events from

1.   In the biblical books, 'Israel' is often a highly ideological term denoting from an insider perspective the true worshippers of the deity Yahweh. In fact, as we shall see, Deuteronomy and the historical books are written from a Judean perspective.

2.   This discreetness may first be explained by the literary fiction of Deuteronomy, according to which the election of Jerusalem is not effective yet, since the people has not entered the land and there is not yet a (Davidic) monarchy. In a more general way Jerusalem is never directly mentioned in the Pentateuch, despite some clear allusions (Gen. 14; Deut. 12). This fact allowed the Pentateuch to become the Sacred Scripture not only of the Judeans but also of the Samaritans (according to whom Yahweh's holy place is the mountain of Gerizim).

the period of the wanderings of the people in the wilderness, including the refusal of the exodus generation to conquer the land as ordered by Yahweh, and the report of the occupation of Transjordanian territories. These events are also related, often in a more explicit way, in the book of Numbers. Deut. 4 insists on the invisibility of Yahweh when he revealed himself to Israel and praises his gift of the law to Israel after he 'stole' his people from Egypt (4.34).

The second introduction is more directly related to the subsequent legal collection, since it contains numerous motivations to respect the divine law transmitted by Moses. Deut. 5 opens this section with the Deuteronomistic version of the Decalogue, the Ten Commandments, which may have been conceived as a kind of summary of the entire legal corpus. Deut. 6.4 contains the central statement of Deuteronomy: '*Hear Israel, Yahweh our God is the One Yahweh. And you shall love Yahweh your God with all your heart, and with all your life and with all your might.*' The second introduction includes a story recalling how Israel broke the covenant that Yahweh concluded with them on the mountain of Horeb (cf. 9.7–10.11: the story of the golden calf, which has a parallel in Exod. 32); it ends with a statement presenting the people with blessings and curses depending on the observance or non-observance of Yahweh's law (Deut. 11, esp. 11.26–32).

Blessings and curses are fully developed at the conclusion of the law collection in Deut. 27–28; it should be noted that ch. 27 differs from the conception of Deuteronomy as a Mosaic discourse since it speaks of Moses in the third person, while 28.69 and 29.1 mark another interruption. Chapters 29–30 conclude Moses' testament; here, he confronts his audience with an alternative: life or death. The audience is of course invited to choose life, that means to obey Yahweh's treaty and to respect his laws.

Deut. 31–34 contains the installation of Joshua as Moses' successor, a song that predicts Israel's rejection of Yahweh after entering the land, Moses' blessing of the twelve tribes (which parallels Jacob's blessing in Gen. 49) and, finally, in ch. 34, his death and his burial by Yahweh himself.

2. Joshua

The book of Joshua is introduced as the immediate sequel of the events described in the last chapters of Deuteronomy (see Josh. 1.1: 'After the death of Moses...'); it represents the fulfilment of the promise of the land which is omnipresent in Deuteronomy. The book may easily be divided into two parts: first, a narrative relating the military conquest of Palestine (Josh. 2–12), followed by a section consisting mainly of lists that enumerate the borders and the territories of the tribes to which Joshua allotted the land (chs 13–22). The book is framed with an introduction (Josh. 1) and a double conclusion (two speeches by Joshua in chs 23 and 24).

Joshua's appointment as Moses' (royal and military) successor (Josh. 1) is followed in chs 2–5 by stories, which prepare in different ways for the conquest accounts in Josh. 6–12. Josh. 2, which interrupts the chronological sequence of 1.11 and 3.2, contains the story of the prostitute Rahab, a prelude to Josh. 6: Rahab saves the life of Joshua's spies who were sent to gather information about Jericho (Josh. 2). Chapters 3–4 report the crossing of the Jordan, an event to which Deuteronomy makes numerous allusions. Josh. 5 relates the circumcision of the desert-generation and the first Passover in the land. The vision of the commander of Yahweh's army by Joshua at the end of ch. 5 introduces the conquest stories in Josh. 6–9: the conquest of Jericho (Rahab's clan is not exterminated), the victory against the population of Ai and Bethel, and the voluntary submission of the population of Gibeon. All these cities are located in 'Benjamin', which is the border region between the kingdom of Judah and the kingdom of Israel. In chs 10–12, the conquest is 'enlarged' by lists enumerating military campaigns of Joshua further into the North and the South.

The information of 13.1 that Joshua had grown old introduces a chronological hiatus with the foregoing stories. The lists of borders and territories that follow in Josh. 13–20 are presented as resulting from the repartition of the conquered land among the different tribes. Josh. 21.43–45 give the impression of a first conclusion of the book,[3] these verses state that all the promises of Yahweh are now fulfilled: 'Thus Yahweh gave to Israel all the land that he swore to their fathers that he would give them ... not one of all their enemies had withstood them, for Yahweh had given all their enemies into their hands. Not one of all the good words that Yahweh had spoken to the house of Israel had

---

3.   There is a much earlier conclusion in 11.23: 'So Joshua took the whole land, according to all that Yahweh had spoken to Moses; and Joshua gave it for an inheritance to Israel according to their tribal allotments. And the land had rest from war.'

failed; all came to pass.' After a chapter which is concerned with the cultic problems encountered by the Transjordanian tribes (are they allowed to build an altar in their territory in spite of the Deuteronomistic ideology of centralization?), Josh. 23 moves to a second conclusion. In his final speech to Israel, Joshua begins by summing up the ideas of 21.43–45. But then he mentions nations that were *not* driven out by Yahweh (contrary to what is stated in 21.43–45), and Joshua even openly evokes the possibility of the loss of the conquered land in case Israel does not keep the pact that Yahweh has prescribed to it. At the end of the conquest, Joshua's farewell address contains an explicit allusion to the exile and the deportation that parallels the last curses of Moses' speech in Deut. 28. The presence of Josh. 24 after ch. 23 is quite puzzling, since this text offers another 'final' discourse by Joshua in Shechem, which contains a summary of the Hexateuch narrative (from the Patriarchs to the conquest). In this speech, Joshua also invites the audience to choose Yahweh as their god and to ward off the other deities. The assembly accepts and Joshua, like a second Moses, concludes a covenant and writes a book (Josh. 24.26; cf. Deut. 31.9).

The book of Joshua concludes then with the death and burial of its hero (and with the death of the priest Eleazar).

A parallel notice on Joshua's end is found in Judg. 2.6–10 (cf. Josh. 24.28–31). This parallel indicates very clearly that the present transition from the book of Joshua to the book of Judges is not original, but, as we will see later, has been heavily reworked.

3. Judges

As Joshua has two (or even three) conclusions, the book of Judges, as it stands now, confronts the reader with two different openings, in 1.1–2.5 and 2.6–3.6. The first prologue is closely related to the conquest events described in Joshua more than to the topics of Judges. It offers an alternative version of the conquest, stating the success of Judah and Joseph but the failure of other tribes in their attempt to drive out the former inhabitants of the land. In 2.1–5 a messenger of Yahweh explains this failure: Israel did not respect the divine injunction to separate completely from the native people of the land. The second prologue is an attempt to create a 'period of the Judges'. In order to obtain a chronological succession for the following stories that deal with charismatic heroes, the author of Judg. 2.6–3.6 constructs a cyclical scheme: after the death of the leader, the people turns away from Yahweh and worships other gods; Yahweh gets angry and punishes Israel by sending other peoples to oppress Israel, who, then, appeals in distress to Yahweh. Yahweh then raises up 'judges' (or 'saviours'), who deliver Israel. But very soon Israel is attracted again by the worship of other gods, and the same story starts anew. The second introduction to Judges in 2.6–3.6 thus gives a frame to the whole collection of 3.7–16.31, and the readers, or the listeners, are thereby instructed as to how they should understand the subsequent narratives on Israel's saviours. There are twelve of them (among whom one woman, Deborah); the actions of seven of these saviours are described in more or less detailed narratives, while for the other five we are just told their names and that they have 'judged' Israel for a certain number of years. The first narrative about Othniel (3.7–11) is very short and stereotyped. It gathers up and anticipates significant elements from the following stories. Othniel is the only Judge coming from Judah; all the others are Northerners. The 'Judges' to whom the authors and redactors pay most attention are: Ehud, the trickster who murders the fat king of Moab (3.12–30); Deborah and Barak, the leaders of an anti-Canaanite war implying some Israelite tribes (Judg. 4–5); Gideon, who fights against the Midianites, and the failure of his son Abimelech to establish a monarchy (Judg. 6–9); Jephthah, his war against the Ammonites and the sacrifice of his daughter (10.6–12.7). The story of Samson and his altercation with the Philistines (Judg. 13–16) is quite unique in comparison to the other Judges. Some of the Samson narratives are burlesques (as is the Ehud story) and offer parallels with Greek mythology, especially with the exploits of Heracles.

The book ends with two appendices. The first (chs 17–18) is concerned with the migration of the tribe of Dan, and contains a critique of the Northern sanctuary in Dan. The second (chs 19–21) deals with the tribe of Benjamin. It tells a sordid story about violation of hospitality by the inhabitants of Gibeah in Benjamin (the narrative has a parallel in Gen. 19). The concubine of a Levite is murdered; the tribes of Israel gather into a coalition against Benjamin, who is defeated. But at the end the survival of the tribe is guaranteed by the rest of Israel through the rape of women from Shiloh. Both appendices are bound together by a refrain, which states that everybody did at the time 'what was right in his eyes' (17.6; 18.1; 21.25).

This remark provides a transition to the books of Samuel and Kings,[4] which are mainly concerned with the rise and fall of the Judean (and Israelite) monarchy.

4. Samuel–Kings

Samuel and Kings were originally only one book each in the Hebrew Bible; they were split into two books at quite a late date. They closely belong together as one may also infer from the Greek headings, which bind them together as the four books of Kingdoms. 1 Samuel starts with the story of Samuel: his birth from a barren woman (the same motif as in the Samson narrative), his call by Yahweh in the sanctuary of Shiloh and his exploits (1 Sam. 1–7). Samuel is presented as a prophet of Yahweh as well as the last judge in Israel, and he is largely involved in the different stories about the appointment of Saul, Israel's first king. 1 Sam. 8–12 offers several different accounts of how Saul rises to kingship, some adopt a quite positive position (e.g., 1 Sam. 9: Yahweh enjoins Samuel to anoint Saul, or 1 Sam. 11: Saul is qualified by his military prowess), while others present a very negative view about the origins of monarchy (1 Sam. 8 and 12: Israel wants to be like the 'other nations' and rejects Yahweh, its real king). Samuel's final discourse in 1 Sam. 12 marks the end of the period of the Judges and the beginning of the monarchical era. This speech provides a summary of events from the exodus, the entrance in the land, the time of the Judges and the origins of the monarchy but it provides also some clues for the understanding of subsequent history, especially by alluding to the possible failure of kingship and the end of the people.

As a matter of fact, this failure already appears in the story of Saul who, despite his relative success at war (1 Sam. 13–15), is rejected by Yahweh who, meanwhile, has changed his mind and chosen David. The divine choice of David from Judah against Saul from Benjamin symbolizes the legitimation of the Judean, Davidic dynasty as against the Northern monarchy.

---

4.   In most of the English Bibles, the reader finds the book of Ruth between Judges and Samuel. This is the order of the Septuagint, the Greek adaptation of the Hebrew Bible. In the canon of the Hebrew Bible, Ruth belongs to the 'Writings', the third part of the Bible.

Two important narrative cycles are devoted to David. The first, which is often called 'the Story of David's Rise' (1 Sam. 16–2 Sam. 5), relates the beginning of David's career, his conflicts with Saul, as well as the allegiance of Saul's son, Jonathan, and of his daughter, Michal, to David. This cycle brings together various traditions about David. According to 16.14–23 David arrives at Saul's court as a musician and a therapist for a depressed Saul. But in 17.55–58 David, after his victory over the Philistine Goliath, is presented to Saul, who does not seem to know him. David's military and amorous successes incite Saul to kill him; David flees to the Philistines and becomes their vassal. After Saul and Jonathan die in a battle against the Philistines (1 Sam. 31–2 Sam. 1), David is consecrated king of Judah in Hebron. He conquers Jerusalem, which becomes his personal fief ('city of David') and the new capital of the United Kingdom. 2 Sam. 6–8 then describes the apex of David's reign: the transfer of the 'ark' (a military symbol for Yahweh's presence in Israel's wars, cf. 1 Sam. 4–6) to Jerusalem, and a divine oracle, transmitted by the prophet Nathan, in which Yahweh promises to David a dynasty that will be established for ever on Israel's throne (2 Sam. 7).

David's depiction in the following cycle (2 Sam. 9–1 Kgs 2) strongly contrasts with his presentation up to this point. In this narrative, usually called the 'Succession to the Throne of David Story' or the 'Court History', David often appears as a weak king, and even as morally incorrect. Having made Bathsheba, Uriah's wife, pregnant, he will send her husband, who is one of his best officers, to death; the same Bathsheba will become the mother of Solomon (2 Sam. 12). David must face revolts, especially on the part of his son Absalom (2 Sam. 13–19), and he has to flee from Jerusalem. After the murder of Absalom by David's general Joab, the king returns to his capital, where he faces another revolt (2 Sam. 20). The story of the succession comes to an end in 1 Kgs 1.1–2.13, after an interruption in 2 Sam. 21–24 (these chapters form an appendix; in the last chapter David is presented as the founder of the future temple; 2 Sam. 24). In 1 Kgs 1, Solomon rises to the throne as the outcome of a *Dallas*-like intrigue led by Nathan and Bathsheba, whereas old David appears to be utterly invalid, without any capacity to control the events.

The following story of Solomon's reign (1 Kgs 3–11) can be divided into two parts. The first part depicts him as the wise king and the builder of the temple. It ends with a long speech by Solomon in 1 Kgs 8, where he ascertains that Yahweh has realized all his promises to

David. Yet, while inaugurating the temple, Solomon already foresees its destruction and the exile of the people. The second part of the Solomon narrative, in 1 Kgs 9–11, presents a more negative view of the king (but there is also the positive story of the Queen of Sheba's visit to Solomon), especially with regard to his attraction to foreign women and foreign deities. The religious and political errors of Solomon provoke the collapse of the 'United Kingdom' after his death (1 Kgs 12–14). Jeroboam, a former civil servant of Solomon, becomes king of Israel, the Northern kingdom; he establishes two yahwistic sanctuaries in Dan and Bethel (that is, on the northern and southern borders of the kingdom of Israel) as an alternative to the Judean temple in Jerusalem.

1 Kgs 15–2 Kgs 17 relates the parallel history of the two kingdoms; the story is told from a clearly Judean perspective. All kings are submitted to an evaluation, which is based on their allegiance to Yahweh and their observance of the commandment of cultic centralization. The Judean kings are also compared to David ('N. acted/did not act as did his father David'). The criterion of cultic centralization explains why no king from Israel can satisfy the ideological standards of the authors or redactors, not even Jehu though he is depicted as a yahwistic revolutionist who brings to an end the dynasty of the Omrides (2 Kgs 9–10). The story of the two kingdoms is told synchronically. As already mentioned, the Northern kingdom appears to have been ruled by wicked kings. Ahab (1 Kgs 16.29–22.40) appears to be the worst of them; he is said to have introduced the cult of the Phoenician Baal, a storm and fertility god. The situation in the North is depicted as anarchic; kings are murdered and dynasties change often. The Southern kingdom, on the contrary, appears to have been ruled all the time by kings from the Davidic dynasty. So every effort is made to present the reign of Athaliah, Ahab's daughter, over Judah (2 Kgs 11) as illegitimate. The synchronic history of the two kingdoms contains numerous prophetic narratives (especially of Elijah and Elisha, 1 Kgs 17–2 Kgs 8). It ends with a long comment of the narrator who indicates the reasons that led to the fall of Samaria and the Northern kingdom, which is transformed into an Assyrian province (2 Kgs 17).

The last chapters (2 Kgs 18–25) relate the story of the kingdom of Judah until its end. Two kings receive particular attention: Hezekiah and Josiah, who both conform to Yahweh's will, in contrast to their predecessor and successors. Hezekiah (2 Kgs 18–20) abolishes the illegitimate cults and cult places; under his reign the Assyrian siege of Jerusalem is abandoned because of Yahweh's intervention. His son Manasseh (2 Kgs 21) is presented as one of the worst kings of Judah, although he was king for 55 years. After the also wicked Amon comes the reign of Josiah, which at first glance appears as the positive outcome of the Judean monarchy, since Josiah, after the discovery of the lawbook in the temple, undertakes a tremendous reorganization of the cult, making Jerusalem the only legitimate sanctuary and destroying the symbols of all illegitimate yahwistic and other cults (2 Kgs 22–23). But even the reform of Josiah cannot prevent the destruction of Jerusalem and Judah by the Babylonians, who punish the revolts of Josiah's successors. According to the author of 2 Kgs 24–25, *all of Judah* went into exile out of its land. The whole story does not end with a final comment, as one would have expected, but with a rather obscure note about the release of the Judean king Jehoiachin from his Babylonian prison; he stays in Babylon but becomes a privileged guest at the table of the king of Babylon (2 Kgs 25.27–30).

This summary of contents shows that in spite of the very different themes and materials which are collected and assembled in Deuteronomy to Kings, these books are nevertheless linked by a chronological principle: from the Mosaic origins to the end of Judah. The time of Moses and Joshua appears as a 'Golden Age', in contrast to the time of the Judges, which is depicted as a rather anarchic and chaotic period. The portrait of the monarchy is profoundly ambiguous. On one hand, one can find texts that insist on the divine legitimation of the Davidic dynasty (in 2 Sam. 7 Yahweh promises that it will last 'for ever'); on the other hand, there are numerous critical remarks about the kings who do not conform to Yahweh's will as exposed in the book of Deuteronomy.

As it stands now, this historical fresco is a story about exile and deportation, as well as about the failure of monarchy. Nevertheless, the same story contains very positive statements about Judean kings, and even quite triumphant views of Israel's possession of the land, which fit badly within a context of exile and deportation. This tension is a first indication for the complexity of the material within the books from Deuteronomy to Kings, which are commonly labelled 'Deuteronomistic History'.

The following history of research will try to show how the theory of a Deuteronomistic History came into life, as well as the current debate about this theory.

Chapter 2

WHAT DOES 'DEUTERONOMISTIC HISTORY' MEAN? A SURVEY OF PAST RESEARCH

Select Bibliography
For a more complete history of research, see:

Alexander, L.V., *The Origin and Development of the Deuteronomistic History Theory and its Significance for Biblical Interpretation* (Ann Arbor: UMI, 1993).

Römer, T., and A. de Pury, 'Deuteronomistic Historiography (DH): History of Research and Debated Issues', in A. de Pury, T. Römer and J.-D. Macchi (eds), *Israel Constructs its History: Deuteronomistic Historiography in Recent Research* (JSOTSup 306; Sheffield: Sheffield Academic Press, 2000), pp. 24–141.

In contrast to the Torah (the Pentateuch), the Deuteronomistic History is not recognized by Jewish or Christian tradition as a separate collection, and the term itself is an invention of modern biblical scholarship. The 'father' of the Deuteronomistic History hypothesis is Martin Noth, who published in 1943 his *Überlieferungsgeschichtliche Studien* (English translation: *The Deuteronomistic History*); he was of course not the first to speak of Deuteronomistic redactions, his new idea has to do with Deuteronomy to Kings as a well-planned historical work, due to one 'author' (sometimes he speaks also of a redactor). In order to get a more accurate picture of the Deuteronomistic History hypothesis we need to sketch, in a brief history of past research, the genesis of the hypothesis and its later developments until the current debate. This sketch can be conveniently divided into three parts: 1. Before Noth; 2. Noth's invention of the Deuteronomistic History; 3. The scholarly discussion since Noth.

1. The Prehistory of the Deuteronomistic History Hypothesis

1.1. The First Steps towards the Idea of a 'Deuteronomistic History'

Select Bibliography

Calvin, J., *Commentaries on the Book of Joshua* (trans. H. Beveridge; Grand Rapids, MI: Eerdmans, 1949).
Schwarzbach, B.E., *Voltaire's Old Testament Criticism* (Etudes de philosophie de l'histoire 20; Geneva: Droz, 1971).
Spinoza, B. de, *A Theologico-Political Treatise. A Political Treatise* (New York: Dover Publications, 1951).

From the beginning, much less attention was paid in Jewish and Christian interpretations of the Bible to the 'Former Prophets' than to the Pentateuch, which is in the Jewish (and also to a certain extent in the Christian) tradition the very centre of the Hebrew Bible. Hence the following books always remained in the shadow of the Pentateuch.

Just as they attributed the Pentateuch to Moses (with a few exceptions such as Deut. 34), the rabbis tried to locate the authors of the Former Prophets among the main characters of these books, or at least among contemporaries of the related events.[1] Thus, the book of Joshua was supposed to have been written by Joshua himself, the books of Judges and Samuel were attributed to Samuel, and 1–2 Kings to the prophet Jeremiah. But the rabbis also took into account a certain number of considerations, which can be seen to anticipate in a certain way the conclusions of modern historical criticism. For instance, since the death of both Joshua and Samuel is reported before the end of their books, the Talmud assumed that later 'redactors' had completed these books. The attribution of Kings to the prophet Jeremiah is also of interest, since it might imply that the rabbis were aware of the stylistic similarities existing between the books of Kings and Jeremiah.

Nevertheless, the rabbis had no real interest in the numerous linguistic, stylistic and ideological affinities between Joshua, Judges, Samuel and Kings. Not much consideration is given either to the above-mentioned fact that the last book of the Pentateuch (Deuteronomy) also serves as an introduction to the story of the conquest related in Joshua. Jewish and Christian commentators were

---

1.   The rabbinic discussion concerning the authorship of biblical books can be found in the Babylonian Talmud, in the tractate *Baba Bathra* 14–15.

mostly busy harmonizing contradictory texts (as for instance the conflicting presentation of the history of kingship in the books of Samuel–Kings and Chronicles) or justifying the morally dubious attitude of some of the biblical heroes (thus Jephthah sacrificing his daughter, Judg. 11.29–40, or David killing the husband of the woman whom he desires, 2 Sam. 11–12). Hence, we have to wait until the sixteenth century to find the very beginnings of a truly *critical* investigation of the Former Prophets.

It is indeed during that time that Humanists and Reformers challenged the traditional view regarding authorship of the biblical books. In his commentary on Joshua, John Calvin rejects the idea that Joshua himself could have written the book bearing his name: it manifests the presence of different styles, and it always addresses Joshua in the third person. Calvin suggests that the priest Eleazar, a contemporary of Joshua, should be regarded as the author of the book, or rather its *compiler*, since he had at his disposal various documents, which he gathered. Why does Calvin opt for Eleazar? Does he simply take over the rabbinic tradition, which attributes to Eleazar the responsibility for completing and supplementing the book of Joshua, or is he already sensitive to the marked 'priestly' character of some of the texts preserved in that book? Whatever the case, it is obvious that Calvin, though denying the authorship to Joshua himself, still seeks to situate the author in the time of the events related by the book.

The Catholic scholar Andreas Masius took a more radical stance. In his critical edition of the Greek and Hebrew texts of Joshua (1574), he states that Ezra should be seen as the final compiler not only of Joshua, but also of Judges and Kings. This means that Masius locates the final redaction of the historical books in the Persian era (fifth–fourth century BCE).

A century later, the Jewish philosopher Baruch Spinoza adopts the same view for the collection going from Genesis to Kings, since he regards the Pentateuch and the Former Prophets as forming a single composition. But Spinoza also points to the fact that the book of Deuteronomy offers the ideological basis for the interpretation of the following history. In his *Tractatus theologico-politicus* (1670), he writes: 'All that is set down in the books we have conduces to the sole object of setting forth the words and laws of Moses, and proving them by subsequent events'.[2] This means that Spinoza has already observed

2.   B. de Spinoza, *Theologico-Political Treatise*, p. 129.

the 'Deuteronomistic' character of the books subsequent to Deuteronomy.

The age of Enlightenment also brings forth the beginning of ideological criticism. The record of the biblical writers is no longer accepted as being divinely inspired but becomes a matter of debate. In his book *The Moral Philosopher* (1737–40), Thomas Morgan analyses the personality and the real motivations of the protagonists featured in the historical books. According to Morgan, Samuel's negative attitude towards monarchy may easily be explained by his selfish fear of losing his power. King David was one of the bloodiest tyrants ever known. On the contrary, King Ahab and his wife Jezebel, who are described in 1 Kgs 16.29–33 and 21 as one of the most wicked couples in the biblical history, are in reality remarkable examples of tolerance and were certainly right when opposing such fanatics as the prophet Elijah. The French philosopher Voltaire adopts a similar position, regarding the extermination of the Canaanites in Joshua or the political manoeuvres of David as being highly immoral.

Thus, at the end of the eighteenth century, the traditional Jewish and Christian view of the Former Prophets is definitely challenged. It has become clear that the authors of Deuteronomy and the Former Prophets cannot be contemporaneous to the related events. There is also some insight regarding the ideological options sustaining the biblical presentation of Israel's history, and there is already – at least in Spinoza's work – the intuition that these ideological options are closely related to and even dependent upon the book of Deuteronomy. Critical exegesis in the nineteenth century will build upon these findings.

1.2. The Discovery of 'Deuteronomism'

Select Bibliography

Colenso, J.W., *The Pentateuch and Book of Joshua Critically Examined* (London: Longman, Green & Co., 1862–79).

Rogerson, J.W., *W.M.L. de Wette, Founder of Modern Biblical Criticism: An Intellectual Biography* (JSOTSup 126; Sheffield: Sheffield Academic Press, 1992).

In a footnote to his 1805 doctoral dissertation, the Swiss scholar M. de Wette identified the book 'found' in the temple under the reign of

Josiah (according to the report of 2 Kgs 22) with the book of Deuteronomy, or its first edition. He suggested that the original Deuteronomy would have been composed in order to legitimate Josiah's new organization of cultic and political matters. Twenty years earlier Voltaire had argued the same idea. Thus, the French philosopher was close to dissociating Deuteronomy from the rest of the Pentateuch and assigning it to an individual author, but it was de Wette who took the decisive step. He advocated the existence of a *Tetrateuch*, containing the books of Genesis, Exodus, Leviticus and Numbers; he argued that the ideological positions of these books are quite distinct from that of the book of Deuteronomy. For the Swiss scholar, Genesis–Numbers should be understood as a collection of various fragments without any authentic historical material, whereas Deuteronomy was a 'mythical' remake out of the material contained in the Tetrateuchal books.

De Wette also advocated a very late date for the book of Joshua. The references to the Mosaic law that it contains (see for instance Josh. 1.1–9) should be explained by the 'Deuteronomic' nature of the book. Together with his colleague J. Vater, de Wette is apparently the first scholar to speak of a 'Deuteronomistic' redaction to explain the formation of the historical books.[3]

De Wette's ideas were taken over by Bishop Colenso, who undertook[4] a detailed examination of Deuteronomy's Hebrew vocabulary. He did not only emphasize the difference of this vocabulary from the language of the Tetrateuch, but also its proximity to the language of the Former Prophets.

1.3. The Elaboration of the Idea of Deuteronomic Editors

Select Bibliography

Driver, S.R., *A Critical and Exegetical Commentary on Deuteronomy* (ICC 3; Edinburgh: T. & T. Clark, 1902).

3.   German scholarship often distinguishes between 'deuteronomic' (dt) as referring to the pre-exilic edition of Deuteronomy, and 'deuteronomistic' (dtr), as referring to the redactor(s) of the (exilic) Deuteronomistic History. We will not follow this distinction, which presupposes as the only 'Deuteronomic' text the Deuteronomic law-book.

4.   In Part 3 of his *The Pentateuch and Book of Joshua Critically Examined* (1863).

Ewald, H., *History of Israel* (London: Longman, Green & Co., 1867–86).

Moore, G.F., *A Critical and Exegetical Commentary on Judges* (ICC 2; Edinburgh: T. & T. Clark, 1908).

Rogerson, J., *Old Testament Criticism in the Nineteenth Century: England and Germany* (London: SPCK, 1984).

In 1843, exactly a hundred years before the publication of Martin Noth's *Studien*, Heinrich Ewald started his six volumes containing *History of Israel*. In the first volume, he elaborated a global hypothesis for the redaction of the books of Genesis to 2 Kings; he designated the collection from Genesis to Joshua as the 'Great Books of Origins', while he called the books of Judges, Ruth (Ewald follows the order of the Greek canon), Samuel and Kings the 'Great book of Kings'. According to Ewald, the latter collection in its 'final' form results from the activity of two Deuteronomic redactors. The first redactor still presupposes the existence of the monarchy, as shown by 1 Sam. 12; he incorporates an older story about David's rise as well as other sources. The reflections of this redactor, Ewald argues, 'show ... an age in which, although the nation was much weakened, yet the kingdom of David and the temple still existed, and the hope of their permanency still lingered. This could be no other than the earliest time after the Reformation by Josiah, when the declining kingdom appeared to be rising into new and glorious life'.[5] The second redactor updated the history of Judah during the Babylonian exile, around 560, shortly after the rehabilitation of the exiled Jehoiachin (2 Kgs 25.27–30). He also inserted the book of Judges as an introduction to the history of the Israelite monarchy; in doing so he wanted to underline that disobedience against Yahweh will certainly provoke divine punishment (Judg. 2.6–3.6). The same redactor also introduced the religious appreciations of each of the Israelite and Judean rulers. According to Ewald, he wanted to answer 'the great and serious question of the age, whence came so much misery upon the people'.[6] In 1861, the Dutch scholar Abraham Kuenen similarly advocated the idea of a double Deuteronomic redaction in Kings.

But let us return to Ewald. It is interesting to note that he ascribes the last modifications in the 'Great Books of Origins' (Genesis–Joshua) to an editor whom he calls the 'Deuteronomist'. This Deuteronomist wrote, according to Ewald, under the reign of Manasseh. He composed

5.   Ewald, *History*, I, p. 157.
6.   Ewald, *History*, I, p. 160.

the books of Deuteronomy and Joshua, but he is not very present in Genesis–Numbers. In Deuteronomy and Joshua, Ewald also allows for some post-Deuteronomistic additions, such as for instance Deut. 33.

If we sum up Ewald's ideas, it appears that Deuteronomistic layers can be discovered in Deuteronomy–Joshua as well as in Judges–2 Kings. But he insists on the break between Joshua and Judges; this means he does not admit the existence of a same Deuteronomistic redaction covering the whole corpus from Deuteronomy to Kings. This refusal may be related to his conviction that the first collection of the Bible is not the *Penta-teuch* but the *Hexa-teuch*, including the book of Joshua.

The concept of a Hexateuch is very tightly related to the elaboration of the 'documentary hypothesis', whose most brilliant advocate was Julius Wellhausen.[7] Drawing together several ideas that had already been advanced earlier, Wellhausen elaborated a formulation of the Documentary hypothesis, which was soon to become somewhat of a 'canonical model' for critical scholarship. Wellhausen isolated two ancient narrative sources, 'J' (the Yahwist) and 'E' (the Elohist). These documents, from the first centuries of Israelite monarchy, were then combined by the 'Jehowist' (JE) into a single work. Wellhausen located the source 'D' (the original book of Deuteronomy) in the seventh century BCE, at the time of Josiah, and 'P' (the Priestly source) at the end of or after the Babylonian exile.[8] According to the Documentary hypothesis, the older sources extended up to Joshua, since it is in this book only that the Israelites eventually take possession of the land promised by Yahweh to the Patriarchs and to Moses.

On the whole, Old Testament critical scholarship in the second half of the nineteenth century was so fascinated by the Documentary hypothesis and by the idea of an original Hexateuch, that critical research on the books of Judges to Kings was pretty much neglected. Therefore, the question of Deuteronomistic redaction(s) inside the Hebrew Bible was mostly limited to the source 'D', which corresponded to the original Deuteronomy and was supposed to have been written at the end of the Judean monarchy. But there were also some texts in Genesis–Numbers, which seemed to have affinities with

---

7.   See especially Wellhausen, J., *Die Composition des Hexateuchs und der historischen Bücher des Alten Testaments* (Berlin: Georg Reimer, 3rd edn, 1899).

8.   For more details see Van Seters, J., *The Pentateuch: A Social Science Commentary* (Trajectories; Sheffield: Sheffield Academic Press, 1999).

Deuteronomistic style and language, as for instance Gen. 15 (compare v. 5 to Deut. 1.10; v. 7 to Deut 1.27, 4.20, etc.) or Lev. 26 (compare v. 15 and 46 to Deut. 11.1 and many other passages). Some authors argued that these texts were inserted by the Jehowist; others, as Colenso, believed that they came from a Deuteronomist, who was 'the *editor* of the Pentateuch and the book of Joshua, which he interpolated throughout, and enlarged especially with the addition of the book of Deuteronomy'.[9]

Wellhausen, in his *Composition des Hexateuchs und der historischen Bücher des Alten Testaments*, offered the following explanations for the Deuteronomistic elements in Judges to Kings: They are due to different redactions from the time of Josiah up to the Babylonian exile; before the intervention of these redactions a scroll of Judges and Samuel already existed but not one of the book of Kings. It is impossible to determine if the same Deuteronomistic redactors edited all these books, or if we have to imagine a different editor for each book. For Wellhausen, this question does not seem very important. He also acknowledges the presence of Deuteronomistic redactions in the Hexateuch, but the question of how the 'Deuteronomistic' texts of Genesis to Joshua relate to those of Judges to Kings is apparently of little or no interest to him.

Wellhausen's model received a broad approval not only in Germany but also in the Anglo-Saxon world. Samuel R. Driver, in his exhaustive commentary on Deuteronomy, offered a detailed list of Deuteronomistic phraseology, and concluded that the influence of Deuteronomy is eminently perceptible in the historical books (p. xci). George F. Moore, commenting on Judges, argued for a redactor belonging to the Deuteronomic school who should be situated in the early sixth century, and to whom the composition of Judg. 2.6–16.31 should be attributed (p. xxiv.).

At the same time, it became progressively obvious that other books in the Hebrew Bible had apparently undergone Deuteronomistic editions. Bernhard Duhm, professor of Old Testament at Basel, ascribed more than half of the book of Jeremiah to Deuteronomistic redactors, who were at work from the sixth down to the first century BCE.[10] Duhm did not have much esteem for those Deuteronomists,

---

9.   Colenso, *The Pentateuch and Book of Joshua Critically Examined*, V, p. 53.

10.   Duhm, B., *Das Buch Jeremia* (KHAT XI; Tübingen–Leipzig: J.C.B. Mohr, 1901).

whom he regarded as rather clumsy scribes whose sole obsession was for Mosaic Law. In spite of his depreciation of their work, Duhm was apparently the first to envisage the possibility that the activity of the 'Deuteronomistic school' could have outlived the end of the exilic period.

At the beginning of the twentieth century, the existence of Deuteronomistic texts in the Penta- (Hexa-)teuch and in the Prophets was widely accepted. But it took another forty years until Martin Noth offered a coherent theory accounting for the presence of these texts.

2. The Elaboration of the Deuteronomistic History Hypothesis by M. Noth

2.1. The Origins of Noth's Thesis

Select Bibliography

Begg, C.T., 'Martin Noth: Notes on his Life and Work', in S.L. McKenzie and M.P. Graham (eds), *The History of Israel's Traditions: The Heritage of Martin Noth* (JSOTSup 182; Sheffield: Sheffield Academic Press, 1994), pp. 18–30.

When writing his *Überlieferungsgeschichtliche Studien*, Noth could build upon the works of de Wette, Ewald, Wellhausen, Driver and others who had defined the 'Deuteronomic style' and advocated Deuteronomistic redactions inside the historical books. But since the immense majority of scholars believed in the existence of a Hexateuch, to explain the continuity between Deuteronomy–Joshua on one hand and the following historical books on the other did not arouse much interest.

Noth was the first to emphasize this continuity when abandoning the idea of a Hexateuch. The new impetus given by Noth resulted from new orientations in Hebrew Bible scholarship, especially the two following. First, a shift occurred at the time of Noth from the source and literary criticism *à la* Wellhausen to the question of the transmission of the biblical traditions (*Überlieferungsgeschichte*). The transmission historical approach is less concerned with the reconstruction of 'ancient sources'; it does not necessarily reject or oppose the Documentary hypothesis, but is interested to explain the development and the formation of larger units as the Pentateuch, Chronicles and the

Deuteronomistic History.[11] Second, the shift in Noth's approach has to do with his work on a commentary of Joshua, for which he used several theories coming from his teacher Albrecht Alt.[12] Alt had argued that Josh. 3–9 was an independent collection of aetiological stories relating the settlement of the tribe of Benjamin. The boundaries list in Josh. 13–19 was based, according to Alt, on a geographical situation before the monarchy even if it was written down much later, whereas Josh. 15 reflects a list of twelve provinces under Josiah. These texts have therefore nothing to do with the priestly document of the Pentateuch, contrary to what the source critics had claimed.

In his 1938 commentary,[13] Noth agreed with Alt's view. This new position implied that the Pentateuch sources did *not* go on in the book of Joshua, and, hence, that there was no *Hexateuch*. Noth solved the problem of the missing end of J or E (without Joshua, these sources do not relate the entry into the land) claiming that their original ending had been amputated when the historical books were attached to the Pentateuch. This denial of the Pentateuchal sources in Joshua opened the way to a complete reappraisal of the composition of the historical books which Noth undertook in his 1943 *Studien*.

2.2. The *Überlieferungsgeschichtliche Studien*

Select Bibliography

Campbell, A.F., 'Martin Noth and the Deuteronomistic History', in S.L. McKenzie and M.P. Graham (eds), *The History of Israel's Traditions: The Heritage of Martin Noth* (JSOTSup 182; Sheffield: Sheffield Academic Press, 1994), pp. 31–62.

Noth, M., *The Deuteronomistic History* (JSOTSup 15; Sheffield: Sheffield Academic Press, 2nd edn, 1991); translation of the first part of

11.   In this sense tradition history, especially in Noth's understanding, comes very close to redaction criticism; see on this Steck, O.H., *Old Testament Exegesis: A Guide to the Methodology* (trans. J.D. Nogalski; SBLRBS 33; Atlanta, GA: Scholars Press, 1998), pp. 66–67.

12.   See especially Alt, A., 'Das System der Stammesgrenzen im Buche Josua (1927)', in *Kleine Schriften zur Geschichte des Volkes Israel* (2 vols.; Munich: C.H. Beck'sche Verlagsbuchhandlung, 1953), I, pp. 191–215; *idem*, 'Josua', in *Kleine Schriften zur Geschichte des Volkes Israel*, I, pp. 176–92; *idem*, 'Judas Gaue unter Josia', in *Kleine Schriften zur Geschichte des Volkes Israel*, II, pp. 276–88.

13.   Noth, M., *Das Buch Josua* (HAT I/7; Tübingen: Mohr, 2nd edn, 1953).

Überlieferungsgeschichtliche Studien. Die sammelnden und bearbeitenden Geschichtswerke im Alten Testament (1943) (Darmstadt: Wissenschaftliche Buchgesellschaft, 3rd edn, 1967).

Noth wrote this small book, which turned out to become one of the most influential contributions to Hebrew Bible scholarship, in 1943, during the Second World War, in Königsberg (at the time Germany's most eastern university).

His main interest was not to delineate precisely which texts in the historical books should be considered as 'Deuteronomistic' and which not. According to him, 'the literary-critical foundation was laid long ago and has produced generally accepted conclusions'.[14] Noth took for granted the existence of a Deuteronomistic redaction in the Former Prophets; what was new in his approach was the way he investigated the possibility that the Deuteronomistic texts belonged to a coherent and unified redaction, due to one redactor, the Deuteronomist (which he abbreviated 'Dtr.').

Evidence for this kind of redaction may be found, according to Noth, in those texts, which he called '*chapters of reflection*'. Noth observed that 'at all the important points in the course of history, Dtr. brings forward the leading personages with a speech, which looks forward and backward in an attempt to interpret the courses of events... Elsewhere the summarising reflections upon history are presented by Dtr. himself ... because there were no suitable historical figures to make the speeches'.[15] Such passages occur in Josh. 1.1–9; 12.1–6; 23.1–16; Judg. 2.11–3.6; 1 Sam. 12.1–15; 1 Kgs 8.14–53; 2 Kgs 17.7–23.

They divide the Deuteronomistic presentation of Israel's history into the following periods: the conquest under Joshua (Josh. 1; 12 and 23), the time of the judges (from Judg. 2.11 to 1 Sam. 12), the instauration of the monarchy (from 1 Sam. 12 to 1 Kgs 8), the history of the kingdoms of Judah and Israel until the fall of Samaria (from 1 Kgs 8 to 2 Kgs 17), the last days of Judah. This delimitation of periods does not concur with the separations between the books such as we find them now in the Former Prophets.

The end of the Deuteronomistic History is identical to the last verses of the books of Kings (2 Kgs 25.27–30), which report the release of Jehoiachin from his Babylonian prison. Since this event can

14.   Noth, *Deuteronomistic History*, p. 15.
15.   Noth, *Deuteronomistic History*, pp. 18–19.

be dated around 562 BCE, Noth concludes that the Deuteronomistic History should have been written shortly after it, around 560 BCE.

As to the beginning of the Deuteronomistic History, Noth hesitates more. Josh. 1 is not a true beginning, strictly speaking, since it alludes to the end of Deuteronomy and presupposes also the settlement of the Transjordanian tribes. The Deuteronomistic History must therefore start somewhere in the Pentateuch, and Noth tries to locate a convenient overture inside the Pentateuch *via negationis*. Thus, he states that 'there is no sign of "Deuteronomistic editing" in Genesis–Numbers'[16] – a view which is less obvious today than it was to Noth. Hence, the book of Deuteronomy offers the most obvious beginning to the Deuteronomistic History, since it contains unmistakable allusions to the Deuteronomistic conquest story in Joshua (cf. Deut. 31.1–13; 34*).

According to Noth, the Deuteronomist (Dtr.) integrated in his history the so-called *Urdeuteronomium* (Deut. 5–30*, that is the first edition of Deuteronomy in the eighth or seventh century BCE) and provided it with a new framework. The book of Deuteronomy, which is presented as Moses' testimony, appears as the hermeneutical key and the ideological basis for reading and understanding the following history.

Starting from Deuteronomy, the Deuteronomistic History relates the story of Israel, from the Mosaic foundations in the wilderness down to the fall of Jerusalem and the Babylonian exile. With this carefully composed piece, Dtr. sought to 'contribute to an understanding of the situation in his own time'.[17] He wanted to show that the end of the kingdom of Judah was caused by the incapacity of the people and their leaders to respect the prescriptions of the Deuteronomic law. Contrary to what was probably a common assumption among the Judeans, the catastrophe of 597/587 did not mean that the national god Yahweh had been defeated by the Babylonian deities. Jerusalem's capture must rather be understood as a sanction of Yahweh against his own people. Philosophers or theologians would characterize such an interpretation of history as a sort of *theodicy*, but (as far as I can see) Noth himself never used this expression.

The way in which Noth further characterizes his 'Deuteronomist' is also of importance. He regards him as a *historian*, comparable to Hellenistic and Roman historians, who also use older traditions which

---

16.   Noth, *Deuteronomistic History*, p. 28.
17.   Noth, *Deuteronomistic History*, p. 122.

they rearrange. Dtr.'s attitude towards his traditions is that of an *'honest broker'*.[18] He integrates in his work all of the older materials available to him, even when they contradict his own theology and his view of past history, which explains why Noth could speak of the Deuteronomistic History as being truly a *Geschichtswerk*, a 'historical work'. Noth is indeed convinced that 'Dtr.'s transmission of old traditional documents and accounts makes his work a most valuable historical source' (p. 121). That means that for Noth Dtr. is as well as a redactor an author who 'brought together material from highly varied traditions' and 'apparently arranged the material according to his own judgement'.[19] As to Dtr.'s social location, 'there is no evidence that Dtr. was commissioned by an individual or by a particular group. Hence the history was probably the independent project of a man whom the historical catastrophes he witnessed had inspired with curiosity about the meaning of what had happened'.[20] In his final footnote, Noth suggests that Dtr. should be located in Palestine, probably in the Mizpah region, the provisional 'capital' of Judah under Neo-Babylonian rule.

Summing up: The Deuteronomistic History, which includes the books from Deuteronomy to Kings, was written according to Noth during the Neo-Babylonian occupation of Judah, about 560 BCE. Dtr. was both an *editor*, since he edited faithfully older documents and materials, but also an *author*, since he constructed a complex view of Israel's history, including a sequence of successive eras, in order to explain the final catastrophe.

One may wonder whether Noth's Deuteronomist does not reflect, at least to some extent, Noth's own social situation: a solitary intellectual facing the possible end of his nation's history. Whatever the possible interactions between Noth's own social and political context and his presentation of the Deuteronomistic History may be, they do not necessarily affect the validity of the Deuteronomistic History hypothesis itself. Yet they may help to understand some of the major modifications, which this hypothesis was soon to undergo, and to situate them, the thesis and its modifications, in the context of Western intellectual history in the second half of the twentieth century.

---

18.   See Noth, *Deuteronomistic History*, pp. 26 and 128.
19.   Noth, *Deuteronomistic History*, p. 26.
20.   Noth, *Deuteronomistic History*, p. 145.

2.3. First Reactions to Noth's Model

Select Bibliography

> Eissfeldt, O., *The Old Testament: An Introduction* (trans. P.R. Ackroyd;
> Oxford: Blackwell, 1965; New York: Harper & Row, 1974).
> Engnell, I., *A Rigid Scrutiny: Critical Essays on the Old Testament* (trans.
> J.T. Willis; Nashville: Vanderbilt University Press, 1962; 2nd edn,
> 1969).

Noth's thesis received an indirect confirmation in the works of Alfred Jepsen and Ivan Engnell. Jepsen wrote in 1939 an essay on the formation of the books of Kings, which appeared only in 1953.[21] In this study, he advocated a prophetic redaction of the books of Kings which would have taken place at about 550 BCE, very much like Noth's Dtr. In a foreword to his book, Jepsen himself emphasized the proximity of his results with Noth's model. Engnell, a Swedish scholar, separated the books of Genesis to Kings into a 'P-work' (the *Priestly* circle: Genesis–Numbers) and a 'D-work' (the *Deuteronomistic* circle: Deuteronomy–Kings), which coincides with Noth's own division.

Since the first edition of the *Überlieferungsgeschichtliche Studien* remained very confidential, the reception of Noth's Deuteronomistic History hypothesis did not really start before the second edition in 1957. From then, it became very common in Hebrew Bible scholarship to speak of the 'Deuteronomistic historiography' or 'history'. Yet if the concept itself was accepted by a large majority of scholars, this was not the case for all of the ideas which Noth had attached to it. Some scholars doubted that Dtr. should be understood as an individual and preferred to think in terms of a group or a scribal school, others found it more convincing to locate Dtr. (who belonged apparently to the Judean intelligentsia) among the deportees in Babylonia; some more authors wondered whether it was likely that Dtr. would have written his long history without any hopes for the future. Other authors were entirely sceptical about the Deuteronomistic History hypothesis as a whole, especially Otto Eissfeldt; he insisted on the specificity of the 'Deuteronomistic' texts in the different books of the Former Prophets as, in his view, the idea of one coherent Deuteronomistic redaction was much too simple to account for the

---

21.   Jepsen, A., *Die Quellen des Königsbuches* (Halle: Niemeyer, 1953; 2nd edn, 1956).

literary complexity of the so-called Deuteronomistic texts. These texts manifest too many differences to be ascribed to a single author–editor (see, e.g., the chronological contradictions in Josh. 1–3 or the various ways Judg. 2.11–3.6 explains why the peoples remain in the land). At the time, these voices remained marginal; yet the popularity of the concept coined by Noth was very soon to be followed by important developments of the hypothesis itself, as well as by the emergence of competing views about the Deuteronomistic History's social and historical setting.

3. Major Modifications and Critics of the Deuteronomistic History Hypothesis

3.1. Frank Moore Cross and the Double Redaction of the Deuteronomistic History

Select Bibliography

Cross, F.M., 'The Themes of the Book of Kings and the Structure of the Deuteronomistic History', in *idem, Canaanite Myth and Hebrew Epic: Essays in the History of the Religion of Israel* (Cambridge, MA: Harvard University Press, 1973), pp. 274–89.

Nelson, R.D., *The Double Redaction of the Deuteronomistic History* (JSOTSup 18; Sheffield: JSOT Press, 1981).

For Noth, Dtr. had a very pessimistic view of Israel's past history; hence, when elaborating his theory, Noth did not pay much attention to those texts which seem to contradict the alleged pessimism of Dtr. For instance, does the divine promise of an everlasting dynasty to David in 2 Sam. 7, which is written in a typically Deuteronomistic style, really fit in the exilic period, when this dynasty apparently had come to an end? And what about the expression 'until this day', which often seems to presuppose the existence of the monarchy (e.g., 1 Kgs 8.8; 9.21)? The end of the Deuteronomistic History is also problematic. Is it really possible to accept 2 Kgs 25.27–30 as a fitting conclusion? In contrast to the foregoing periods, there is no concluding speech or comment.

On the basis of such and other observations, Frank Moore Cross advocated in a 1968 article that the first edition of the Deuteronomistic History had to be located under the reign of *Josiah*. In analysing the books of Samuel and Kings, Cross discovered two major themes in the Deuteronomistic History: Yahweh's commitment to the Davidic dynasty and the 'sin of Jeroboam', that is the building of yahwistic shrines in Dan and Bethel after Israel's declaration of independence from the House of David (cf. 1 Kgs 12). These two themes converge in the account of Josiah's reign. In 2 Kgs 23.15, it is said of Josiah: 'The altar at Bethel, the high place made by Jeroboam son of Nebat, who had caused Israel to sin – even that altar and high place he demolished'. Furthermore, 2 Kgs 22.2 makes explicit that Josiah is also the worthy successor of David.

For Cross, these observations make little sense after the fall of Judah and the end of the monarchy; they can only be explained by positing a first Deuteronomistic redaction in the time of Josiah. In this view, the Josianic edition of the Deuteronomistic History ended in 2 Kgs 23.25: 'Neither before nor after Josiah was there a king who turned to Yahweh as he did – with all his heart and with all his soul and with all his strength, in accordance to all the Law of Moses.' This verse refers to Deut. 6.4–5, which probably constituted the original beginning of the book of Deuteronomy. After the fall of Jerusalem, the Josianic Deuteronomistic History was completed by a *second* Deuteronomistic redactor, who updated the account of Kings by inserting 2 Kgs 23.26–25.30; he also introduced into the Deuteronomistic History those texts which allude to the exile (e.g., Deut. 28.36–37, 64–68; Josh. 23.11–16; 1 Sam. 12.25, etc.).

The model of a double redaction of the Deuteronomistic History quickly became dominant in the United States and in English-speaking scholarship. An impressive number of Cross' students consolidated their master's theory. So for instance Richard Nelson, who tried to show in a 1973 dissertation (published in 1981) that the style of 2 Kgs 23.26–25.30 is quite different from that of the rest of the book of Kings, its 'rubber stamp character' clearly suggesting a secondary, exilic redactor[22].

This reformulation of the Deuteronomistic History hypothesis reverses its understanding by Noth. For certain, Cross agreed with Noth on the sharp distinction between the Tetrateuch and the

---

22.   See also Richard E. Friedman, who came in his own work to very similar conclusions: Friedman, R.E., *The Exile and Biblical Narrative: The Formation of the Deuteronomistic and Priestly Works* (HSM 22; Chico, CA: Scholars Press, 1981).

Deuteronomistic History, but a Josianic Deuteronomistic History implies a totally different ideology from the one Noth had assigned to Dtr. It becomes, with Cross, 'a propaganda work of the Josianic reformation ... in David and in his son Josiah is salvation'.[23]

3.2. Rudolf Smend and the Multiple Exilic Redactions of the Deuteronomistic History

Select Bibliography

Dietrich, W., 'Martin Noth and the Future of the Deuteronomistic History', in S.L. McKenzie and M.P. Graham (eds), *The History of Israel's Traditions: The Heritage of Martin Noth* (JSOTSup 182; Sheffield: Sheffield Academic Press, 1994), pp. 153–75.

Smend, R., 'The Law and the Nations. A Contribution to Deuteronomistic Tradition History', in G.N. Knoppers and J.G. McConville (eds), *Reconsidering Israel and Judah: Recent Studies on the Deuteronomistic History* (trans. P.T. Daniels; SBTS 8; Winona Lake, IN: Eisenbrauns, 2000), pp. 95–110.

Things turned out quite differently in German scholarship. In an article published in 1971, R. Smend, himself a former assistant of Noth, laid out the foundations of what would become the Smend (or 'Göttingen') school. His starting point was the observation that some Deuteronomistic texts are obviously composite. Noth had already identified some 'Deuteronomistic' texts as secondary additions, but he was not interested in identifying more precisely the origin and location of these additions. Smend began his critical reappraisal of Noth's hypothesis by a study of Josh. 1.1–9. In this speech, Yahweh addresses Joshua as a king or as a military chief, who is about to wage war. Yahweh's discourse apparently comes to an end in v. 6; in v. 7, Yahweh starts afresh to speak to Joshua, but this time in order to admonish him to study the Law. Apparently, these verses are a later attempt to correct the military language and ideology of Joshua in focusing on the obedience of the Mosaic Law. Smend found similar additions in Josh. 13.1bß–6; 23 and Judg. 1.1–2.5; 2.20–21, 23. These passages advocate, contrarily to other Deuteronomistic texts about the conquest of Canaan, the idea that this conquest was not fully achieved and that other peoples

---

23.   Cross, *Canaanite Myth*, p. 289.

remained in the land. Smend ascribed these later additions to a common redactional layer, which he designated as 'nomistic' (*DtrN*) because of its emphasis on the obedience to the Law. The first (exilic) edition of the Deuteronomistic History he labelled *DtrH* (the Deuteronomist *Historian*).

Walter Dietrich, a student of Smend, discovered another Deuteronomistic layer, characterized by its insistence on prophecy; he therefore designated it as *DtrP* (the *prophetic* Deuteronomist).[24] According to Dietrich, most of the prophetic stories and oracles in Samuel and Kings do not belong to the first edition of the Deuteronomistic History, but stem from this later redactor. This redactor is eager to show that everything Yahweh did announce through the prophets finally came true. For this reason *DtrP* provided for every prophetic oracle he introduced a notice of accomplishment (see for instance 1 Kgs 14.7–13* and 1 Kgs 15.29 or 2 Kgs 21.10–14 and 2 Kgs 24.2). In two studies published in 1975 and 1977, Timo Veijola applied this new model of three successive Deuteronomistic redactions to the books of Samuel.[25] According to him, the diachronic model advocated by the Göttingen–school could explain satisfactorily the problem of the complex (and even apparently contradictory) position of Dtr. towards the monarchical institution. Whereas *DtrH* still regarded monarchy positively (1 Sam. 9–10), *DtrP* took a critical stance towards the Davidic dynasty (cf. 2 Sam. 12); *DtrN*, finally, while also rejecting the monarchical institution as such, tried to whitewash the founders of the Judean dynasty, David and Solomon (cf. 1 Sam. 8.6–22; 1 Kgs 1.35–37; 2.3, 4aß).

The Smend school is close to Noth in its exilic setting of the different Deuteronomistic strata. But the idea of an author-redactor is given up. Smend for instance considered *DtrN* as a sort of siglum, which should probably be subdivided into $DtrN^1$, $DtrN^2$, and so on. That idea generates an inflation of Deuteronomistic layers, which theoretically contradicts the idea of a unified, coherent Deuteronomistic History.

24.   Dietrich, W., *Prophetie und Geschichte* (FRLANT 108; Göttingen: Vandenhoeck & Ruprecht, 1972).

25.   Veijola, T., *Die ewige Dynastie: David und die Entstehung seiner Dynastie nach der deuteronomistischen Darstellung* (Annales Academiae Scientiarum Fennicae, Series B, 193; Helsinki: Suomalainen Tiedeakatemia, 1975); *Das Königtum in der Beurteilung der deuteronomistischen Historiographie: eine redaktionsgeschichtliche Untersuchung* (Annales Academiae Scientiarum Fennicae, Series B, 198; Helsinki: Suomalainen Tiedeakatemia, 1977).

3.3. The 'Neo-Nothians'

Select Bibliography

McKenzie, S.L., *The Trouble with Kings: The Composition of the Books of Kings in the Deuteronomistic History* (SVT 42; Leiden: Brill, 1991).

McKenzie, S.L., 'The Trouble with Kingship', in A. de Pury, T. Römer and J.-D. Macchi (eds), *Israel Constructs its History: Deuteronomistic Historiography in Recent Research* (JSOTSup 306; Sheffield: Sheffield Academic Press, 2000), pp. 286–314.

Van Seters, J., *In Search of History: History in the Ancient World and the Origin of Biblical History* (New Haven: Yale University Press, 1983).

In spite (or rather perhaps precisely because) of these refinements, some scholars have recently expressed their disagreement regarding the different developments of the Deuteronomistic History hypothesis, advocating instead a return to Noth's model of a single Dtr. in the exilic period.

This is the case in particular of John Van Seters, although he refines Noth's model in two important and related points: the conception of Dtr. as a 'creative author', and the question of the later additions to Dtr. In Noth's mind, as we have noticed, Dtr. was mostly an 'honest broker', who faithfully retained in his own work a considerable amount of ancient traditions; for Van Seters, on the contrary, Dtr. should rather be seen as an author who made a very free use of the documents at his disposal in order to construct his presentation of Israel's history, so that, in most cases, the attempt to reconstruct these documents is entirely useless. This brings us to the second aspect in which Van Seters' approach differs from that of Noth. Whereas for Noth the contradictions and the tensions which are found in Deuteronomy to Kings are mostly due to Dtr.'s respect for his sources, which he copies even if they disagree with his own view of Israel's history, most of the ideological and theological divergences inside the Deuteronomistic History should be explained, in Van Seters' opinion, by later additions to Dtr.'s work. This is especially the case for the so-called 'History of David's Succession', or 'Court History' in 2 Sam. 2–4*; 9–20*; 1 Kgs 1–2*. This story presents David as a murderer (2 Sam. 12), as well as a very weak and irresolute king. Such a picture is in complete contradiction to the Deuteronomistic portrayal of David, since for Dtr. he is the model to which all further kings are compared. Thus, the Court History should be identified, according to Van Seters, as a late and purely fictional anti-Davidic addition to the Deuteronomistic History, written around 550 BCE. Consequently, Van Seters' Deuteronomistic History is much shorter than Noth's, since several of the texts which are often labelled as 'Deuteronomistic' are now ascribed to later, post-deuteronomistic additions (e.g., Josh. 2; 1 Kgs 13*).

Steve L. McKenzie holds a position close to that of Van Seters, since he also maintains the idea of a single, exilic, Deuteronomistic author. In his 1996 article (published in English in 2000) devoted to 1 Sam. 8–12, he argues for a setting of the Deuteronomistic historian in Mizpah shortly after 587/586, which might explain the presence in the Deuteronomistic History of texts expressing an ongoing interest in the Davidic dynasty.[26] Similarly to Van Seters, McKenzie also eliminates an important number of texts from the first edition of the Deuteronomistic History (for instance, most of the prophetic stories in Kings).[27]

The approach of Van Seters and McKenzie reaffirms the coherence of the Deuteronomistic work, even if their Deuteronomistic History is now more limited than in Noth's model. The main problem with this approach, however, is that most of the post-deuteronomistic additions to the Deuteronomistic History lack a precise location and give therefore the impression of floating in limbo. Another question is how these layers relate to Deuteronomistic editing in the Tetrateuch or in some books of the Later Prophets.

26.   In his *Trouble with Kings*, McKenzie was still advocating a first edition under Josiah; in his contribution to *Israel Constructs its History*, he locates the Dtr. Historian in Palestine shortly after the events of 587.

27.   For the 'Court History', he only considers the Bathsheba-story in 1 Sam. 12 to be a post-deuteronomistic addition, cf. McKenzie, S.L., 'The So-called Succession Narrative in the Deuteronomistic History', in A. de Pury and T. Römer (eds), *Die sogenannte Thronfolgegeschichte Davids: Neue Einsichten und Anfragen* (OBO 176; Freiburg (Switzerland) and Göttingen: Universitätsverlag and Vandenhoeck & Ruprecht, 2000), pp. 123–35.

3.4. The Deuteronomistic History and Other Deuteronomistic Redactions

Select Bibliography

Albertz, R., *Israel in Exile: The History and Literature of the Sixth Century* BCE (trans. D. Green; Studies in Biblical Literature 3; Atlanta, GA: Society of Biblical Literature, 2003).

Blenkinsopp, J., *The Pentateuch: An Introduction to the First Five Books of the Bible* (ABRL; New York: Doubleday, 1992).

Curtis, A.H.W., and T. Römer (eds), *The Book of Jeremiah and its Reception – Le livre de Jérémie et sa réception* (BETL 128; Leuven: Peeters, 1997).

Van Seters, J., 'The So-called Deuteronomistic Redaction of the Pentateuch', in J.A. Emerton (ed.), *Congress Volume Leuven 1989* (SVT 43; Leiden: Brill, 1991), pp. 58–77.

Today, it is frequently argued that Deuteronomistic redactions can also be found in the Tetrateuch (Genesis to Numbers) and in some of the prophetic books. Thus, some scholars consider the so-called Yahwistic document (J), which was traditionally located in the tenth century BCE, to be in fact the work of a Deuteronomist of the second or third generation,[28] although other authors deny such a characterization.[29] Another model explains the formation of the Pentateuch as a compromise between a D(tr) and a P(riestly) composition, considering an important part of the non-priestly texts as the product of a Deuteronomistic milieu.[30] If the presence of a Deuteronomistic redaction in the Pentateuch is taken for granted, a related question to be answered (but not in this volume!) would be whether there ever was an attempt to create a 'great history' of origins, going from Genesis to Kings, and, if so, when (at which stage in the composition of the Pentateuch and of the Former Prophets) and by whom.

More pointedly, the debate about Deuteronomistic redactions and 'Deuteronomism' in the Pentateuch raises an important question regarding the criteria defining a text as 'Deuteronomistic'. The only way to avoid arbitrary definitions is to combine stylistic and ideological

---

28. See Rose, M., *Deuteronomist und Jahwist: Untersuchungen zu den Berührungspunkten beider Literaturwerke* (ATANT 67; Zürich: Theologischer Verlag, 1981).

29. Especially J. Van Seters.

30. See Blum, E., *Studien zur Komposition des Pentateuch* (BZAW 189; Berlin and New York: de Gruyter, 1990); and also Albertz and Blenkinsopp.

criteria. If we do so, it appears very difficult to find many Deuteronomistic texts in the Patriarchal narratives of Genesis. The rather peaceful cohabitation between Abraham and his neighbours, who are often also his relatives, contradicts the Deuteronomistic view of strict separation from the people of the land, which may even include their extermination (cf. Deut. 7.1–5). The only text that comes close to the Deuteronomistic style and ideology in Genesis is the narrative of ch. 24. The story about Abraham's servant who must find a wife for Isaac in Abraham's Mesopotamian 'family' most probably reflects concerns from the Persian period, when parts of the former deportees considered themselves and the Babylonian *Golah* (the Jewish community that remained in Mesopotamia after the fall of the Babylonian empire) as the only 'true Israel'.[31] But this story alone does not make Genesis a Deuteronomistic book. The situation is very different in the book of Exodus, where we find numerous Deuteronomistic texts and features, as for instance 'the list of peoples' in the story of Moses' call (Exod. 3.8) or the prescriptions of Exod. 23.23–33 for the separation from, and expulsion of, foreign peoples. These observations might indicate the possibility of a 'Deuteronomistic' History running from Exod. 2(?) to the end of 2 Kings.[32] Further research has to be done on this question. What seems quite clear nowadays is the fact that there is a major break between the books of Genesis and Exodus; these books contain in fact two competing origin myths (the genealogical myth and the Exodus myth), which had been combined perhaps very late by priestly redactors.[33]

We should briefly mention the problem of Deuteronomistic redactions in the prophetic books. That there is a 'Deuteronomistic' redaction in the book of Jeremiah is quite widely accepted, whereas the question is very much disputed for the book of Isaiah.[34] One may observe some

31.   See e.g. Rofé, A., 'An Inquiry into the Betrothal of Rebeka', in E.Blum *et al.*, (eds), *Die Hebräische Bibel und ihre zweifache Nachgeschichte* (FS R. Rendtorff; Neukirchen–Vluyn: Neukirchener Verlag, 1990), pp. 27–39.

32.   This solution is advocated by Schmid, K., *Erzväter und Exodus: Untersuchungen zur doppelten Begründung der Ursprünge Israels innerhalb der Geschichtsbücher des Alten Testaments* (WMANT 81; Neukirchen–Vluyn: Neukirchener Verlag, 1999).

33.   For a presentation of the debate see Carr, D.M., 'Genesis in Relation to the Moses Story. Diachronic and Synchronic Perspectives', in A. Wénin (ed.), *Studies in the Book of Genesis: Literature, Redaction and History* (BETL 155; Leuven: Leuven University Press–Peeters, 2001), pp. 273–95.

34.   See different contributions in Curtis and Römer, *The Book of Jeremiah and its Reception.*

ideological and even editorial links between Isaiah and the Deuteronomistic History, especially between Isa. 36–39 and 2 Kgs 18–20, but, on the other hand, there is little evidence in Isaiah for the presence of Deuteronomistic terminology. The book of Ezekiel is also a difficult case, since it reveals a mixture of Deuteronomistic and priestly influences, both on the level of language and theological issues (see especially ch. 20). In the book of the Twelve, Hosea, Amos as well as Micah are the most likely candidates for having undergone a Deuteronomistic redaction,[35] but it is not quite clear if the 'Deuteronomistic' texts in these books come from the very beginning of Deuteronomism or from a late period. In any case, there is enough evidence for a Deuteronomistic edition of parts of the prophetic corpus, which may also explain why the books of Joshua to Kings were considered by Jewish tradition as the first part of the 'Prophets' (*Nebiim*).

3.5. Recent Criticisms of the Deuteronomistic History Hypothesis

Select Bibliography

Auld, A.G., 'The Deuteronomists and the Former Prophets, or "What Makes the Former Prophets Deuteronomistic ?"', in L.S. Schearing and S.L. McKenzie (eds), *Those Elusive Deuteronomists: The Phenomenon of Pan-Deuteronomism* (JSOTSup 268; Sheffield: Sheffield Academic Press, 1999), pp. 116–26 = *Samuel at the Threshold Selected Works of Grame Auld* (SOTSM), Hants and Burlington, VT: Ashgate, 2004), pp. 185–92.

Knauf, E.A., 'Does "Deuteronomistic Historiography" (DtrH) Exist?' in A. de Pury, T. Römer and J.-D. Macchi (eds), *Israel Constructs its History: Deuteronomistic Historiography in Recent Research* (JSOTSup 306; Sheffield: Sheffield Academic Press, 2000), pp. 388–98.

---

35.   For Hosea see Yee, G.A., *Composition and Tradition in the Book of Hosea: A Redaction Critical Investigation* (SBLDS 102; Atlanta, GA: Scholars Press, 1987); for Amos, Micah (and Jeremiah), Alvarez Barredo, M., *Relecturas deuteronomisticas de Amos, Miqueas y Jeremias* (Publicaciones del Instituto Teologico Franciscano 10; Murcia: Espigas, 1993). There might also be a case for Deuteronomistic redaction in Zechariah, see Person Jr, R.F., *Second Zechariah and the Deuteronomic School* (JSOTSup 167; Sheffield: Sheffield Academic Press, 1993). For a Deuteronomistic collection as forerunner of the book of Twelve, see Albertz, R., 'Exile as Purification. Reconstructing the "Book of the Four"', in P.L. Reddit and A. Schart (eds), *Thematic Threads of the Book of Twelve* (BZAW 325; Berlin and New York: de Gruyter, 2003), pp. 232–51.

The multiplication of numerous Deuteronomistic layers, especially in works of scholars of the Göttingen school, is already a real challenge to the idea of a coherent Deuteronomistic work. And it is hardly astonishing that recently the existence of a Deuteronomistic History has come under heavy attack and quite a lot of scholars seem now tempted to give up the idea of a unified Deuteronomistic History. One point of the debate is the understanding of 'historiography', the other point is the question of the coherence of the so-called Deuteronomistic History.

3.5.1. Deuteronomistic History and Historiography

Quite frequently Noth's 'deuteronomistisches Geschichtswerk' is translated as 'Deuteronomistic Historiography', and it is no wonder that such an expression has generated strong objections. We cannot deal in detail with the quite passionate and sometimes also ideological debate whether there exists any biblical historiography at all.[36] We will restrict ourselves to the problem of the definition of historiography.

If we adopt the Greek conception of *historia*, it seems indeed very difficult to characterize such works as the Deuteronomistic History as 'historiography'. According to Thucydides,[37] a historian should only use reliable sources, avoid miraculous explanations based on divine interventions, and try to give objective descriptions of the facts that happened in the past. In this respect, it is quite appropriate to describe the Former Prophets as being still 'mythical', since, for instance, narratives of divine intervention occur continuously in the Deuteronomistic History. Another difference between the biblical and the Greek histories concerns the conception of *authorship*. All the histories in the Hebrew Bible are anonymous works, which indicates that they have another function than the works of the Greek authors. In these histories, the individuality and singularity of the narrator are not put forward; they are hidden, since the authors of the biblical stories endeavour to offer a gnomic vision of the past, that is, one which is beyond any alternative, critical interpretation.

---

36.   See for instance Thompson, T.L., 'Israelite Historiography', *ABD* 3 (1992), pp. 206–12.

37.   Thucydides 1.21–22; C.F. Smith (trans.), *Thucydides* (LCL; Cambridge, MA: Harvard University Press, 1956), pp. 37–41.

So what should we call such a work as the Deuteronomistic History? Following J. Van Seters, who adopts the definition of the Dutch historian Huizingua according to whom 'History is the intellectual form in which a civilization renders account to itself of its past',[38] it is possible to qualify the Deuteronomistic work. as historiography. If, on the contrary, one wishes to stress the differences between the histories in the Hebrew Bible and Greek or modern historiography, we should rather speak of a '*narrative history*'; by which is meant 'the organization of material in a chronologically sequential order and the focusing of the content into a single coherent story, albeit with subplots'.[39] There is in fact a clear sequential structure in the Dtr. History, as Noth has clearly pointed out: the foundation (Deuteronomy), the Conquest (delimited by Josh. 1 and 23), the time of the Judges (delimited by Judg. 2.6–19 and 1 Sam. 12), the origins of the monarchy (delimited by 1 Sam. 12 and 1 Kgs 8), the history of the two kingdoms (delimited by 1 Kgs 9 and 2 Kgs 17) and the history of Judah until its fall (with an 'open end' in 2 Kgs 25). This is truly a history telling which constructs a chronology and creates its past.[40] Apart from the Deuteronomistic History, the other biblical example for such a 'narrative history' would be the work of the Chronicler, which apparently tries to offer an alternative vision of Israel's history, with another sequential organization and a much more optimistic ideology.[41] To avoid misunderstandings, it seems preferable to speak of a Deuteronomistic *History* instead of a Deuteronomistic *Historiography*. But still the question remains if such a History did ever exist.

---

38.   Quoted in Van Seters, *In Search of History*, p. 1.

39.   Stone, L., 'The Revival of Narrative: Reflections on a New Old History', *Past and Present* 85 (1979), pp. 3–24, here p. 3. Quoted by Barstad, H.M., 'History and the Hebrew Bible', in L.L. Grabbe (ed.), *Can a 'History of Israel' Be Written?* (JSOTSup 245; Sheffield: Sheffield Academic Press, 1997), pp. 37–64, here pp. 54–55.

40.   See also Barstad, 'History', p. 55.

41.   See on this Japhet, S., 'Postexilic Historiography: How and Why?' in A. de Pury, T. Römer and J.-D. Macchi (eds), *Israel Constructs its History: Deuteronomistic Historiography in Recent Research* (JSOTSup 306; Sheffield: Sheffield Academic Press, 2000), pp. 144–73.

3.5.2. Do the Books from Deuteronomy to Kings Reveal a Coherent Deuteronomistic Redaction?

C. Westermann[42] takes up older critics against Noth, arguing that the different books which constitute the so-called Deuteronomistic History do not bear the marks of the same Deuteronomistic style or ideology. Judges, contrarily to Kings, presents a cyclical view of history, while Samuel shows very few clear characteristics of Deuteronomistic language. Therefore Westermann claims that each book of the Former Prophets stems from a different social and historical context. Even if there were some redactors, they transmitted faithfully the old oral traditions; therefore the texts in the historical books should be considered as stemming almost from eye-witnesses of the related events. But Westermann's idea of 'oral tradition' does not conform to the results of anthropological and sociological researches, which clearly show that the writing down of what one may call 'oral tradition' means transformation in form and content of the selected material.[43]

E. Würthwein[44] and A.G. Auld argue that the oldest kernel of Deuteronomistic editing is to be found in the books of Kings. Later, in a process including several stages, the books of Samuel, Judges, and finally, Joshua were progressively added; Deuteronomy and the Tetrateuch came still later and were influenced by texts and figures from the Former Prophets. E.A. Knauf comes close to this position since he also believes that only the books of (Samuel and) Kings could be labelled as 'Deuteronomistic History'. He does not consider Deuteronomy as a fitting opening for the following historical book; since

---

42.   Westermann, C., *Die Geschichtsbücher des Alten Testaments: Gab es ein deuteronomistisches Geschichtswerk?* (ThB.AT 87; Gütersloh: Kaiser, 1994).

43.   See Kirkpatrick, P.G., *The Old Testament and Folklore Study* (JSOTSup 62; Sheffield: Sheffield Academic Press, 1988); Wahl, H.M., *Die Jakobserzählungen: Studien zu ihrer mündlichen Überlieferung, Verschriftung und Historizität* (BZAW 258; Berlin and New York: de Gruyter, 1997). See also the very important work of Niditch, S., *Oral World and Written Word: Ancient Israelite Literature* (Library of Ancient Israel; Louisville, KY: Westminster John Knox Press, 1996) and her rejection of the 'romantic notion of an oral period in the history of Israel' (p. 134).

44.   Würthwein, E., 'Erwägungen zum sog. deuteronomistischen Geschichtswerk. Eine Skizze', in *idem, Studien zum deuteronomistischen Geschichtswerk* (BZAW 227; Berlin and New York: de Gruyter, 1994), pp. 1–11.

according to the Deuteronomistic ideology Israel's history starts with the Exodus it would seem much more logical to start with that story. But if one adopts the idea that this 'greater Deuteronomistic History' would always have included the books of Exodus and Numbers, other problems arise. How should we explain, then, the presence of texts like Deut. 1–3, which recapitulate the events in Exodus and Numbers? If Deuteronomy had always followed Exodus and Numbers, there would simply be no reason for Deuteronomy to open with a summary of the events reported in the previous books. Finally Knauf argues that the so-called Deuteronomistic History (Deuteronomy–Kings) is never attested in the historical summaries or in the 'historical' Psalms, contrary to the Pentateuch (e.g., Pss. 74; 95), the Hexateuch (Pss. 105; 114) or the 'Primary History' covering the books from Genesis to Kings (e.g., Pss. 78; 106). But, if all of these collections are documented in the Psalms, none mentions *all* of the narrative traditions they contain, except for the late Ps. 105. So it seems rather dubious that one might claim that these collections are firmly attested in the Psalms. For sure, there are some late texts, which try to summarize or even to create a Hexateuch (Josh. 24) or a 'Primary History' (Neh. 9). But we also have in Ps. 136 a summary of the Tetrateuch (which ends with the conquest of Transjordan, as does the book of Numbers); this Psalm seems to consider that Deuteronomy belongs to the following books. Finally, 2 Kgs 17.7–23 could well be understood as a summary of the Deuteronomistic History. It is true that the text starts with the Exodus tradition. But since no other theme from the Tetrateuch is alluded to, the opening verse may perfectly be taken as a summary of the book of Deuteronomy: 'the people of Israel had sinned against Yahweh their God, who had brought them up out of the land of Egypt … and they had feared other gods' (v. 7). The identification of Yahweh as the God who led Israel out of Egypt and the warning against other gods are two main themes of Deuteronomy.[45] Verse 8 alludes to the conquest; there are allusions in the following verses to the time of the Judges and of Samuel; vv. 16–17 refer to events related in the book of Kings. We may conclude, then, that 2 Kgs 17.7–23 presupposes or summarizes the *extent* of the Deuteronomistic History.[46]

45. See e.g., Deut. 5.6–7, 6.12–14, 29.14–15.
46. For more details on 2 Kgs 17 see V.2 and Römer, T., 'The Form-Critical Problem of the So-called Deuteronomistic History', in M.A. Sweeney and E. Ben Zvi (eds), *The Changing Face of Form Criticim for the Twenty-First Century* (Grand Rapids, MI and Cambridge: Eerdmans, 2003), pp. 240–52.

Contrary to Rösel[47] and others who argue that there exist no Deuteronomistic themes which link together the books of Deuteronomy to Kings, one cannot deny the existence of such themes. There are some of those features, which are almost entirely lacking in the Tetrateuch. This is the case of the *ᵉlōhim ᵃḥērim*, the 'other gods'. This expression is a Deuteronomistic standard occurring in all the Deuteronomistic History; in the Tetrateuch it is only attested two or three times in the book of Exodus.[48] The theme of the worship of other gods and rejection of Yahweh runs through all the books from Deuteronomy to Kings, and offers a major explanation for the catastrophe of the exile and the destruction of both Israel and Judah.

The exile itself, the deportation out of the land given to Israel, is another 'comprehensive *Leitmotiv*' in the Deuteronomistic History. Except Lev. 26.27–33, which is a very late text, there is no direct allusion to the exile in the Tetrateuch. Of course, a lot of the texts in this corpus may be understood in the light of the events of 597/587, as for instance Exod. 32, Num. 13–14 and many more, but these texts never mention the exile explicitly. Only in the book of Deuteronomy is Israel's vanishing from the land clearly addressed (see, e.g., Deut. 28.63–64). And from there, the announcement of the deportation occurs repeatedly especially in the Deuteronomistic discourses and comments. Related to this is the use of the root *šmd* ('to be exterminated'), which is frequently attested in Deuteronomy and the *Nebiim*, but not in the Tetrateuch.[49]

Deut. 28.63 and 68 make the following announcements: '... you shall be plucked off the land that you are entering to possess... Yahweh will bring you back in ships to Egypt by a route that I promised you would never see again...' These threats are fulfilled at the end of the books of Kings: 'So Judah was exiled out of its land... Then all the people [who had not been deported to Babylonia] set out and went to Egypt...' (2 Kgs 25.21, 26). The books from Deuteronomy to Kings are thus tightly bound, to the extent that *together* they explain why

47.   Rösel, H.N., 'Does a Comprehensive "Leitmotiv" Exist in the Deuteronomistic History?', in T. Römer (ed.), *The Future of the Deuteronomistic History* (BETL 147; Leuven: Leuven University Press–Peeters, 2000), pp. 195–211.

48.   Exod. 20.3 (= Deut. 5.7); 22.13; Exod. 34.14 (singular). Outside the Deuteronomistic History the expression occurs 18 times in the Deuteronomistic parts of Jeremiah, once in Hosea (3.1) and then in the Chronicles.

49.   In the Tetrateuch only in Gen. 34.30; Lev. 16.33; Num. 33.52.

Israel and Judah could not escape from the fate that was announced by Moses from the very beginning.

There is also a form-critical argument for the unity of Deuteronomy–Kings. As far as Deuteronomy is deliberately composed as a single and huge discourse of Moses at the end of his life, it provides the very pattern for the speeches and testaments in the remainder of the historical books (esp. Josh. 23; 1 Sam. 12; 1 Kgs 8).

These observations still allow considering the books of Deuteronomy to Kings as forming a 'Deuteronomistic History', but in a different way from Noth's.

4. The Present State of Discussion: A Time for Compromise?

Select Bibliography

O'Brien, M.A., *The Deuteronomistic History Hypothesis: A Reassessment* (OBO 92; Freiburg (Switzerland) and Göttingen: Universitätsverlag and Vandenhoeck & Ruprecht, 1989).

Provan, I.W., *Hezekiah and the Book of Kings: A Contribution to the Debate about the Composition of the Deuteronomistic History* (BZAW 172; Berlin and New York: de Gruyter, 1988).

Considering the diversity of the models of the Deuteronomistic History which have been advocated in the last half-century and the recent rejection of the hypothesis, a student of the Hebrew Bible might wonder how he or she should handle these conflicting conceptions. It is true that, for a long time, there has been very little debate between the schools of Cross and Smend; their positions came close to a religious war of sorts, which made it difficult to evaluate critically both models. And it is also true that the weak points of the theory underlined recently by some scholars have often been too easily neglected.

Each of the positions presented above nevertheless contains valuable insights. The Crossian model provides a fitting explanation for those texts which seem to presuppose a monarchical ideology, and are rather optimistic regarding the future of the state and of the land. Texts such as 2 Sam. 7 (which Noth did not take much into consideration), or the conquest accounts in Josh. 6–11 do not seem yet to reflect the experience of the exile but fit better within the late pre-exilic period, at a time when Assyrian hegemony was declining and the kingdom of Judah could obtain some political autonomy (that is, towards the end of the seventh century BCE, especially under Josiah). Nevertheless, a Josianic setting for most texts of the Deuteronomistic History as advocated by Cross fails to explain satisfactorily the numerous allusions to the destruction of Jerusalem and the Babylonian exile which can be found in the Deuteronomistic History, allusions which cannot be simply explained by the exilic 'updating' of a previous document. The Göttingen school is right when it emphasizes how much the disaster of the exile permeates most of the Deuteronomistic History, as is particularly clear in the continuous warnings given by Yahweh to the people and its kings. Also, the identification of three (or even more) redactional layers by the Göttingen school may point to the oversimplification of a two-edition hypothesis. At the same time, the multiplication of Deuteronomistic layers, especially in German scholarship, is in a certain way linked to recent criticism of the Deuteronomistic History theory; in fact, there are indeed differences between the Deuteronomistic editing in Judges and in Kings for instance, and those differences should be taken seriously.

So we should consider if the points highlighted by the different scholarly positions allow for the possibility of a new and promising compromise. In his study of the books of Kings, Iain W. Provan claims that the major concern of the Deuteronomistic school is about the abolition of the *bamot* (open-air sanctuaries), which was realized, according to the biblical record, by Hezekiah. In Provan's view, the Josianic edition of the Deuteronomistic History should end therefore with 2 Kgs 18–19. Furthermore, this first edition did not consist of Deuteronomy to Kings, but only included a first version of the books of Samuel and Kings. The books of Deuteronomy, Joshua and Judges were added later, during the Neo-Babylonian period. The primitive Deuteronomistic History was therefore limited to the story of the Israelite and Judean monarchies. This coincides with the above-mentioned position of Auld, Knauf and others.

Norbert Lohfink[50] has postulated the existence of a conquest narrative, which would have been limited to the books of Deuteronomy and Joshua (Deut. 1–Josh. 22*). He designates this original conquest narrative as 'DtrL' ('L' standing for *Landeroberung*, 'conquest'), and

---

50.   Lohfink, N., 'Kerygmata des Deuteronomistischen Geschichtswerks' (first published 1981), in *idem, Studien zum Deuteronomium und zur deuteronomistischen Literatur II* (SBA.AT 12; Stuttgart: Katholisches Bibelwerk, 1991), pp. 125–42.

considers that it would have been written under Josiah as propaganda for the king's expansionist policy.

Taken together, these observations may support the idea that the Neo-Assyrian period (more specifically the seventh century BCE) should be regarded as the starting point for the Deuteronomistic literary production. The existence of a Deuteronomistic scribal activity in the time of Josiah does not mean yet that we can trace back to that time the elaboration of the Deuteronomistic History in its present form, extending from the Mosaic foundation (Deuteronomy) down to the fall of Judah (2 Kings). Instead, it is much more likely that such a 'history' was not conceived before the exilic period, in an attempt by the former royal scribes to deal with the national and theological crisis of 597/587. As we will see, there are also some indications that this History underwent a new redaction in the Persian period.

If the Deuteronomistic scribes were already active under the reign of Josiah, their literary activity must be linked in one way or another to the concerns of the royal court: it was not, therefore, a sophisticated exercise in history writing, but rather a literature of *propaganda*. A first version of Samuel–Kings* might thus have been composed in order to reinforce the legitimacy of Josiah, presenting him as the true successor of David, while a document written in the spirit of the Assyrian conquest accounts (Deuteronomy–Joshua*) would have backed Josiah's policy by legitimizing Judah's possession of the land in the name of Yahweh himself. Such a compromise between the different views on the composition of the Deuteronomistic History seems promising. The presentation that follows is, in part, an attempt to explore this direction of research.

Chapter 3

THE DEUTERONOMISTIC HISTORY FROM THE ASSYRIAN TO THE PERSIAN PERIOD

1. Who Were the 'Deuteronomists'?

Select Bibliography

Davies, P.R., *Scribes and Schools: The Canonization of Hebrew Scriptures* (Library of Ancient Israel; Louisville, KY: Westminster John Knox Press, 1998).

Jamieson-Drake, D.W., *Scribes and Schools in Monarchic Judah: A Socio-Archaeological Approach* (JSOTSup 109; Sheffield: Sheffield Academic Press, 1991).

Lohfink, N., 'Was There a Deuteronomistic Movement?', in L.S. Schearing and S.L. McKenzie (eds), *Those Elusive Deuteronomists: The Phenomenon of Pan-Deuteronomism* (JSOTSup 268; Sheffield: Sheffield Academic Press, 1999), pp. 36–66.

Niditch, S., *Oral World and Written Word: Ancient Israelite Literature* (Library of Ancient Israel; Louisville, KY: Westminster John Knox Press, 1996).

Person Jr, R.F., *The Deuteronomic School: History, Social Setting, and Literature* (Studies in Biblical Literature 2; Atlanta, GA: Society of Biblical Literature, 2002).

According to Noth, Dtr. was an individual, who, without any institutional links, wrote his history, apparently for his own concerns, in order to explain the ruin of Judah and Jerusalem in 587; Deuteronomistic History was 'probably the independent project of a man whom the historical catastrophes he witnessed had inspired with curiosity about the meaning of what had happened, and who tried to answer this question in a comprehensive and self-contained historical account'.[1] In

1.   Noth, M., *The Deuteronomistic History* (JSOTSup 15; Sheffield: Sheffield Academic Press, 2nd edn, 1991) p. 145.

regard to the ancient Israelite or Judean society this is an anachronistic position. As evident from socio-archaeological and historical research, literacy in agrarian societies as were Judah and Israel was restricted to a very small percentage of the population, which according to some scholars did not exceed one per cent in Egypt or Mesopotamia. Of course, more people probably were able to write down their names and maybe some more words or even basic letters; but the capacity of writing scrolls was limited to a small group of higher officials: priests and scribes.[2] In monarchic Judah, those 'intellectuals' cannot be located elsewhere than in the palace and the royal sanctuary, the temple of Jerusalem. There is no evidence for a widespread educational system in monarchic Judah neither for writing as a 'leisure-activity' or as a non-institutional occupation. In Palestine such a phenomenon does not occur before the Hellenistic period; the book of Qoheleth may indeed reflect the individualization of writing.

There is quite a consensus about the fact that Judah did not become a developed monarchic state before the eighth century BCE. There is archaeological evidence for the growth of Jerusalem at that time;[3] these changes imply a more developed royal administration with records, archives and so on. In a certain way the rise of Judah and Jerusalem results also from the destruction of Israel's capital Samaria by the Assyrians and its transformation into an Assyrian province. One often reads about refugees from the North that arrived in Jerusalem. Here also one should beware of too anachronistic conceptions of refugees. Nevertheless, some inhabitants from Israel may have arrived after 722 in Judah. The growth of Jerusalem results primarily from the vacuum created by the incorporation of Israel and the Aramean States into the Assyrian empire, and it certainly implied more and more powerful officials.

The 'Deuteronomists' should therefore be located among the high officials of Jerusalem, probably among the scribes, even if one should not exclude that officials from other groups (priests, 'ministers') did support their political and ideological views.

2.   See especially the important work of Jamieson-Drake, who shows that rudimentary writing capacities among the population might be assumed for Judah since the eighth century BCE.

3.   See Auld, A.G., and M. Steiner, *Jerusalem I: From the Bronze Age to the Maccabees* (Cities of the Biblical World; Cambridge: Lutterworth Press, 1996), p. 39.

That brings us to the following question: should we speak of a Deuteronomistic 'movement', a Deuteronomistic 'party', or a Deuteronomistic 'school'; or are there other terms to be preferred? As Lohfink emphasizes, 'movement' implies a large part of the population taking part[4] in it and this will hardly fit for the Deuteronomists. If the idea of a 'party' is taken in the narrow sense of a political party with numerous members then it should be avoided; if one takes 'party' more loosely for a group of like-minded individuals, then it might be appropriate for the Deuteronomists. If the expression 'Deuteronomistic school' is taken primarily as referring to an educational institution it would be misleading, but if it denotes a (small) group of authors, redactors or compilers who share the same ideology and the same rhetoric and stylistic techniques then one may speak of a 'Deuteronomistic school' (as one speaks also of a school of artists or philosophers). Others may prefer more neutral terms such as 'group' or 'circle'; nevertheless the expression 'school' recalls more clearly the scribal and intellectual setting; for that reason this term will be preferred, but is not to be used exclusively.

How should we imagine the writing activities of those (Deuteronomistic) scribes? The task of the scribes is to keep archives and tax-records for the needs of the court and the urban elite; in antiquity sanctuaries and palaces were also recipients of taxes. Scribes did also keep annals, were involved in diplomatic correspondence, and compiled laws. We know that they also kept records of memorable events, for instance, of prophetic activities in palaces and temples. They had also to compose propaganda, inscriptions or texts. But their capacity for writing also conferred on a them certain independence from the king, who was not always able to write, and, as we may infer from Egyptian texts, they may have considered themselves as intellectually superior.[5] It is clear that scribes could also write of their own initiative and try, by their writings, to influence the politics of the court.

The scrolls (of papyrus or sometimes of leather) they wrote on were kept in archives or 'libraries' located in the palace or the temple. There is no evidence, for the monarchic times, of scrolls that were kept by private individuals. And we should not imagine hundreds of scrolls circulating all over the country. The first location of books is in the

---

4.   Lohfink is inclined to allow the idea of a Deuteronomistic movement for the time under Josiah; but this is a quite romantic idea, based on a certain reading of 2 Kgs 22–23.

5.   See also Davies, *Scribes*, p. 19.

palace and the sanctuary and those scrolls probably existed in a single copy.[6] These scrolls or parts of them may have been read on special occasions to the king or to the people gathered in the sanctuary (see for instance Jer. 36[7]). The scrolls were probably also used for teaching the scribes 'history' and writing. From time to time new copies of those scrolls were made, either because the papyrus was too damaged, or because of the necessity of updating or correcting the former scroll. Anyway, we should not imagine the copying of scrolls on the pattern of the monks' work in medieval monasteries. Copying a scroll always meant transformation. One may, following Person, imagine a hierarchical organization of the Deuteronomistic guild where lower scribes wrote down what the few higher ranked scribes dictated to them.[8] The very common idea that copying included a slavish conservation of the older texts does not apply to scribal practices in antiquity. The examples from the recopying of the Gilgamesh epic (where we have some older documents conserved) or of Assyrian inscriptions clearly indicate a very free attitude of the scribes towards the older texts. That means that we cannot reconstruct exactly the older texts that have been re-edited in later times, even if some biblical scholars still think they can. We must therefore be content with the outlines of the hypothetically reconstructed older documents.

Should we call the Deuteronomistic scribal guild authors or redactors? As Noth had rightly observed they were both. They did use in some cases other documents either to gather information (see the frequent references to royal annals in the books of Kings) or to integrate them in their work (this could be the case for the 'book of saviours' which was used to create the period of the Judges); they may have also written down so-called 'oral traditions'. They probably also combined smaller independent scrolls into one scroll (this happened in a certain way also to the Gilgamesh epic: older, independent heroic stories were arranged chronologically and edited as one story in a series of tablets[9]). Since the Hebrew Bible contains anonymous texts and literature (with the exception of Qoheleth?) we should take care not to introduce a modern, anachronistic and individualistic concept of

6.   See Lohfink, 'Movement', p. 48.
7.   Even if this text was written in the Persian period, it may reflect practices from the time of the monarchy.
8.   Person, *School*, p. 150.
9.   See Tigay, J.H., *The Evolution of the Gilgamesh Epic* (Philadelphia, PA: University of Pennsylvania Press, 1982).

authorship. For Palestinian scribes from the eighth to the fourth century BCE no clear distinction between author and redactor can be made.[10]

Do we possess any further indications about the origins and the composition of the Deuteronomistic school? There is one text in the Hebrew Bible, which is often used to reconstruct the so-called reform of Josiah: 2 Kgs 22–23.

2. The Foundation Myth of the Deuteronomistic School in 2 Kgs 22–23: Book-finding and Cultic Reform

Select bibliography

Barrick, W.B., *The King and the Cemeteries: Towards a New Understanding of Josiah's Reform* (SVT 88; Leiden: Brill, 2002).

Handy, L.K., 'Historical Probability and the Narrative of Josiah's Reform in 2 Kings', in S.W. Holloway and L.K. Handy (eds), *The Pitcher is Broken: Memorial Essays for Gösta W. Ahlström* (JSOTSup 190; Sheffield: Sheffield Academic Press, 1995), pp. 252–75.

Lohfink, N., 'The Cult Reform of Josiah of Judah: 2 Kings 22–23 as a Source for the History of Israelite Religion', in P.D. Miller Jr, P.D. Hanson and S.D. McBride (eds), *Ancient Israelite Religion: Essays in Honor of Frank Moore Cross* (Philadelphia, PA: Fortress Press, 1987), pp. 459–75.

2 Kgs 22–23 plays a central role in the discussion about the origins of the Deuteronomistic school. These chapters relate how a scroll was found in the eighteenth year of Josiah's reign in the temple of Jerusalem during renovation works. The discovery by the priest Hilkiah and the reading of this scroll to the king by the high official Shaphan provokes a very strong reaction. Josiah seems heavily affected by the curses of

10.   Recently J. Van Seters has fustigated the frequent reference to redactors in biblical scholarship. According to him, the idea of redactors is a major flaw in current Hebrew Bible criticism (see for instance Van Seters, J., 'The Redactor in Biblical Studies: A Nineteenth Century Anachronism', *JNSL* 29 [2003], pp. 1–19). I agree with Van Seters, that one should not use the term redactor for the editors of the 'final form' of a text, since such a final form never existed. But one may and even should use the term in the broader sense to designate the creative reworking and editing of older documents (see for instance *The Chambers Dictionary*).

the book; he sends Hilkiah, Shaphan and other officials to the prophetess Huldah to enquire about the meaning of the scroll. And Huldah speaks to the delegation as if she were Jeremiah (compare 2 Kgs 22.16–17 with Jer. 19.14 and 7.20); but she refers also to important texts from the Deuteronomistic History as Deut. 6.12–15; 31.29; Judg. 2.12–14a. In doing so she confirms the divine judgement, which Yahweh will bring upon Jerusalem and Judah. As for King Josiah, she delivers a more positive message: since he has been attentive to the words of the book he will be buried in peace (2 Kgs 22.18–20). After his officials have transmitted the message, Josiah himself reads the book for the 'whole people' and engages in a treaty with Yahweh (2 Kgs 23.1–3). Then Josiah starts to undertake important cultic modifications in Jerusalem and Judah. He eliminates the cultic symbols and the priests of the deities Baal and Asherah, and of the 'celestial army', which alludes to the veneration of sun, moon and stars. He also defiles and destroys the *bamot*, open sanctuaries (the 'high places') for the veneration of Yahweh, as well as the *tophet*, apparently a place for human sacrifices. According to 23.15 he even demolishes the altar at Bethel, the former official Yahwistic sanctuary of Israel. These acts of destruction have their positive counterpart in the above-mentioned conclusion of a (new?) treaty between Yahweh and the people, and in the celebration of a Passover (vv. 21–23). Both rituals are mediated by Josiah, and presented as prescriptions from the unfolded scroll.

Early Jewish commentators, as well as some Church Fathers, already identified the book mentioned in 2 Kgs 22–23 as the book of Deuteronomy, since the acts of Josiah and the ideology of centralization, which sustains his 'reform', seem to agree with the prescriptions of the Deuteronomic Law (cf. e.g., Deut. 17.1–3 and 2 Kgs 23.4–5; Deut. 12.2–3 and 2 Kgs 23.6, 14; Deut. 23.18 and 2 Kgs 23.7; Deut. 18.10–11 and 2 Kgs 23.24). This identification was then used in the nineteenth and twentieth centuries as a way of locating the primitive edition of Deuteronomy at the time of Josiah, in the last third of the seventh century. According to the *pia fraus* ('pious lie') theory, as advocated by Wellhausen and others, the first edition of Deuteronomy was written in order to promote the Josianic reform, disguised as Moses' testament and hidden in the temple so as to be quickly discovered.

This theory takes the story of the unfolded book as reflecting a historical fact, which is not devoid of difficulties. 2 Kgs 22–23 is above all the 'foundation myth' of the Deuteronomists, and cannot be used naively as an eye-witness report of the so-called reform. The narrative, as it stands now, already reflects on the destruction of Jerusalem and the Babylonian exile (especially in the speeches by the prophetess Huldah, in 22.16–17); therefore in the present text of 2 Kgs 22–23, as T.R. Hobbs puts it, 'the important point about the reign and the reform of Josiah is their failure'.[11] The 'cleansing' of the temple was indeed of not much use, since it was destroyed a few decades later. But the discovery of the book offered the possibility to *understand* this destruction, and to worship Yahweh *without any temple*.

The book-finding motive is indeed a very common concept in ancient literature.[12] and is usually employed in order to legitimate changes in religious, economical or political matters. That means that the story about the restoration of the temple and the discovery of the book in 2 Kgs 22 is most probably a complex literary construction, based on Near Eastern motifs. One should indeed distinguish in 2 Kgs 22–23 several stages of composition. As for 2 Kgs 22, it is quite obvious that the restoration report in vv. 3–7 depends literally on 2 Kgs 12.10–16.[13] The notice about the priest Hilkiah finding the book in v. 8 is introduced quite abruptly, and interrupts the first scene (see vv. 3–7, 9). Thus, as it has often been argued, it is very likely that one should distinguish in 2 Kgs 22 between two stories: the restoration report (*Instandssetzungsbericht*) and the narrative about the discovery of the book (*Auffindungsbericht*). It is possible that the discovery report (22.8, 10, 11, 13*, 16–18, 19*, 20*; 23.1–3) is a later insertion, which one may ascribe to a postexilic redactor.[14]

The origin of the 'book-finding' motif is probably to be situated in the deposit of foundation tablets in Mesopotamian sanctuaries, which

11. Hobbs, T.R., *2 Kings* (WBC 13; Waco, TX: Word Books, 1985), p. xxv.

12. See the compelling paper by Diebner, B.-J., and C. Nauerth, 'Die Inventio des הַתּוֹרָה סֵפֶר in 2 Kön 22: Struktur, Intention und Funktion von Auffindungslegenden', *DBAT* 18 (1984), pp. 95–118.

13. See especially Hoffmann, H.-D., *Reform und Reformen: Untersuchungen zu einem Grundthema der deuteronomistischen Geschichtsschreibung* (ATANT 66; Zürich: Theologischer Verlag, 1980), pp. 169–270.

14. As advocated by Levin, C., 'Joschija im deuteronomistischen Geschichtswerk', *ZAW* 96 (1984), pp. 351–71; p. 355 = Levin, C., *Fortschreibungen. Gesammelte Studien zum Alten Testament* (BZAW 316; Berlin and New York: de Gruyter, 2003), pp. 198–216; p. 201. One may also argue that both motifs fit quite well together and could therefore be the work of one scribe of the exilic or more probably the Persian period.

are often 'rediscovered' by later kings undertaking restoration works. The Egyptian variant of this motif occurs for instance in the final rubric of the sixty-fourth chapter of the Egyptian Book of the Dead, which was standardized not earlier than during the Saitic period (664–525 BCE). Chapter 64 is presented as having been found in the Sokaris temple, and as going back to the very origins of Egypt.[15]

In Babylonian royal inscriptions, the discovery-reports are often variations of the following pattern: 1. An important person (king, prince) wants to undertake political or cultic changes, which are often presented as a restoration of an initial state; 2. He is afraid of opposition; 3. He or one of his loyal servants is sent to a holy place; 4. There, he discovers a written document of divine origin; 5. This discovery gives divine impulse to the projects of the monarch.

Of special interest are Nabonidus' inscriptions, who strived to appear as the discoverer of numerous documents. All his reports follow the same outline. In the cylinder from Sippar, Nabonidus tells the following story.[16] He wanted to rebuild the temple of Ibarra (belonging to Shamash) in Sippar:

> (19) a former king (= Nabuchodonosor) had searched for the ancient foundation stone without any success. (20) On his own initiative he had built a new temple for Shamash, but it was not built (good enough) for his reign... (22) The walls sagged and risked a break-down... (26) I supplicated him (= Shamash), offered him sacrifices and was searching for his decisions. (27) Shamash, the very high Lord, had chosen me from the earliest days on... (32) I made investigations and gathered the

---

15.   This text exists in the longer and in the abbreviated version of ch. 64. The Papyrus of Nu contains the following text: 'This chapter was found in the city of Khemennu ... under the feet of the god during the reign of His Majesty, the King of the North and the South, *Men-kau-Rā*... triumphant, by the royal son *Heru-ṭā-ṭā-f*, triumphant; he found it when he was journeying about to make an inspection of the temples ... he brought it to the king as a wonderful object when he saw that it was a thing of great mystery, which had never [before] been seen or looked upon. This chapter shall be recited by a man who is ceremonially clean and pure...' (quoted from Wallis Budge, E.A., *The Book of the Dead*, Vol. II [London: Routledge & Kegan Paul, 2nd edn, 1956], pp. 221–22. For variants, see pp. 217 and 221).

16.   Translated from F.E. Peiser, in *Keilschriftliche Bibliothek: Sammlung von assyrischen und babylonischen Texten in Umschrift und Übersetzung*, III/2 (ed. E. Schrader; Berlin: H. Reuther, 1890), pp. 80–121, esp. pp. 108–13. A similar story is related in Nabonidus' cylinder from Abû Happa, see pp. 103–105.

ancients of the town, the Babylonians, the architects, (33) the wise men... (34) ... I told them: 'Look for the ancient foundation-stone, (35) take care of the sanctuary of the Judge Shamash...'. (36) The erudite persons looked for the ancient stone of foundation, imploring Shamash, my Lord, and praying to the great Gods, (37) they inspected the apartment and the rooms and they saw it. They came to me and told me: (38) 'I have seen the ancient foundation-stone of Naram-Sin, the former king, the real sanctuary of Shamash, the dwelling place of his divinity'. (39) My heart exulted and my face was radiant.

According to this text, the foundation stone contains the document of the 'original temple', and enables Nabonidus to undertake his restoration works.

It seems quite clear that the authors or the redactors of 2 Kgs 22 resort to the same literary convention. This confirms the assumption that 2 Kgs 22–23 is to be read as the foundation myth of the Deuteronomistic group. The foundation stone is in 2 Kgs 22–23 replaced by the book, which becomes the 'real' foundation for the worship of Yahweh. And the mediators of this 'book-religion' are neither the king nor the priest and their sacrificial cult, but the scribes who produce and read those books. Therefore we should not too easily locate the story of the book-finding and the following reform into the end of the seventh century BCE, as is commonly done. It is easily understandable that some scholars argue that the whole idea of a Josianic reform is a late invention.[17]

True, we do not have primary evidence for a so-called Josianic reform[18] (that is, we have no document that can clearly be dated as stemming from Josiah's reign and proving the existence of a political and cultic reorganization). Nevertheless, there are some indicators that point to cultic and political changes in Judah at the end of the seventh century BCE. According to 2 Kgs 23, Josiah suppressed numerous elements linked to an astral cult, which was an important part of the Neo-Assyrian

17.   See Handy, L.K., and Niehr, H., 'Die Reform des Joschija. Methodische, historische und religionsgeschichtliche Aspekte', in W. Groß (ed.), *Jeremia und die 'deuteronomistische Bewegung'* (BBB 98; Weinheim: Beltz Athenäum, 1995), pp. 33–56.

18.   For the distinction between primary and secondary evidence see Knauf, E.A., 'From History to Interpretation', in D.V. Edelman (ed.), *The Fabric of History: Text, Artifact and Israel's Past* (JSOTSup 127; Sheffield: Sheffield Academic Press, 1991), pp. 26–64.

religious ideology. The references to the horses and chariots of Shamash, the Sun-God (23.11) and to the *kemarim*-priests[19] serving 'the Sun, the Moon, the constellations, and all the host of the heavens' (23.5), have historical plausibility in the Assyrian period. Their elimination from the temple of Jerusalem is not necessarily a sign of an anti-Assyrian insurrection; it may simply denote the fact that Assyrian influence in Syria and Palestine had significantly dwindled in the last decades of the seventh century. C. Uehlinger has pointed out that there is a clear change in Judean glyptic from the seventh to the sixth century. During the seventh century, seals from the upper class and the officials are strongly marked by astral motifs. On the other hand, in a corpus of about 260 seals, to be dated at the beginning of the sixth century, there is complete lack of astral symbols and deities, which clearly indicates that around 600 BCE, astral motifs had come out of fashion among the Jerusalemite elite.[20]

The temporary vacuum in the last decades of the seventh century BCE (very soon filled by Egypt) created in Syria-Palestine by the fading away of the Assyrian power structures also gives some plausibility to the hypothesis that Josiah or his counsellors undertook some political and cultic reorganization.[21] The attempt to centralize cult, power and taxes (the sanctuaries were also tax-offices) in Jerusalem has a good historical plausibility in this context. The relative independence of Judah around 620 BCE perhaps put forth the conviction in some circles that Josiah was the inaugurator of a great and independent Judean kingdom.[22] It is often argued that Josiah annexed the Assyrian provinces established upon the former kingdom of Israel. There is however little evidence for this. 2 Kgs 23.15 tells of the destruction of the sanctuary of Bethel; but if this notice is historical at all, which is most uncertain, it does not indicate

19.   This rare term in the Hebrew Bible is probably linked to the Assyrian word *kumru* which designates foreign priests; for more details see Hobbs, *2 Kings*, p. 333.

20.   Uehlinger, C., 'Gibt es eine joschijanische Kultreform? Plädoyer für ein begründetes Minimum', in W. Groß, (ed.), *Jeremia und die 'deuteronomistische Bewegung'* (BBB 98; Weinheim: Beltz Athenäum, 1995), pp. 57–90; pp. 65–67.

21.   According to 2 Kgs 22.1, Josiah was eight years old when he began to reign. If this is historical information, it means that during the first years of his reign, his counsellors (the Deuteronomists?) governed instead of him.

22.   See Ahlström, G.W., *The History of Ancient Palestine from the Palaeolithic Period to Alexander's Conquest* (JSOTSup 146; Sheffield: Sheffield Academic Press, 1993), p. 778.

an occupation of the Samaritan provinces of Samerina, Magidu[23] and Gal'aza. It is nevertheless possible that Josiah and his counsellors made the claim of being the rightful heirs of 'Israel'. They might have tried to enlarge the northern border, and Josiah was probably successful in annexing the small territory of Benjamin (this is probably reflected in some texts of the book of Joshua, as we will see).

Summing up: The biblical presentation of Josiah and his reign cannot be taken as a document of primary evidence. On the other hand, some indicators suggest nevertheless that some attempts to introduce cultic and political changes took place under Josiah. His reform was certainly not based on the discovery of a book, but the first edition of Deuteronomy may well have been written under Josiah. 2 Kgs 22–23 may even provide some information about names or families we may associate with the Deuteronomists. All the names in these chapters are probably not late inventions,[24] and so we may conclude that Hilkiah and especially Shaphan and his family belonged to the Deuteronomistic group.[25]

The narrative in 2 Kgs 22–23 was obviously edited in successive stages. The kernel from the Assyrian period (approximately 22.1–7*, 9, 13aα; 23.1, 3–15*, 25aα) focused on the removal of Assyrian cult symbols and on the centralization of Yahweh's worship in the restored royal sanctuary. The story of the temple renovation, the consultation of the prophetess and the oracle announcing the divine judgement in ch. 23 were added after 587 BCE in order to explain the collapse of Judah and Jerusalem. The last revision, probably including the motif

23.   According to Stern, the fact that Josiah is killed by the Egyptian king in Megiddo may indicate that Josiah did rule this area for a short time (Stern, E., *Archaeology of the Land of the Bible*. II. *The Assyrian, Babylonian, Persian Periods 732–332* BCE [ABRL; New York: Doubleday, 2001], p. 68). But one should better assume that Megiddo was at this time under Egyptian control, see Ahlström, *History of Ancient Palestine*, p. 765.

24.   A seventh-century seal from Judah is referring to Hilkiah who might be the same person mentioned in 2 Kgs 22, see Elayi, J., 'Name of Deuteronomy's Author Found on Seal Ring', *BAR* 13 (1987), pp. 54–56.

25.   2 Kgs 22 mentions Shaphan and Ahikam, son of Shaphan (v. 12, see also 25.22. It is debated if this is the same Shaphan as the scribe). The Shaphan family also plays an important role in Jer. 36, where a descendant of Shaphan 'finds' the 'book of Jeremiah' and reads it to the king. According to Barrick Hilkiah was Josiah's mentor and was probably Shaphan's uncle (see the interesting but somewhat speculative paper by Barrick, W.B., 'Dynastic Politics, Priestly Succession and Josiah's Eight Years', *ZAW* 112 [2000], pp. 564–82).

of the book discovery, was made during the Persian period The aim of this redaction was, as we will see in more detail, to replace the temple cult by the reading of the book.

The analysis of the history of the composition of the Deuteronomistic History remains an essential step in order to understand its origins and its transformations. True, the composition of the Deuteronomistic History is widely debated today; nevertheless, it is possible to discern within several texts of the Deuteronomistic History three main redactional layers, corresponding to *three successive editions* of the Deuteronomistic History, each of which can be located in a different historical and social context. This threefold composition is most clearly manifest at the very beginning of the Deuteronomistic History, in Deut. 12, the opening of the Deuteronomic law code.

3. The Three Different Viewpoints about Centralization in Deut. 12 as an Example of the Threefold Edition of the Deuteronomistic History

Select Bibliography

Levinson, B.M., *Deuteronomy and the Hermeneutics of Legal Innovation* (New York and Oxford: Oxford University Press, 1997).

Richter, S.L., *The Deuteronomistic History and the Name Theology:* šakken šᵉmô šām *in the Bible and the Ancient Near East* (BZAW 318; Berlin and New York: de Gruyter, 2002).

Deut. 12 is a very extensive statement about cult centralization. As we will see, the origin of such an ideology should be located in the context of the social and economic changes that some of the families related to the court attempted to undertake during the reign of King Josiah. As it stands now, however, Deut. 12 cannot be entirely situated at the end of the seventh century BCE. Instead, several indications suggest that the original law of centralization has been successively reworked.

Deut. 12 insists indeed several times on the fact that Yahweh has chosen for himself only one place (*māqôm*) 'to put his Name there' (vv. 4–7, 11–12, 13–14, 26–27). If we start from this fourfold insistence on the unique place chosen by the divinity, we may notice how the first three statements are at the centre of three sequences, which are all structured in the same way. In these three cases, the main commandment is preceded by a negative statement: vv. 2–4 (4): not to act towards Yahweh in the way of the nations; vv. 8–10 (8): not to act as today; v. 13: not to offer holocausts in all places. Furthermore, the sequence ends each time with a call to rejoice (vv. 7, 12, 18). These observations thus point to three distinct units, delimited as follows: vv. 2–7/ 8–12/ 13–18(19[26]). The 'you' in the last unit is formulated in the singular whereas the other ones mainly use the plural. The first unit is manifestly linked with vv. 29–31, whereas vv. 13–18 are taken up in vv. 20–28. Such delimitation allows for the identification of three different ideologies about the unique sanctuary.

It is generally acknowledged that inside Deut. 12.1–19, vv. 13–18 constitute the kernel to which first vv. 8–12, then vv. 2–7 were added. This redactional process suggests successive editing, which may be compared to the modern practice of successively prefacing new editions to commercially successful books.

Deut. 12.13–18 addresses quite wealthy landowners who possess slaves and cattle. Verses 8–12 should be considered as the first 'actualization' of the commandment during the time of the Babylonian exile. Here the fiction of a discourse placed in Moses' mouth and directed to a group which has not yet entered the land plays an important role (cf. v. 10). Verses 2–7 probably stem from the first century of the Persian period. The aggressive obsession of strict separation from the 'foreign nations' has parallels in the ideology of the books of Ezra and Nehemiah, which sharply distinguish the 'true Israel' (the Babylonian Golah and those returned to Jerusalem) from the 'people of the land'.

This hypothesis for the chronological succession of the three versions of the law of centralization is confirmed by the development of the centralization formula:

> v. 14: The place (*māqôm*) that Yahweh will choose in one (*eḥad*) of your tribes;
> v. 11: The place (*māqôm*) that Yahweh, your God, will choose as a dwelling (*šakken*) for his name;

26.　　The concern for the Levite in v. 19 may stem from a late redaction close to the ideology of Chronicles which, at the end of the Persian period, defends the status of the Priestly class of the Levites, cf. Dahmen, U., *Leviten und Priester im Deuteronomium: Literarkritische und redaktionsgeschichtliche Studien* (BBB 110; Bodenheim: PHILO, 1996), p. 379.

v. 5: The place (*māqôm*) that Yahweh, your God, will choose out of all your tribes to put his name there to make it dwell.[27]

It is manifest that the original formulation (v. 14) was gradually developed and reinterpreted by the scribes responsible for the successive editions of Deut. 12. The exilic edition (v. 11) introduces the motif of the divine *name* dwelling inside the sanctuary (instead of the deity itself), which may already be taken to be a reinterpretation after the capture of Jerusalem in 587/586 of the traditional motif of the deity's presence – materialized by its statue – in the temple. The last formulation (v. 5) looks like a combination of the former two (vv. 14 and 11).

3.1. Deut. 12.13–18: Practical Consequences of the Centralization at the End of the Seventh Century BCE

The oldest text in Deut. 12 first opposes the totality (*b⁽ᵉ⁾kol-māqôm*) of sacred places to the only sanctuary that Yahweh will choose for himself in 'one' tribe. This precision makes it difficult to read the centralization formula in a distributive manner, so as to understand that at each period God would choose for himself another sanctuary. Thus, the *māqôm* in Deut. 12 does not point at anything else than the temple of Jerusalem, and the 'one' tribe cannot mean any other than (the kingdom of) Judah.[28] The same ideology is to be found in Ps. 78, which is closely related to Deuteronomistic ideology: according to this Psalm, Yahweh explicitly refuses to choose Ephraim (the North) but chooses instead 'the tribe of Judah, the mountain of Zion which he loves' (v. 68). The author of Deut. 12.13–18 takes up the Jerusalemite tradition of Yahweh's election of temple–mountain and transforms it into an *exclusive* election, incompatible with any other sanctuary.

Thus, the Deuteronomistic ideology of centralization tends to show that the former kingdom of Israel has no divine legitimation. On the other hand, Deut. 12 also stands in opposition to the opening of the so-called 'Covenant Code', Exod. 20.22–26. According to this text,

---

27.   The masoretic vocalization of the root is problematic. The original form of the verb most probably was an infinitive of the intensive/factitive form as rendered above.

28.   See Mayes, A.D.H., *Deuteronomy* (NCB Commentary; Grand Rapids, MI and London: Eerdmans and Marshall, Morgan & Scott, 1981), p. 227.

altars should be built in the totality of the places (*bᵉkol-māqôm*) in which Yahweh will make his name to be remembered (v. 24). It is often assumed that this is an older conception, which the Deuteronomists try to correct, but it is also possible that Exod. 20.22–26 reflects an anti-Deuteronomistic reaction from the periphery, which may be contemporaneous with Deut. 12.13–18 or even later. Exod. 20.22–26 can therefore be read as legitimating the existence of other sanctuaries (Bethel, or even Mizpah) during the Babylonian occupation, or even as reflecting the view of the intellectuals from the Jewish diaspora, arguing for Yahweh's presence outside of Jerusalem and Judah. But this does not mean that the whole 'Covenant Code' (Exod. 20.22–23.18) should be understood as contemporaneous of the first edition of the Deuteronomic Code or even later.[29] Exod. 20.26–26 is quite clearly a later addition to the Covenant Code, whose original opening is still preserved in 21.1. There is much evidence to support that the first edition of Deut. 12–26 was composed in order to actualize and probably also to replace the Covenant Code.[30] This attempt of urbanizing and modernizing the older law collection points to the context of political and economic changes that Judah underwent during the seventh century BCE, and this is quite clearly the social and historical context of Deut. 12.13–18. The idea of centralization, which is expressed here, means a concentration of political and religious power in the capital. The concentration of religious power in Jerusalem required the cultic unification of the national deity Yahweh. Such an attempt at unification finds a clear expression in Deut. 6.4–5; the first edition of Deuteronomy probably started with this statement insisting on the unity of Yahweh. It is possible that Deut. 6.4–5[31] was, in the first edition of the book, immediately followed by Deut. 12.13–18. The common emphasis on the words 'totality' (*kol*) and 'one' (*eḥad*) makes it possible to read them as a unit:

> Hear Israel, Yahweh is our god; Yahweh is one (*eḥad*). You shall love Yahweh your god with all (*bᵉkol*) your heart, with all (*bᵉkol*) your life and with all (*bᵉkol*) your strength. Be careful not to offer your holocausts in every (*bᵉkol*) place you see. Only at the place that Yahweh will choose in one (*eḥad*) of your tribes you shall offer your holocausts,

29.   For this view see Van Seters, J., *A Law Book for the Diaspora: Revision in the Study of the Covenant Code* (Oxford: Oxford University Press, 2003).

30.   This is almost a scholarly consensus, see especially Levinson.

31.   Verses 6–9 already presuppose an exilic or even postexilic background.

and there you shall observe everything (*kol*) that I command you (Deut. 6.4–5; 12.13).

It may be astonishing that Deut. 12.13–18 is mainly concerned with the practical consequences of the centralization law ('profane' slaughtering) and that there is not much insistence on the explanation of the necessity of centralization. So it could be possible, as Lohfink assumes, that the version of Deut. 12.12–18 has replaced a somewhat older form of the centralization law, which we are unable to reconstruct.[32] But it is not necessary to adopt this assumption; it seems also quite logical that the (theoretical) closing down of the local butcheries in the sanctuaries required new regulations for the killing of animals outside of Jerusalem. The allowing of slaughter without priestly involvement is an attempt to annihilate definitely the influence of the priesthood outside Jerusalem. This new conception of slaughtering does not abrogate the prohibition of consuming blood, which is a very common taboo of antique religions; and there is of course also a reminder that this new law does not mean fewer taxes and offerings (tithe, firstborn, vows), which must all be brought now to the Jerusalem temple (v. 17).

The theme of profane slaughter is taken up again in 12.20–28 with somewhat of a restriction: 'If the place where Yahweh your god has chosen to put his name is too far away from you, then you may slaughter animals from the herds and flocks that Yahweh your god has given to you...' (v. 21). It is often argued that the allusion to the enlargement of the territory in this text reflects Josiah's annexation of territories which formerly belonged to Israel, but that point is far from being assured: historically speaking, the actual expansion of Judah under Josiah was most likely quite modest, limited in the North to the small territory of Benjamin.[33] Moreover, the narrative of 2 Kgs 23.15–20 (which refers to such an expansion) never takes up the terminology of Deut. 12.20. The use of *g^ebûl* ('border, territory') in Deut. 12.20–28 can hardly refer to the Promised Land, which in the current Deuteronomistic terminology is called *'adamà* or *'ereṣ*. Therefore the best hypothesis may be to understand this text as an

32.   Lohfink, N., 'Fortschreibung? Zur Technik von Rechtsrevisionen im deuteronomischen Bereich, erörtert an Deuteronomium 12, Ex 21,2–11 und Dtn 15,12–18', in T. Veijola (ed.), *Das Deuteronomium und seine Deutungen* (Schriften der Finnischen Exegetischen Gesellschaft 62; Helsinki and Göttingen: Finnische Exegetische Gesellschaft and Vandenhoeck & Ruprecht, 1996), pp. 127–71.

33.   Stern, *Archaeology*, II, pp. 138–42.

allusion to the diaspora situation in postexilic times: the temple is rebuilt, but the Jews in Babylon or in Egypt cannot get there each time they slaughter. According to A. Rofé, Deut. 12.20–28 wants to harmonize the Deuteronomistic law of centralization with the legislation of Lev. 17,[34] which seems less concerned with the idea of centralization than with the condemnation of profane slaughter. This observation confirms the setting of 12.20–28 in the Persian period. The two passages dealing with the practical consequences of cultic centralization, vv. 13–18 and 20–28, presuppose the existence of the Jerusalemite temple: in 12.13–18, the *first* temple, in 12.20–28, the *second* temple. This is not the case with Deut. 12.8–12, where the original prescription of 12.13–18 is now actualized in order to fit a new historical context.

3.2. Deut. 12.8–12: An Exilic Reinterpretation of the Concept of Centralization

Deut. 12.8–12 clearly addresses an audience that is supposed to stay away from the land; that means that the addressees of this instruction are manifestly the deportees. They are identified as the generation of the desert to whom entrance into the country is promised under certain conditions. Here the literary fiction of Deuteronomy as Moses' testament becomes for the first time transparent, since v. 10 evokes the coming crossing of the Jordan. The Deuteronomistic redactor opposes in this text the situation of 'today', where everybody does 'what is right in his own eyes', and entering into the 'rest' ($m^e nuḥâ$) (v. 9). What is, in this context, the meaning of this term? In a number of texts (Isa. 66.1; Pss. 95.11; 132.8, 14), the word refers to the Jerusalem temple. More important still, however, Deut. 12.9 prepares for 1 Kgs 8.56, a passage from Solomon's prayer, as has often been noted.

> Deut. 12.9: You have not yet come into the *rest* and the possession that Yahweh your God is *giving* to you.
> 1 Kgs 8.56: Blessed be Yahweh who has *given rest* to the people Israel according to all … that he spoke through his servant Moses.

---

34.   Rofé, A., 'The Book of Deuteronomy: A Summary', in *idem*, *Deuteronomy: Issues and Interpretation* (Old Testament Studies; London and New York: T. & T. Clark, 2002), pp. 1–13; p. 8 (article published 1986 in Hebrew, trans. H.N. Bock).

Only in these two texts do we read that Yahweh gives a rest to Israel; this implies a very clear connection to the books of Kings.

This strong link indicates that the same exilic redactors reworked Deut. 12 and 1 Kgs 8. As a result of this editing it appears now that Yahweh has definitely given the land only after the building of the temple. Even if the conquest comes to an end in Josh. 21.43–45 and 23, the exilic Deuteronomists present the temple as a microcosm, which symbolizes Yahweh's presence in the land that he had granted to Israel. For this reason, the expression of the land given to the fathers appears inside the Deuteronomistic History for the first time in 1 Kgs 8 (vv. 34, 40, 48; in the books of Deuteronomy and Joshua the formula was about the land sworn to the fathers; after the temple building the divine oath is realized). This symbiotic relation between land and temple is also reflected in the use of the word *māqôm* ('place'). In the first edition of Deuteronomy, *māqôm* is used in the traditional meaning of 'sanctuary'; in 12.11 it may well include a reference to the land. This is clearly the case in the exilic conclusion of the law code in 26.9; this verse states: '(Yahweh) brought us to this *māqôm*. He gave us this land.'

Since temple and land are closely interrelated, the destruction of the temple in 587 BCE and the deportation of the Judean elite (to which the Deuteronomists belonged) explain why the situation during this time is considered as anarchic (12.9). The cryptic expression of v. 9 may allude to cultic activities in the ruins of the temple, in Mizpah, or in Bethel during the time of Babylonian occupation (cf. Jer. 41.4–6).

Even if the temple remains a central symbol, the Deuteronomists must nevertheless face the problem of yahwistic worship outside of Judah among the deportees. Therefore, they enlarge the centralization formula, adding that Yahweh chooses the *māqôm* 'to make dwell his name'. There exists an Akkadian parallel to this expression (*šakanu šumšu*), which expresses a juridical claim of possession. In the context of exilic Deuteronomistic ideology, the formula implies a certain 'secularization'[35] of the temple: Yahweh does not dwell in the temple but in the sky (cf. also Deut. 26.15 and 1 Kgs 8). Although he may have his name dwell there, the divine presence no longer depends on the temple itself. After the deportation of the Judean elite to Babylon,

---

35.   Mettinger, T.N.D., *The Dethronement of Sabaoth: Studies in the Shem and Kabod Theologies* (trans. F.H. Cryer; ConBOT 18; Lund: Gleerup, 1982), pp. 36–37.

and the foundation of important Jewish colonies in Egypt there was no more geographical unity for the worshippers of Yahweh. Thus, the question about the meaning of cult centralization in a context of diaspora arose. This is the question, which the author of Deut. 12.2–7 tries to answer.

3.3. Deut. 12.2–7: Cult Centralization and the Rejection of 'Illegitimate' Cults in the Persian Period

Deut. 12 is framed by two aggressive texts (2–7; 29–31[36]). The theme of the unique sanctuary becomes here mainly a pretext for an ideology of strict separation from the 'nations' dwelling in the land. A comparable ideology is to be found in Deut. 7.1–6, 22–26 and 9.1–6. Adepts of the 'Göttingen School' (see the history of research) often attribute these texts to *DtrN*, which is to be dated around the end of the exile or, more likely, at the beginning of the Persian period.[37] Indeed, vocabulary and content corroborate this dating, as for instance the idiom 'to seek Yahweh' (v. 5), typical of the book of Chronicles.

This violent language is typical for a minority group which is afraid to lose either its identity or its power. If such a group feels itself in danger it will create ideological strategies to survive and such strategies often imply a very sharp opposition to the 'others'. In Deut. 12.2–7 the nations from which the addressees must separate are either figuring the globalization of the Persian empire, or more probably the 'people of the land', that is the Judean population who had not been deported by the Babylonians. Some representatives of the Babylonian Golah considered this population as not belonging to the 'true Israel'; consequently they were opposed to any (sexual or other) relations between the members of the Golah and the 'autochthonous' population (cf. Ezra. 9.1–3; Neh. 9.2; Neh. 13). The prescriptions in Deut. 12.2–4 indicate that the population that had remained in Judea was probably more 'conservative' in its religious practices than the deported intelligentsia and had not been quite eager to follow the Deuteronomistic cult

---

36. These two texts may well be attributed to the same redactor, even if 12.29–31 does not mention the law of centralization.

37. See on this Pakkala, J., *Intolerant Monolatry in the Deuteronomistic History* (Publications of the Finnish Exegetical Society 76; Helsinki and Göttingen: Finnish Exegetical Society and Vandenhoeck & Ruprecht, 1999), pp. 94–99.

centralization. The mention of all the places (*kol hammᵉqōmôt*) in v. 2 indicates the existence of local sanctuaries outside Jerusalem and the exhortation to eliminate the statues and names of other gods from 'this place' in v. 4 points to some 'unorthodox' cults in Jerusalem (see also Ezek. 8; Jer. 44.15–19, which bear witness to a continuing popular religiosity). The assertion of the centralization in vv. 4–6 is used to reinforce the ideological opposition between 'Israel' and the '*goyim*'.[38] If Deut. 12.2–7 presupposes the existence of the second temple, then it is noteworthy that contrary to Deut. 12.13–18, no allusion is made to a possibility of slaughter outside the temple. Nevertheless, Deut. 12.2–7 was not written to replace but to actualize the original statement; this actualization also took place in 12.20–27 which, as we have seen, was also written in the Persian period. It is therefore possible to ascribe vv. 2–7 and 20–27 to the same redactor who provided a 'frame' for the older texts in order to make the centralization ideology fit to a new historical context.

3.4. The Three Editions of Deut. 12 and Scribal Activity in the Deuteronomistic History

To sum up briefly our investigation on Deut. 12: This chapter reflects three stages of Deuteronomistic scribal activity.

- 12.13–18 was written about 620 BCE; this text provides an ideological legitimation for the politics of centralization under Josiah and delineates its practical implications.
- 12.8–12 is the outcome of an exilic redaction, which inserts the law of centralization in the larger context of a Deuteronomistic History extending from Joshua to 2 Kings (see in particular the links to 1 Kgs 8). It maintains the importance of the temple, even at a time when the latter is partially destroyed.
- Finally, 12.2–7 and 12.20–27 represent the last revision, probably from the Persian period. Verses 2–7 reveal an ideology of segregation. The main issue of the law of centralization has now become the prohibition and destruction of what are regarded as illegitimate cults.

38.　In Deut. 12.2, this term, which usually means 'nation', takes already the sense of 'pagan', like in post-biblical Hebrew.

A similar threefold redaction can be found in other texts of the Deuteronomistic History, for instance Josh. 7–8; 1 Sam. 8–12; 1 Kgs 8; 2 Kgs 22–23. Of course the model of three successive redactions of the Deuteronomistic History is somewhat schematic. In particular, we should probably reckon with redactional interventions not directly related to one of these three main editions. It is indeed quite plausible that in the context of Deuteronomistic scribal activity revisions were made on only one scroll or section of the Deuteronomistic History. It is quite possible for instance that a particular redactor updated the Judges but not the other parts; one must allow therefore for revisions, which did not encompass the totality of the Deuteronomistic History. However, it is often difficult to locate those redactions precisely, and they may tell us little about the general intention of the main editors of the Deuteronomistic History. Thus, the identification of the three main redactional layers within the Deuteronomistic History, corresponding to three distinct social, political and historical contexts (Neo-Assyrian, Neo-Babylonian and Persian), appears as the best working hypothesis. It is along the lines of this model, therefore, that the enquiry about the Deuteronomistic History will be undertaken in the following chapters.

Chapter 4

DEUTERONOMISTIC EDITING IN THE ASSYRIAN PERIOD AND ROYAL PROPAGANDA

1. The Beginning of Deuteronomistic Literary Production in the Seventh Century BCE

Select Bibliography

Na'aman, N., 'The Kingdom of Judah under Josiah', *Tel Aviv* 18 (1991), pp. 3–71.

Sweeney, M.A., *King Josiah of Judah: The Lost Messiah of Israel* (Oxford: Oxford University Press, 2001).

As already mentioned, Noth himself never considered the possibility of Deuteronomistic activity before the exile – a position still assumed by most German scholars. Yet a global exilic setting for all the Deuteronomistic texts in Deuteronomy to Kings makes it difficult to explain the following observations: the optimistic tone in some conquest stories, as well as the positive view of the Davidic dynasty, and the praise of the kings Hezekiah and Josiah in particular. These features suggest that some parts of the Deuteronomistic History (DH) at least originated in a period when the Judean kingship had not yet come to an end. Some scholars advocate the reign of Hezekiah for the beginning of Deuteronomistic literary activity, since he is presented as the most outstanding king since David (2 Kgs 18.1–6).[1] He is also said to have removed the open sanctuaries (*bāmôt*), which the foregoing Davidic kings who were otherwise judged positively had left in place

---

1.   See for instance Halpern, B., *The First Historians: The Hebrew Bible and History* (San Francisco, CA: Harper & Row, 1988) and Eynikel, E., *The Reform of King Josiah and the Composition of the Deuteronomistic History* (OTS; Leiden: Brill, 1996).

since Solomon (Asa: 1 Kgs 11.14; Jehoshaphat: 1 Kgs 22.44; Joash: 2 Kgs 12.4; Amaziah: 2 Kgs 14.4; Azariah: 2 Kgs 15.35). It is clear that Hezekiah's reign constitutes a first climax in the DH. But it is quite difficult to assume that there was a first edition of the DH that ended somewhere in 2 Kgs 18–20*. First of all the statement 'that there was no one like him among all the kings of Judah after him, or among those who were before him' (18.5) only makes sense in a time later than Hezekiah's.[2] 2 Kgs 18.5–6 is probably an addition from a redactor who looks back on the whole history and is unhappy with Josiah's shameful death. Driven by an ideology of retribution he therefore tries to rank Hezekiah before Josiah. Historically, there might have been a 'Zionist' and a nationalist revival under Hezekiah because of the aborted siege of Jerusalem by the Assyrians in 701. Hezekiah was probably also the first Judean king to benefit from the collapse of the Northern kingdom in 722. But on the other hand he had to submit to the Assyrian king Sennacherib and to pay a heavy tribute out of the temple's treasure (2 Kgs 18.14–16). Hezekiah had to suffer the destruction of the fortified city of Lachish and about fifty more Judean settlements; most of the southern part of the kingdom was destroyed and seems to have been rebuilt only under his successor Manasseh, who was a loyal vassal to the Assyrians.[3] There might have been a first attempt at 'cult-central-ization' under Hezekiah, due to the fact that important sanctuaries outside of Jerusalem had become unavailable.[4] Nevertheless, there was still such overwhelming Assyrian pressure during Hezekiah's time, that it seems more appropriate to locate the beginning of the Deuteronomistic literature under Josiah, unless one wants to make of the Deuteronomists an 'underground movement'. This sounds nice, but

---

2.   Consequently, Provan, I.W., *Hezekiah and the Book of Kings: A Contribution to the Debate about the Composition of the Deuteronomistic History* (BZAW 172; Berlin and New York: de Gruyter, 1988) postulates a first edition of the DH, ending with Hezekiah, but locates this edition under Josiah's reign.

3.   See on this Stern, E., *Archaeology of the Law of the Bible. II. The Assyrian, Babylonian, Persian Periods 732–332* BCE (ABRL; New York: Doubleday, 2001) pp. 130–31.

4.   Swanson makes the very interesting suggestion that historically the so-called reform of Hezekiah may have consisted in removing Egyptian cult symbols (the serpent) to symbolize his submission to Assyria; see Swanson, K.A., 'A Reassessment of Hezekiah's Reform in Light of Jar Handels and Iconographic Evidence', *CBQ* 64 (2002), pp. 460–69.

is not very realistic. Therefore, the most plausible solution remains to situate the origins of the Deuteronomistic school under Josiah;[5] this also complies with the Deuteronomistic self-understanding as expressed in 2 Kgs 22–23. Even this account cannot be taken as a historical source (at least in its present state): it clearly intends Josiah to stand out among the Judean kings as the 'new David' (2 Kgs 23.25); as to the high officials mentioned in this narrative they may well refer to the leading figures of the Deuteronomists. Above all, the end of the seventh century offers the most plausible historical setting for the emergence of Deuteronomistic literature.

Although any detailed reconstruction of Josiah's reign, which depends heavily on the narrative of 2 Kgs 22–23, is subject to caution, there is evidence enough of a change in the political situation of the Levant in the seventh century BCE. From the ninth century onwards, the influence of the Neo-Assyrian empire has been continuously growing in the region, and since the reign of Tiglath-Pileser (745–727), all kingdoms in Syria and Palestine are *de facto* under Assyrian domination. The Northern kingdom (Israel), which had a more developed economy and political structure than Judah and was therefore more attractive, was very quickly forced to become a vassal state. It definitely lost its political autonomy in 722, when its capital city, Samaria, was captured and the whole kingdom was integrated into the Assyrian provinces. The end of the Northern kingdom caused important demographic and social changes in Judah. Archaeological investigations clearly suggest a rise in population and an extension of the city of Jerusalem in the second half of the seventh century, probably after 722: 'In a matter of few decades – surely within a single generation – Jerusalem was transformed from a modest highland town of about ten or twelve acres to a huge urban area of 150 acres of closely packed houses, workshops, and public buildings. In demographic terms, the city's population may have increased as much as fifteen

---

5.   Of course, scribal activity certainly existed under Hezekiah (see Prov. 25.1), and one may, for instance, postulate a first edition of Kings under his reign (Moenikes, A., 'Beziehungssysteme zwischen dem Deuteronomium und den Büchern Josua bis Könige', in G. Braulik [ed.], *Das Deuteronomium* [Österreichische Bibelstudien 23; Frankfurt am Main: Peter Lang, 2003], pp. 69–85, argues for a scroll covering 1 Kgs 15.8–2 Kgs 19*). But it is difficult to reconstruct the extent and the contents of such a scroll.

times, from about one thousand to fifteen thousand inhabitants'.[6] These changes may be related to the arrival of refugees from Israel, but above all to the fact that Judah became integrated in the Assyrian 'world market'. These changes implied a reorganization of social and political structures in the Southern kingdom. Judah underwent an 'economic revolution',[7] the traditional system of clan-based and agricultural economics was opposed to a more and more centralized state power. We may therefore assume that Judean administration experienced an important development during the seventh century and became gradually professionalized. All these observations suggest that for the first time, the royal court in Jerusalem must have attained a certain degree of complexity. This development was probably achieved under the reign of Manasseh, whom the exilic edition of the DH depicts as the worst king in the history of Judah (2 Kgs 21), but who managed to maintain a peaceful situation by remaining loyal to the Assyrian empire. This non-controversial acceptance of Assyrian domination during the long reign of Manasseh (55 years according to 2 Kgs 21.1) must have played a significant role in the diffusion of Neo-Assyrian culture and propaganda in Judah. It is indeed very plausible that a copy of Manasseh's vassal treaty with the Assyrian king was kept in Jerusalem;[8] the Jerusalem scribes were undoubtedly aware of Assyrian propaganda and literary production.

The accession of Josiah to the throne in 639 coincided with a major political change in the region. The internal and external conflicts by which the Assyrian empire was confronted (struggles for succession to the throne and troubles on the north-eastern border) caused the diminution of its military presence in Syria-Palestine. This situation allowed the kingdom of Judah to aspire to a certain political autonomy, or at least to encourage nationalistic dreams among certain circles. If

---

6.   Finkelstein, I., and N.A. Silberman, *The Bible Unearthed: Archaeology's New Vision of Ancient Israel and the Origin of its Sacred Texts* (New York: Free Press, 2001), p. 243.

7.   According to an expression used by Finkelstein, *Bible Unearthed*, p. 246.

8.   The Assyrians kept one copy of each treaty in one of the three *pirru*, tax collection points (which were in Kahlu, Ninive and Dur Sarrukin), and probably handed over another copy to their vassals, cf. Steymans, H.U., 'Die neuassyrische Vertragsrhetorik der "Vassal Treaties of Esarhaddon" und das Deuteronomium', in G. Braulik (ed.), *Das Deuteronomium* (Österreichische Biblische Studien 23; Frankfurt am Main: Peter Lang, 2001), pp. 89–152, pp. 96–97.

there is any truth in the biblical report according to which Josiah came to the throne at the age of eight (2 Kgs 22.1), this probably means that the real power was in the hands of priests, scribes and of some important families at the royal court. The Deuteronomistic school probably participated in this coalition of members from these different social groups, with a clear nationalistic and Zionist orientation. Let us remember that the Shaphan family probably played a prominent role among the Deuteronomists since they are expressly mentioned in 2 Kgs 22 and Jer. 36. Interestingly, they are implicated in both texts in the transmission of a scroll containing instructions to which the king has to conform, which may be taken as reflecting the influence this family exercised inside the royal court.

If the origins of the literary activity of the Deuteronomistic school are to be located in this socio-historical context the Deuteronomistic work was first meant to support and encourage the nationalistic and expansionist politics of the 'Zionist party' in Jerusalem; thus it was merely a work of literary *propaganda*. The first Deuteronomistic scrolls did not need to have the thematic and chronological consistency of the thoroughgoing DH later published in the exile. Therefore, one should not think of a *unified* literary work under Josiah, but rather of a collection of different documents (scrolls) expressing the preoccupations of the nationalistic party, which may have been assembled in a library of a sort. As we will see in detail, these documents consisted in a collection of laws concerned with the political, economic and religious reorganizations of the Judean society at the end of the seventh century (mainly preserved in Deut. 12–25*); a conquest account mirroring certain military ambitions and territorial claims by Josiah and his generals (Josh. 3–12*); and a chronicle of the kings of Judah and Israel legitimating the Davidic dynasty and presenting Josiah as a David *redivivus* (Samuel*–Kings*). All of these different documents have parallels in the Mesopotamian court literature, and clearly reflect the influence of Neo-Assyrian culture among Judean scribes. Deuteronomy is very close to Assyrian law codes; Josh. 3–12* has interesting parallels in Neo-Assyrian conquest accounts; and the books of Kings are influenced by the literary genre of the Royal Chronicles.

Such parallels are another argument for seeing the origins of the Deuteronomistic literature in a *royal* context. The Assyrian texts also confirm the literary *independence* of the documents which came to form later the DH. This conclusion is further supported by literary-critical observations. The book of Judges presents scarce Deuteronomistic editorial activity, which sometimes differs considerably from the Deuteronomistic redactions of the foregoing and following books; and there is no conclusive reason to attribute any of the Deuteronomistic redaction in the book of Judges to the time of Josiah.

The summarizing speeches in Deuteronomy–Kings creating and linking the successive periods in the history of Israel and Judah clearly point to an exilic, or even postexilic, date; these texts frequently mention or allude to the loss of the land and to deportation; they also continuously stress the consequences of the disobedience of the people. Therefore, the existence of Deuteronomistic writings at the end of the seventh century does not imply that they were already arranged in a chronological sequence. However, some of the documents inside the Deuteronomistic library were probably already part of a larger tradition dealing with Israel's origins. This is clearly the case in the first editions of the books of Deuteronomy (if the legal instructions were already placed in the mouth of Moses, a point to which we will come back later) and of Joshua (Joshua being the successor of Moses). Blum, Otto and others have made a suggestive case for the existence of a Mosaic tradition in the seventh century,[9] and it is very tempting to assume that this tradition must also have belonged to the Deuteronomistic library. In that case, this *vita Mosis* probably served as an anti-Assyrian manifesto, as far as it presents Moses in opposition to Sargon, the (supposed) founder of the Assyrian monarchy (see in particular the narrative of the birth of Moses in Exod. 2); the liberation from forced labour in Egypt would then allude to the attempts, under the reign of Josiah, to get rid of the exigencies imposed by the Assyrian empire upon its vassals.

Now that we have suggested the possibility and the nature of Deuteronomistic literary activity in the second half of the seventh century, and briefly situated this activity in its socio-historical setting, we may review the different documents that we attributed to the Deuteronomistic library under the reign of Josiah.

---

9.   Blum, E., *Studien zur Komposition des Pentateuch* (BZAW 189; Berlin and New York: de Gruyter, 1990); Otto, E., 'Mose und das Gesetz. Die Mose-Figur als Gegenentwurf Politischer Theologie zur neuassyrischen Königsideologie im 7.Jh. v. Chr.', in *idem* (ed.), *Mose: Ägypten und das Alte Testament* (SBS 189; Stuttgart: Katholisches Bibelwerk, 2000), pp. 42–83. See also Römer, T., *Moïse 'lui que Yahvé a connu face à face'* (Découvertes 424; Paris: Gallimard, 2002).

2. The First Edition of Deuteronomy in the Assyrian Period

Select bibliography

Levinson, B.M., *Deuteronomy and the Hermeneutics of Legal Innovation* (New York and Oxford: Oxford University Press, 1997).

O'Brien, M.A., 'The Book of Deuteronomy', *CRBS* 3 (1995), pp. 95–128.

Parpola, S., and K. Watanabe, *Neo-Assyrian Treaties and Loyalty Oaths* (SAA 2; Helsinki: Helsinki University Press, 1988).

Römer, T., 'The Book of Deuteronomy', in S.L. McKenzie and M.P. Graham (eds), *The History of Israel's Tradition: The Heritage of Martin Noth* (JSOTSup 182; Sheffield: Sheffield Academic Press, 1994), pp. 178–212.

In its present form, the book of Deuteronomy is the result of a long redactional process, which is indicated by the following points: the book has at least two prologues (chs 1–3[4] and 5–11) and several conclusions (chs 26; 27–28; 30–34). Numerous laws in the core of the book (chs 12–26) do not presuppose the historical introductions (esp. chs 1–4; 9–10), which tend to integrate Deuteronomy into a larger historical perspective, with several allusions to parallel episodes in Exodus and Numbers. These chapters underwent several stages of editions, as can be shown by inconsistent statements[10] or changes of style. In this context, one has to mention the so-called *Numeruswechsel*; this term designates the frequent alternation of second person singular and plural forms of address.[11] This criterion is often used in order to determine the successive stages of growth within Deuteronomy: thus, it is often claimed that the texts in the *plural* belong to exilic redactors, whereas texts recurring with a *singular* form of address should be seen as belonging to the original book of Deuteronomy.[12] But this view is certainly oversimplified, as can be seen in the following example:

10. See for instance Deut. 10: the report of Moses sojourning on the Mountain of Yahweh seems to come to an end in vv. 6–9, which relate the departure of the people, the death of Aaron and institutions concerning the Levites; nevertheless in vv. 10–12, Moses is again on the mountain. Verses 6–9 are clearly later additions (which are to be distinguished in vv. 6–7 and 8–9).

11. This phenomenon is unfortunately not apparent in current English translations of the Hebrew Bible. In the following example we will use 'thou', 'thee' to designate the second person singular.

12. This view was put forward by G. Minette de Tillesse, 'Sections "Tu" et sections "Vous" dans le Deutéronome', *VT* 12 (1962), pp. 29–87.

> These are the statutes and ordinances *that you must diligently observe* in the land that Yahweh, the God of thy fathers, has given thee *to occupy all the days that you live on earth* (Deut. 12.1).

It is impossible to reconstruct here an original sentence in the singular and it does not make much sense either to postulate for this verse three redactional levels.

Consequently, some scholars consider the combination of singular and plural forms as a purely *stylistic* device. There are indeed numerous texts in Deuteronomy where it is impossible to postulate a new stratum for each change of form of address; and the phenomenon of *Numeruswechsel*, which in the Hebrew Bible is not limited to Deuteronomy (see also Exod. 23.20–33; Lev. 19), also appears in non-biblical texts, in the Sefire inscription, as well as in Assyrian treaties. The following example comes from a treaty of Esarhaddon:[13] '(92) Thou shall keep absolute loyalty with respect to Assurbanipal ... on behalf of whom Esarhaddon, king of Assyria, has concluded (this) treaty with you.'

In Deuteronomy, the oscillation between singular and plural pronouns *may* indicate in some cases the presence of different diachronic strata, probably in the earliest stages of development (see III.3 above on Deut. 12). For later redactors, the combination already existed, and they could easily have imitated it.

2.1. Deuteronomy and Assyrian Treaty Literature

The conclusion of vassal treaties is a quite common feature in the Near East since the second millennium BCE. In those treaties the suzerain king puts down different stipulations to which the vassal kings have to conform. The central idea is to constrain the vassals to an absolute loyalty to their lord. Curses, and often also blessings, are an important part of those treaties; they provide motivations for the necessity of submission. The book of Deuteronomy undoubtedly resembles such treaties. Since treaties occur already under the Hittite emperors (second half of the second millennium BCE), some scholars have used this analogy to claim a second-millennium date for Deuteronomy. This

---

13.   For an English translation see Parpola and Watanabe, *Neo-Assyrian Treaties*, pp. 28–58

apologetic view is impossible: there is no social location during the second part of the second millennium BCE for editing such a document in Judah or Israel (which do not even exist at the time).

On the contrary, there are clear links between Deuteronomy and the Neo-Assyrian loyalty oaths, and these links even suggest literary dependency. Especially important are the *adê* (loyalty oaths) of Esarhaddon written in 672 BCE. This document focuses on the recognition by the vassal kings of Assurbanipal as the legitimate successor to Esarhaddon and opens with a list of divine witnesses. The following stipulations of loyalty insist on 'love' for Assurbanipal and the necessity for future generations to keep the commandments:

> (266–68) You shall love Assurbanipal ... king of Assyria, your lord, as yourself.
> (195–97) You shall hearken to whatever he says and do whatever he commands, and you shall not seek any other king or other lord against him.
> (283–91) This treaty ... you shall speak to your sons and grandsons, your seed and your seed's seed which shall be born in the future.

These stipulations are very close to Deut. 6.4, a text that is very often considered as the original opening of Deuteronomy:

> Hear, Israel: Yahweh is our God, Yahweh is One. You shall love Yahweh your God with all your heart, with all your life and with all your might ... Keep these words that I am commanding you today on your heart and teach them to your sons (Deut. 6.4–7a).

As we have already seen, the original Deuteronomic code opened with the centralization law in 12.13–18; this law is linked to the next chapter, Deut. 13, by the same ideology of centralization. Interestingly Deut. 13 also parallels stipulations from the Esarhaddon vassal treaty, which warns against instigators of insurrection.[14] The opening verse 13.1, 'You must diligently observe everything I command to you; do not add to it or take anything from it', is probably inspired by similar

---

14.   For these parallels see esp. Dion, P.E., 'The Suppression of Alien Religious Propaganda in Israel during the Late Monarchical Era', in B. Halpern and D.W. Hobson (eds), *Law and Ideology in Monarchical Israel* (JSOTSup 124; Sheffield: Sheffield Academic Press, 1991), pp. 147–216, and Otto, E., *Das Deuteronomium: Politische Theologie und Rechtsreform in Juda und Assyrien* (BZAW 284; Berlin and New York: de Gruyter, 1999), pp. 14–90.

statements in the Esarhaddon treaty: (57) 'You shall neither change nor alter the word of Esarhaddon, king of Assyria.'

The original text of Deut. 13 was concerned with high treason against Yahweh:

> (2a) If appears among you an ecstatic or a visionary (3*) and he says to you: 'Let us follow other gods and let us serve them' (4a) you shall not take heed of the words of the ecstatic or the visionary. (5) But Yahweh, your God, you shall follow, him alone you shall fear, his commandments you shall keep, his voice you shall obey, him you shall serve, to him you shall hold fast. (6aα) And this ecstatic or visionary shall be put to death for having spoken treason against Yahweh, your God. (7abα) If anyone secretly entices you, your brother, your mother's son, or your son or your daughter, or the wife of your heart, or the friend you love as yourself, saying: 'Let us go and serve other gods', (9) you must not yield to him or follow him. Show him no pity or compassion and do not conceal it. (10) But you shall surely kill him.[15]

This commandment is best understood as an adaptation from prescriptions of Esarhaddon:

> (108–123*): If you hear any evil, improper, ugly word which is not seemly or good to Assurbanipal ... from the mouth of your brothers, your sons, your daughters, or from the mouth of a prophet, an ecstatic, an inquirer of oracles, or from the mouth of any human being at all, you shall not conceal it, but come and report it to Assurbanipal...
> [See also 201–11, esp. 'you shall not listen to him or let him go away, but you must guard him strongly until one of you, who loves his lord ... goes to the palace', and 502 'speaking treason against Assurbanipal']
> (138–40) If you are able to seize them and put them to death, then you shall destroy their name and their seed from the land.

The author of Deut. 13 who copied from Esarhaddon's treaty meant to apply the ideology of an absolute and exclusive loyalty to the relation between Yahweh and 'Israel';[16] in Deuteronomy, Yahweh

---

15.   For the reconstruction of this text see, although with some differences, Otto, *Deuteronomium*.

16.   The term Israel from the tenth to the seventh century BCE was the designation of the 'Northern Kingdom' whose capital was Samaria. When Israel ceased to exist as a political unity, it became an ideological term for the 'people of Yahweh' and was probably claimed by Josiah (the same happened to the 'Holy Roman Empire').

takes over the position of the Assyrian king. Another part of Deuteronomy is also adapted from the same treaty: the list of curses in Deut. 28.20–44.[17] Let us restrict ourselves to the following examples:

Deut. 28

> (24) Yahweh will change the rain of your land into powder, and dust shall come down from the sky until you are destroyed.
>
> (26) Your corpse shall be food for every bird of the sky and animal of the earth, and there shall be no one to frighten them away.
>
> (27) Yahweh will strike you with the boils of Egypt, with ulcers, scurvy, and itch, of which you cannot be healed.
>
> (28) Yahweh will strike you with madness, blindness, and confusion of mind.

Vassal Treaty of Esarhaddon

> (530) Just as rain does not fall from a brazen heaven so may rain and dew not come upon your fields and your meadows; instead of dew may burning coals rain on your land.
>
> (425–27) May Ninurta, the foremost among the gods, fell you with his fierce arrow; may he fill the plain with your blood and feed your flesh to the eagle and the vulture.
>
> (419–21) May Sin, the brightness of heaven and earth, clothe you with leprosy and forbid you entering into the presence of the gods and of the king. Roam the desert like the wild ass and the gazelle.
>
> (422–24) May Shamash, the light of heaven and earth, not judge you justly. May he remove your eyesight. Walk about in darkness.

These and other parallels[18] only allow the conclusion that a copy of this treaty was available in Jerusalem, which strongly influenced the

---

17. Steymans, H.U., *Deuteronomium 28 und die adê zur Thronfolgeregelung Asarhaddons: Segen und Fluch im Alten Orient und in Israel* (OBO 145; Freiburg (Switzerland) and Göttingen: Universitätsverlag and Vandenhoeck & Ruprecht, 1995).

18. For instance, Deut. 28.38–44 correspond to the themes of VTE 490–93: food, drinks, ointment, home. For more details and other parallels see Steymans, *Deuteronomium* and Otto, E., 'Die Ursprünge der Bundestheologie im Alten Testament und im Alten Orient', *Zeitschrift für Altorientalische und Biblische Rechtsgeschichte* 4 (1998), pp. 1–84, pp. 41–43.

first edition of Deuteronomy. Otto thinks that Deut. 13* and 28* first existed independently as a loyalty oath for Yahweh before they were combined with other texts of the Law code. But one may perceive Assyrian influence also in other chapters of Deuteronomy,[19] so that this assumption remains quite speculative.

2.2. Content, Concerns and Ideology of the First Edition of Deuteronomy

The first edition of Deuteronomy started with Deut. 6.4–5(6–7a) and ended with the curses of Deut. 28. In its centre stood the centralization and loyalty laws in chs 12* and 13*; as well as the following prescriptions, which in a certain way can be understood as consequences of the ideology of centralization. Most of these laws actualize the older prescriptions of the Covenant Code and adapt them to the new social and economic situation under Josiah. Deut 14.21–29[20] centralizes the payment of the yearly taxes (the 'tithe'), which were formerly collected by the local sanctuaries. The social prescriptions in Deut. 15* may be understood as a compensation for the loss of economic power by the local sanctuaries, but in a more general way the chapter applies to all the poor within the Judean society. This social concern results from the perturbation of the traditional clannish and familial structures after the destruction of the Judean countryside by the Assyrians, the deportation of parts of the rural population and the installation of peasants in fortified towns under Hezekiah. Judah's development under Manasseh and Josiah was linked to the growth of urban population, whereas the population of the countryside experienced economic difficulties which could no more be resolved by the appeal to clannish solidarity. Therefore the central power had to be concerned about social cohesion.

In Deut. 16.1–17 the law of centralization is applied to the three major annual festivals (Passover, festival of weeks, tabernacles) as shown by the quotation from 12.17–18 in 16.5–6 (see also vv. 11 and

---

19.   We have seen that Deut 6.4–7 also depends on the same treaty of Esarhaddon.

20.   Deut. 14.1–20 is a later insertion, which, in a priestly style, gives complementary information about clean and unclean animals.

15). The law about judges (*šōpheṭîm*) and state officers (*šōṭerîm*)[21] in 16.18 and 17.8–13*[22] most probably reflects the creation of professional judges, who may have existed before in Jerusalem, but who now also control any jurisprudence outside the capital. This law is motivated by a desire of control and standardization.

The origin and intention of the law about the king (Deut. 17.14–20) are heavily disputed. It is often said to have belonged to the Josianic edition of Deuteronomy.[23] According to Dutcher-Walls this law reflects a corporate power strategy; it reveals the attempt of the Deuteronomists who belong to the Judean elite to limit the king's power. The restriction of royal power should be understood as the attempt to create 'a careful balance between being loyal to Yahweh and being loyal to Assyria, that is, that the king can be both a good servant of Yahweh and a good vassal to Assyria'.[24] In the ancient Near East, high officials, especially scribes, could undoubtedly exercise some control on the king, who very often was unable to read or to write, and this is certainly also true of Josiah. But the presence of such a 'law' in

21.   It is quite possible that this title and function were taken over from the Assyrian administration, cf. Gertz, J.C., *Die Gerichtsorganization Israels im deuteronomischen Gesetz* (FRLANT 165; Göttingen: Vandenhoeck & Ruprecht, 1994), pp. 82–84.

22.   16.19–17.7 interrupt the law about the judges and are later additions. 16.19–20 is a general exhortation (addressed in the second pers.) about the necessity to pursue justice; 17.1–8 presents a case of worship of other gods and is inspired by Deut. 13. In 17.8–13, vv. 9b and 10 were added later as well as the transformation of the priest into a levitical priest (v. 9a). For a diachronic analysis of these texts see Gertz, *Gerichtorganization*, and Morrow, W.S., *Scribing the Center: Organization and Redaction in Deuteronomy 14:1–17:13* (SBLMS 49; Atlanta, GA: Scholars Press, 1995).

23.   See among recent publications Knoppers, G.N., 'The Deuteronomist and the Deuteronomic Law of the King: A Reexamination of a Relationship', *ZAW* 108 (1996), pp. 329–46; Levinson, B.M., 'The Reconceptualization of Kingship in Deuteronomy and the Deuteronomistic History's Transformation of the Torah', *VT* 51 (2001), pp. 511–34, and Dutcher-Walls, P., 'The Circumscription of the King: Deuteronomy 17:16–17 in Its Ancient Social Context', *JBL* 121 (2002), pp. 601–16.

24.   Dutcher-Walls, 'Circumscription', p. 616. In former publications, she underlines the existence of conflicting factions among the elite class in agrarian societies (see esp. Dutcher-Walls, P., 'The Social Location of the Deuteronomists: A Sociological Study of Factory Politics in Late Pre-Exilic Judah', *JSOT* 52 [1991], pp. 77–94).

the Josianic edition of Deuteronomy would be astonishing: it has no parallels in other Near Eastern law codes. And even if the 'Josianic reform' was strongly supported by the Deuteronomists, they would not so openly restrict the king's power in an 'official' publication. The 'king's law', as it now stands, is not a law but much more an introduction to the story of the failure of monarchy as related in the exilic edition of the books of Samuel and Kings;[25] consequently we will come back to this text when dealing with the exilic edition of the DH. The stipulations about priestly income and the possibility for the local Levites to enrol in the staff of the central sanctuary (18.1–8*) stem from the Josianic edition of Deuteronomy, whereas the law about prophets is probably due to the exilic redactor. The institution of cities of asylum in 19.2a, 3b, 4–6, 11–12[26] is a logical consequence of the centralization law; traditionally the local sanctuaries were places of asylum. Their (theoretical) closing down necessitated substitutes for this function. The laws of warfare in ch. 20 probably did not belong to the first edition of Deuteronomy, even if the prohibition against the destruction of fruit trees (20.19–20) may be understood as polemic against an Assyrian practice. The function of Deut. 20 is less legal than programmatic. It prepares the conquest accounts in the book of Joshua. The social and cultic laws in 21.1–4, 5–9*, 15–21*; 22*; 23.18–26;[27] 24.1–25.16* are quite common in ancient Near Eastern law codes (see the parallels with the Covenant Code, the Code of Hammurabi and also with Assyrian Law Codes[28]). They fit well with royal ideology according to which the king is the protector of the poor

25.   An exilic setting of Deut. 17. is also advocated by Otto, E., 'Von der Gerichtsordnung zum Verfassungsentwurf. Deuteronomische Gestaltung und deuteronomistische Interpretation im "Ämtergesetz" Dtn 16,18–18,22', in I. Kottsieper *et al.* (eds), '*Wer ist wie du, Herr, unter den Göttern?*': *Studien zur Theologie und Religionsgeschichte Israels* (Festschrift O. Kaiser; Göttingen: Vandenhoeck & Ruprecht, 1994), pp. 142–55.

26.   For this reconstruction of the original law, see Gertz, Gerichtsorganization, pp. 118–27.

27.   The 'law' against male and female (cultic) prostitutes in vv. 18–20 is understandable in the context of an ideology of exclusive yahwism, since those prostitutes are associated with the goddess Ishtar (maybe Asherah in Judah). A similar concern may be detected in the prohibition of transvestism in 22.5, which is also related with the cult of Ishtar. Since this verse interrupts the theme of behaviour towards animals in vv. 1–4 and 6–7, 22.5 might be a later addition.

28.   For details see Otto, *Deuteronomium*.

and the weak in his kingdom. Deut. 26.2*, 3a, 10–11* conclude the first edition of the Deuteronomic prescriptions. These verses refer back to main themes of the overture in Deut. 12.13–18: the one sanctuary chosen by Yahweh (cf. 26.2 and 12.18) and the offering of the first fruits at the sanctuary, which is a sign of Yahweh's bounty (26.10–11 and 12.17–18). Thus the whole law code is dominated by the ideology of centralization. The code ended with the curses in Deut. 28* (see above)[29] and perhaps with the invocation of heaven and earth as (divine) witnesses in 30.19a.

The Deuteronomic law code of the seventh century can be understood as a programme for the reorganization of the Judean state in order to provide more power to its centre. The numerous parallels with Assyrian documents, especially the Esarhaddon treaty, concord with the strong influence of Assyrian culture on all the states of the Levant. But the fact that the Deuteronomistic scribes did in some cases almost copy the Esarhaddon treaty may also reveal a subversive or a polemical intention. Presenting Deuteronomy as a treaty between Yahweh and Judah ('Israel'), they also underline the fact that Judah's suzerain is not the Assyrian king and the deities he represents but Yahweh the 'only' (national) god of Judah–Israel. A quite similar intention can be detected in the first edition of the book of Joshua.

3. Political and Military Propaganda in the Book of Joshua

Select Bibliography

Nelson, R.D., *Joshua: A Commentary* (Old Testament Library; Louisville, KY: Westminster John Knox Press, 1997).

Rowlett, L.L., *Joshua and the Rhetoric of Violence: A New Historicist Analysis* (JSOTSup 226; Sheffield: Sheffield Academic Press, 1996).

Van Seters, J., 'Joshua's Campaign of Canaan and Near Eastern Historiography', *SJOT* 2 (1990), pp. 1–12.

Younger, K.L, Jr, *Ancient Conquest Accounts: A Study in Ancient Near Eastern and Biblical History Writing* (JSOTSup 98; Sheffield: JSOT Press, 1990).

29.   If the Josianic edition of Deuteronomy is mainly inspired by Esarhaddon's treaty, we may assume that, following the Assyrian model, it only contained curses but no blessing.

3.1. The Problem of Composition in Joshua

The book of Joshua can easily be divided into two main parts, containing very different types of materials. Josh. 2–12 is mainly a narrative relating the preparation and realization of the conquest, while most of chs 13–22 contains lists with the territories and boundaries of the tribes of Israel after their settlement. The whole book is framed by speeches of Yahweh and Joshua (Josh. 1; Josh. 23–24). The age and provenance of the various materials contained in these two sections are widely debated today, but, in any case, the obvious difference of genre clearly suggests that chs 2–12 and 13–22 must have undergone a separate development. The framing speeches (Josh. 1 and 23–24) are generally attributed to the Deuteronomistic editions of the book; but Josh. 24 is, as we will see, probably even later (postexilic).

The origins of the lists preserved in Josh. 13–19 (20–21) are difficult to determine. Most scholars located them in the context of royal administration, and some even attributed parts of the lists of the tribal territories to the time of Judges.[30] On the other hand, some scholars, in particular due to the presence of Priestly style and terminology in these chapters, see all the lists in Josh. 13–21 as late creations from the postexilic period.[31] One has to agree that the biblical view of Israel's organization in twelve tribes is a late projection without any historical basis; a setting for a list including twelve tribes earlier than the Israelite monarchy should therefore be abandoned. However, one may wonder whether it is entirely satisfying to attribute all the lists in Josh. 13–21 to authors of the Babylonian or Persian period; we may not exclude that some of them come from royal archives and may reflect attempts at territorial reorganization under Josiah. Josh. 15.20–62 and 18.21–28 could reflect the districts of Judah about 620 BCE including Benjamin. But it is clear that the present form of these lists comes from a much later period, as already indicated by the combination of Priestly and Deuteronomistic styles in these chapters.

The narrative section in Josh. 2–12 must also have undergone a complex genesis. In any case, it is clear that the traditional view concerning the origins of the conquest account cannot be maintained

---

30.   Especially Alt; for more details see the above history of research.

31.   Cf. Van Seters, J., *In Search of History: History in the Ancient World and the Origin of Biblical History* (New Haven, NY: Yale University Press, 1983), pp. 331–37.

any longer. This view was based on the observation that the detailed conquest accounts in Josh. 6–9 are taking place in the territory of Benjamin. A. Alt and M. Noth drew the conclusion that these accounts were originally local traditions from the end of the second millennium BCE; their purpose was to explain the settlement of the tribe of Benjamin. Later, a Judean editor would have collected and revised these aetiologies, applying to them a pan-Israelite perspective.

Since in the present narrative the hero, Joshua, comes from the North, from the tribe of Ephraim, Alt and Noth had to suppose that an original Benjaminite hero had later been suppressed and replaced by Joshua. This is entirely speculation. Moreover, the existence of a widespread literary activity in southern Palestine at the beginning of the first millennium has been challenged by socio-archaeological investigations. Finally, Alt and Noth's reconstruction presupposes a conception of the *exogenous* origin of Israel (by conquest or slow infiltration), which seems impossible to maintain. There is no reasonable doubt that the emergence of early Israel (mentioned in the victory stele of Pharaoh Merneptah at the end of the thirteenth century BCE) was an outcome of socio-economic changes in Canaan. Most of the early Israelites were local people who settled in the highlands of Canaan.[32]

As to the 'Benjaminite setting' of Josh. 6–9, which still needs explanation, it appears that the Neo-Assyrian and Neo-Babylonian conquest accounts offer a much safer start for this investigation than some dubious considerations on the supposed tribal origins of Israel.

3.2. Neo-Assyrian Conquest Accounts and their Significance for the First Edition of Joshua

Conquest accounts are quite common in the ancient Near East, and play an important role in court ideology; such accounts can be found in Hittite, Egyptian and Mesopotamian literature. We have several witnesses from Neo-Assyrian literature in particular, where conquest accounts seem to have been one of the major genres used for royal propaganda.[33] It is clear that these accounts are not 'realistic' or

---

32.   On the question of the Israelite origins see Finkelstein and Silberman, *Bible Unearthed*, pp. 97–122.

objective descriptions of historical events. They reflect the nationalistic and militaristic self-understanding of the Assyrians and belong to strategies of 'psychological warfare', as can be seen already from the presence of manifold stereotypes in these accounts. Interestingly, Neo-Assyrian conquest accounts in particular reveal numerous parallels with the stories in Josh. 6–12; this phenomenon can only be explained by literary dependence.

The elements occurring most frequently in the Assyrian accounts are the following:

> a. The conquest of certain strategic places is told at great length, whereas other defeated places or lands appear in summarizing statements.
> b. Before waging war, the king receives a salvation oracle from the tutelary deity.
> c. The accounts also stress the voluntary submission of foreign peoples, some of which have even come from afar to surrender to the king.
> d. Enemies are often organized in impressive coalitions.
> e. The Assyrian army is nevertheless always victorious due to the miraculous interventions of the Assyrian gods.
> f. Complete victory frequently implies putting to death enemy kings, who try in vain to escape.

All these elements can also be found in the book of Joshua.

> a. Josh. 6–12 relates in detail the conquest of Jericho and Ai-Bethel (chs 6–8), whereas the subsequent victories are told in a more enumerative manner (10.28–12.24).
> b. Josh. 10.8 contains an oracle of salvation for Joshua, delivered by Yahweh at the edge of a decisive battle: 'Fear not, for I have handed them over to you; not one of them shall stand before you' (see also Josh. 1.3–6; 11.6). This oracle is very close to numerous oracles given to Esarhaddon by prophets of the goddess Ishtar, assuring him of future victory, as in the following example (SAA 9 1.1). 'Esarhaddon, king of the lands, fear not … I am Ishtar of Arbela, I will flay your enemies and deliver them up to you. I am Ishtar of Arbela, I go before you and behind you'.[34]

33.   These texts are conveniently collected and discussed in Younger, *Ancient Conquest Accounts*.

34.   Quoted from Nissinen, M., *Prophets and Prophecy in the Ancient Near East* (Writings from the Ancient World 12; Atlanta, GA: Society of Biblical Literature, 2003), p. 102.

c. The motif of voluntary submission from foreign peoples is also attested in Josh. 9 where the Gibeonites, wishing to become vassals of the Israelites, pretend to come from far away. They are integrated and 'protected' by the Israelite army, as are the vassals of Assyria.

d. Josh. 10.1–5 describes an impressive coalition of five 'Amorite' kings, which Joshua will defeat with the help of Yahweh.

e. Josh. 10.10–11 has a parallel in a text of the Assyrian king Sargon II, called 'Letter to the God'. This text relates the victory of the Assyrian army thanks to an intervention of the storm god Hadad. Both texts relate a great slaughter of the enemies on the descent or ascent of a mountain and both stories are followed by divine military intervention. 'The rest of the people, who had fled to save their lives ... Adad, the violent, the son of Anu, the valiant, uttered his loud cry against them; and with flood cloud and stones of heaven, he totally annihilated the remainder'.[35] Josh. 10.11 reports in a similar way: 'As they fled before Israel, while they were going down the slope of Beth-horon, Yahweh threw down huge stones from heaven on them as far as Azekah, and they died; there were more who died because of the hailstones than the Israelites killed with the sword.'

f. The campaigns of King Sennacherib all include the annihilation of the fugitives and the death of the enemy kings or governors: 'And the mighty princes feared my battle array; they fled their abodes, and like bats (living in) cracks (caves), they flew alone to inaccessible places ... the governors (and) nobles who had sinned I put to death; and I hung their corpses on poles around the city'.[36] These texts are very close to Josh. 10.16 and 26: 'Meanwhile, these five kings fled and hid themselves in the cave at Makkedah (...) Joshua struck them down and put them to death, and he hung them on five trees. And they hung on the trees until evening.'

These parallels suggest that the conquest accounts in the book of Joshua were directly influenced by the genre and ideology of Neo-Assyrian warfare accounts; therefore, they are hardly earlier than the eighth or seventh century BCE.[37] As a matter of fact, it is no surprise

35.   Younger, *Ancient Conquest Accounts*, p. 210.

36.   Quoted from Younger, *Ancient Conquest Accounts*, pp. 221 and 223. The report of Assurbanipal's campaign against the Elamites also contains interesting parallels to Josh. 10, for the text see Nissinen, *Prophets*, pp. 146–50.

37.   As already mentioned, military accounts are not limited to Assyrian and Babylonian texts, but can be found in nearly the whole ancient Near East. The themes of the deity chasing the defeated enemies before his people, and of the ban on the captives (who are supposed to be put to death), occur also, for instance, in the stele of the Moabite king Mesha (around 840 BCE). Nevertheless, the most precise and direct parallels to the conquest accounts of the Hebrew Bible are within the Neo-Assyrian documents.

that the royal scribes in Jerusalem knew of the Neo-Assyrian documents, and chose to imitate them in their attempt to create a literature of conquest legitimizing Judah's national autonomy, for the Assyrians had developed remarkable propaganda strategies. Documents (such as those we discussed above), inscriptions, all sorts of iconographic resources (drawings, bas-reliefs, etc.) and even rituals were mobilized in order to manifest the military supremacy of the Neo-Assyrian king. This is the case in the frequent representations showing a city's siege in which Assyrian soldiers are often pictured as being several times taller than their opponents and sometimes even as tall as the city itself, thus clearly suggesting the overwhelming superiority of the Assyrian army. It would not be a mere exaggeration to speak of a 'psychological warfare', suggesting to the besieged populations that resistance is hopeless and that their local gods are of no help. This Assyrian strategy is reflected in the Hebrew Bible, in 2 Kgs 18–19. These chapters relate Jerusalem's siege under Hezekiah (701 BCE); according to this story, the Assyrian king sends a high official. He delivers a speech to the inhabitants of the Judean capital telling them that the gods of the nations are unable to resist the Assyrian ruler and asking them to give up their national god and to surrender to the Assyrian supremacy. The deportation of the gods of the captured cities into Assyrian temples, which are well attested, also had the function of visualizing the dominance of Assyria and of its gods over the defeated countries. Therefore, the Jerusalemite scribes could not ignore this massive propaganda, and it is only logical that it constituted their main source of inspiration when they composed the first version of the conquest accounts in Joshua.

3.3. The Function of the First Conquest Account in Josiah's Time (Josh. 5–12*)

As we have already seen, the most favourable social and political context for the beginnings of the Deuteronomistic literary activity is the time of Josiah. Like Deuteronomy, the first edition of Joshua would have served very well the national policy of Josiah and his advisers. This edition probably consisted almost exclusively of narratives of battle and conquest; imitating the genre of Assyrian propaganda, it was aimed at affirming Judah's political and military independence, at a time when Assyrian influence was declining in the region.

As a result, the Judean god Yahweh was presented as taking over the main characteristics of the Assyrian national god Assur and as being, therefore, the warrant for the political autonomy of his people.

It is no longer possible to reconstruct the precise extent of the primitive version of the book of Joshua. It may have started with Joshua's investiture in Josh. 5.13–14, although it is obvious that the text as it stands now cannot constitute the original beginning of the story of Joshua; nevertheless, this short episode provides a good introduction to the following accounts, since Joshua is divinely designated as military leader. This text also has a close parallel in the report of Assurbanipal's campaign against Elam; this campaign is preceded by a vision in which a prophet sees the goddess Ishtar armed and standing in front of the king telling him that she will fight for him in his war against the Elamites:

> Ishtar who dwells in Arbela entered, having quivers hanging from her right and left and holding a bow in her hand. She had drawn a sharp pointed sword, ready for battle. You stood before her and she spoke to you like a mother who gave birth to you … You said to her: 'Wherever you go, I will go with you!' But the Lady of Ladies answered you: 'You stay here in your place! … until I go accomplish that task'.[38]

In the book of Joshua, the vision was originally followed by 6.2, which introduces the story of Jericho's conquest.[39] This story opens the cycle of the conquests in Josh. 5–12* with an exemplary account, showing how Israel's victories are all due to Yahweh's miraculous intervention. The story was probably originally limited to the following verses: 6.2a, 3, 4b*, 5, 11, 14–15, 20b–21, 27. It reports the main elements for a successful conquest according to the Jerusalemite scribes: the mediation of Joshua, who stands here for the king as intermediary between the national deity and the people and who clearly alludes to *Josiah*, the obedience of the people, and the execution of the ban on the captured city as a sign of consecration of the victory to God. The conquest of Jericho was initially immediately followed by

38.   Quoted from Nissinen, *Prophets*, pp. 147–48.

39.   Yahweh's reply in 5.15 cannot be the original answer to Joshua's question in 5.14. But his declaration in 6.2 would offer a good answer to this question, and follows smoothly after 5.14, so that it is likely that 5.15 and 6.1 are later interpolations. 5.15 apparently sought to establish a parallel between Joshua and Moses, cf. Exod. 3.5.

the conquest of Ai in Josh. 8*, the story of Achan being most likely a later interpolation. But whereas Josh. 6* emphasized divine intervention in the capture of the city, in the story of Ai's conquest the accent is put upon the military strategies used by Joshua and the army of Israel. Thus, the core of the episode is formed by the description of the ambush by which Joshua managed to defeat the inhabitants of Ai and Bethel. The original version probably included 8.1–2*, 10–12, 14–16, 19b, 20–21, 23, 25, 27, 29.

The mention in this narrative of *Bethel* alongside Ai is particularly remarkable (cf. 8.12). At first sight, this mention is surprising in a story relating the conquest of Ai. However, this makes perfect sense in the context of Josiah's reign, since this town along with Jericho and Gibeon (the submission of which is related in Josh. 9*) represent major cultural and political centres in the Benjaminite region, and would logically have been the most immediate targets for Josiah's politics of national and territorial expansion. It is difficult to know how successful Josiah's campaign was. According to 2 Kgs 23.15, Josiah destroyed the sanctuary in Bethel, but this notice may be a late fiction without any historical basis. Yet, even if we have no historical record for the annexation of Benjamin under Josiah, Benjamin would have constituted the first step for a campaign aiming at conquering some of the Northern territories under the Neo-Assyrian hegemony. The fact that under Neo-Babylonian rule, Benjamin and Judah could be grouped in a single administrative entity (the capital of which was most probably Mizpah) would also suggest that the Neo-Babylonian conquerors already perceived these two regions as forming somehow a political and territorial unity; this situation is also reflected in some biblical texts, for instance Jer. 17.26; 32.44; 33.13.

The story of the treaty with the inhabitants of Gibeon in Josh. 9 is not a conquest account strictly speaking, yet it reflects both an actual practice in the Neo-Assyrian policies of conquest and occupation and a literary device frequent in the scribal tradition of propaganda, where foreign peoples are depicted as surrendering spontaneously to the Assyrian king. According to the Neo-Assyrian ideology, the conclusion of such treaties warranted protection for the peoples surrendering, which became thus the vassals (in administrative language: the 'friends') of the Assyrian king. In the original episode of Josh. 9, which may have included 9.3–6, 8b and 9–15a*, the Gibeonites are represented in a similar fashion: having heard of the reputation of Joshua after his victory over Jericho and Ai, they choose to surrender to him. Joshua is here presented in the manner of the Assyrian suzerain who receives the allegiance of his vassals and protects them in return, as is shown in the following story (Josh. 10). In this chapter, Joshua acts as a suzerain defending the Gibeonites who had become his vassals against impressive coalitions of enemies, who are finally defeated. The idea of large coalitions of enemies whose kings are finally put to death (10.1–5 and 16–27) is a favourite theme in the Neo-Assyrian conquest accounts, as well as the pronouncement of a divine oracle announcing the victory (10.8) and the intervention of the deity itself (10.10–11). But the Deuteronomistic authors of Josh. 10* go even further than their literary model; they describe on this occasion Joshua's control even over the sun and the moon themselves (10.12–13) which are important Assyrian deities, thus implying the superiority of Yahweh (and his chosen leader) over the Assyrian pantheon.

Thus, Josh. 6–10* presents the reader with three different types of conquest accounts: one in which the city, its inhabitants and possessions are annihilated (Josh. 6*); one in which the city is destroyed but some booty is seized (Josh. 8*); and a third type in which the people choose to surrender and become vassals. The first type appears as a sort of Deuteronomistic 'ideal' of war, which can also be found in the Mesha stele for instance. This monument, which celebrates the victory of a Moabite king against Israel, affirms that 'all Israel' was exterminated and put to the ban in honour of Kemosh, the national god of Moab. Nevertheless Mesha indicates a little later the number of captives whom he has taken, which shows that the ban on Israel was not complete and had therefore mostly a symbolical and ideological significance. A similar structure can be observed when we move from Josh. 6 to Josh. 8. The latter account also suggests that the destruction of the city was not absolute, since the livestock is taken away by the Israelites as booty. Finally, chs 9–10* suggest that there is an alternative to destruction in case of submission to the Israelite army. It is tempting to interpret the alternative constructed by these chapters in the context of Josianic propaganda directed towards the former kingdom of Israel, especially if Joshua is a sort of cipher for Josiah himself as some authors have suggested. The conquest account of Josh. 6–10* would thus invite the Northern inhabitants to accept Josiah as their new master.

Without excluding entirely the possibility that some of the material preserved in the lists of Josh. 13–19 comes from the seventh century, and might have belonged to the Josianic edition of Joshua, we have already seen that chs 13–19 in their present form are of a much later origin. If the first edition of Joshua did not contain texts such as Josh. 15* or 18* it was possibly closed by the statement in 11.23 ('So Joshua took the whole land ... and gave it for an inheritance to Israel according to their tribal allotments. And the land had rest from war'), which is a fitting conclusion. Otherwise, the ending of the Josianic edition should probably be found in Josh. 21.43–45*;[40] above all, these verses insist on the fact that Yahweh has given the entirety of the land to the people of Israel and defeated all their enemies.[41]

Thus, the original version of the book of Joshua borrows from royal Assyrian ideology in order to construct a military narrative legitimizing Israel's occupation of the land. This narrative stands in opposition to other myths of Israel's origins, which can be found in the Patriarchal narratives (Gen. 12–36), and in some psalms as well as in Hosea. In all these traditions, Israel's occupation of the land is described in a pacific way, whether Israel is seen as a native population as in the oldest stories of Genesis or as coming from outside and being led into the land by Yahweh (Hos. 13.4–6). In this respect, the original version of Joshua is laying the foundation of the nationalistic ideology characteristic of the Deuteronomistic school towards the end of the Judean monarchy. It is quite possible that the so-called 'conquest tradition' is nothing else than an invention by Deuteronomistic scribes.

4. Judges, Samuel and Kings

4.1. The Book of Judges

As we already mentioned, Judges is the book within the Former Prophets, which has the fewest typically Deuteronomistic passages. These texts (Judg. 2.6–3.6; 6.11–18; 10.6–16) are generally regarded

---

40.   As we shall see later, most of chs 20–24 belongs to later, exilic or postexilic, redactions.

41.   It is possible that the reference to the divine promise to the fathers in these verses is a later insertion, intended to create a redactional link between the books of Joshua and Deuteronomy. The original text of Josh. 21.43–45 would have been limited therefore to v. 43* (without 'which he had sworn to give to their fathers') and 44. Whether the books of Deuteronomy and Joshua already formed a coherent composition at the time of Josiah is a matter of debate.

as rather late compositions, and cannot therefore be attributed to the royal scribes at the end of the seventh century. This does not necessarily mean that the whole book of Judges is a later creation. The observation that all of the Judges except one (Othniel) came from the North has led to the convincing hypothesis that there is behind the present book of Judges a collection of accounts about Israelite 'Saviours' originating from the Northern kingdom. Although this collection was slightly reworked by the Deuteronomistic school when the book of Saviours was integrated at a later time inside the Deuteronomistic History, it is only too logical to assume that it was not used by the royal scribes at the time of Josiah, since the Northern orientation of this collection did not suit at all their own Judean nationalistic policy. This implies that, at the time of Josiah, there was still no Deuteronomistic 'history' properly speaking, since the books from Deuteronomy to Kings were not related to each other by a coherent chronological framework and the succession of different distinct periods. The Deuteronomistic work at that time was instead a rather loose collection, telling the story of Israel's origins (Deuteronomy and Joshua) and of the Davidic monarchy up to Josiah (Samuel and Kings).

4.2. The Books of Samuel

Select Bibliography

Dietrich, W., and T. Naumann, *Die Samuelbücher* (Erträge der Forschung 287; Darmstadt: Wissenschaftliche Buchgesellschaft, 1995).

McCarter, P.K., 'The Books of Samuel', in S.L. McKenzie and M.P. Graham (eds), *The History of Israel's Tradition: The Heritage of Martin Noth* (JSOTSup 182; Sheffield: Sheffield Academic Press, 1994), pp. 260–80.

McCarter, P.K., *I Samuel: A New Translation with Introduction, Notes and Commentary* (AB 8; Garden City, NY: Doubleday, 1980).

McCarter, P.K., *II Samuel: A New Translation with Introduction, Notes and Commentary* (AB 9; Garden City, NY: Doubleday, 1984).

Several units are commonly distinguished within the books of Samuel. 1 Sam. 1–3 (1.1–4.1a) reports Samuel's birth and service at the local sanctuary of Shiloh. 1 Sam. 4–6 (4.1b–7.1) relates the loss of Yahweh's 'ark' (probably a battle palladium) in a fight against the Philistines. In 1 Sam. 7–15, the instauration of kingship in Israel (8–12) and the first years of Saul, Israel's first king (13–15), are described. The introduction of the character of David in 1 Sam. 16, who will ultimately replace Saul on the throne of Israel, marks the inauguration of a new section, usually designated as the 'History of David's Rise' (HDR), starting at 1 Sam. 16 and traditionally concluded at 2 Sam. 5, when the Judean David is made king over 'all Israel' (cf. v. 3. Chapters 5–8 of 2 Samuel relate various central episodes of David's reign: the capture of Jerusalem, David's future capital (2 Sam. 5), the return of Yahweh's ark to Jerusalem (2 Sam. 6), David's eagerness to build a temple for the ark to reside within and the promise of an everlasting dynasty which David receives in return from Yahweh (2 Sam. 7), and, finally, David's battles and administration (2 Sam. 8).

Chapters 9–20 of 2 Samuel are usually described as the 'Succession Narrative' (SN), since David's children and the problem of his succession have become the main focus of the story (in particular in the narrative on Absalom's attempt to replace his father on the throne, 2 Sam. 13–20). Finally, 2 Sam. 21–24 presents a collection of various traditions on David, which constitutes a sort of 'appendix' to David's reign and to the books of Samuel as a whole.

As this brief summary suggests, the books of Samuel are among the least unified and the least homogeneous within the Former Prophets. 1 Sam. 1.1 offers a good introduction to the new era, which begins after the period of the Judges, but the story in 1 Sam. 1–6 has little to do directly with the introduction of the monarchical government in Israel. The division into two books is also somewhat artificial: the conclusion of 1 Samuel in ch. 31 with Saul's death conforms to biblical usage (cf. Gen. 50; Deut. 34; Josh. 24; etc.), but it breaks the HDR in two. The end of 2 Samuel is especially problematic: the SN is manifestly continued in 1 Kgs 1–2, with the report on David's succession and death, which should have formed the logical conclusion to the books of Samuel. Instead of this, 2 Sam. 21–24 interrupts the SN. These chapters form a loose collection of traditions on David with little thematic connections, even though the present arrangement of the material is not devoid of coherence.[42] The artificiality of the division between the books of Samuel and Kings is also manifest in the fact that the Greek tradition groups Samuel–Kings in a single collection (1–4 Kingdoms). These observations

42.   The arrangement of 2 Sam. 21–24 presents an inverted structure:
  A 21.1-14: Plague (drought)
     B 21.15-22: Heroes of David
        C 22: Psalm of David
        C' 23.1-7: David's last teaching
     B' 23.8-39: Heroes of David
  A' 24: Plague (pestilence)

confirm the traditional view that the books of Samuel do not result from the work of a single author or redactor, but rather from the integration of several collections of traditions. The opinion that most of these traditions were written down very shortly after the event during the tenth or ninth century BCE is still very popular. But this view should definitely be given up.[43] There is no contemporaneous extra-biblical evidence for a united and huge Davidic and Solomonic empire, and Jerusalem at that time was no more than a modest hill-country village. The quest for the historical David or Solomon is as difficult as for King Arthur. There is perhaps one mention of David outside the Bible, in an inscription discovered in 1993 in Dan, dating from the ninth or eighth century BCE and referring to the 'house of David'. If this interpretation is correct,[44] it shows that, as Omri for the North, David was considered as the founder of the Judean dynasty. But this does not allow locating the stories in Samuel shortly after David's reign. In their written form most of the stories presuppose the collapse of the Northern kingdom in 722, which is alluded to in the fate of King Saul. The authors probably knew about older traditions, for instance the Philistine menace. Nevertheless these kinds of memories do not allow interpreting the collections in the books of Samuel in the context of the tenth century.

Among these collections, few are likely to have been part of the Josianic library. Although the Ark Narrative in 1 Sam. 4.1b–7.1, which contains very few traces of Deuteronomistic language, probably preserves an older tradition (the importance of the Shiloh sanctuary indicates a Northern origin and the kernel of 1 Kgs 8 possibly relates the installation of the ark in the Jerusalemite temple), the present arrangement of 1 Sam. 1–6 already seems to reflect the destruction of the temple of Jerusalem in 587/586 BCE. The redactional comment upon the loss of the ark in 4.21 ('The Glory is banished from Israel') is very close to the description of the departure of the Glory from the temple in Ezek. 8–10, suggesting that the story of the loss of the ark

43.   See also the archaeological and historical arguments in Finkelstein and Silberman, *Bible Unearthed*, pp. 128–45.

44.   The alternative meaning would refer to a sanctuary of a deity 'Dod'; nowadays this view is adopted by a minority of scholars, for a discussion see Cryer, F.H., 'Of Epistemology, Northwest-Semitic Epigraphy and Irony: The *bytdwd*/House of David Inscription Revisited', *JSOT* 69 (1996), pp. 3–17, and Na'aman, N., 'Beth-David in the Aramaic Stela from Tel Dan', *BN* 79 (1995), pp. 17–24; Athas, George, *The Tel Dan Inscription. A Reappraisal and a New Interpretation* (*Copenhagen International Seminar* 12), London / New York, Sheffield Academic Press, 2003.

foreshadows the later destruction of the Jerusalem temple. Also, the fact that Samuel is raised as a priest in the sanctuary of Shiloh, but ultimately becomes a prophet (3.19–4.1a) and survives the destruction of the sanctuary *in his office of prophet* and intercessor for 'all Israel' (cf. 1 Sam. 7.2–14) also recalls the replacement of the temple by the prophetic word as a medium of access to the divine will, a central theme of the Deuteronomistic theology in the exilic and postexilic periods. It is also difficult to imagine that all of 1 Sam. 7–15, which contains several texts very critical towards kingship as an institution (see in particular 1 Sam. 8; 10.17–27; 12), would have been composed by the scribes of Josiah, even if these chapters certainly preserve earlier traditions on Saul, perhaps of Benjaminite origin (1 Sam. 9.1–10.16*; 11*; 13–14*). The birth story of Samuel in ch. 1 was perhaps originally the opening of a Saul-story, since the word play on šāʾal ('ask', see 1 Sam. 1.20), fits better the name of šāʾûl (Saul), than šᵉmûʾēl (Samuel). Be that as it may, the original tradition about Saul was probably related as a foundation story of the Northern monarchy.

The question of the composition of the SN is presently disputed, since some authors would consider it being a late (exilic or early postexilic) composition altogether.[45] In any case, David's presentation in the SN, where he appears as a rather weak, if not faulty, character (2 Sam. 11–12), makes it rather unlikely that the SN would have been part of the Josianic library. It is nevertheless possible that a shorter account of the court history, without the 'scandalous chapters' 2 Sam. 11–12; 15–17* and 19*[46], did already exist in the seventh century. The

---

45.   Cf. in particular Van Seters, J., 'The Court History and DtrH: Conflicting Perspectives on the House of David', in A. de Pury and T. Römer (eds), *Die sogenannte Thronfolgegeschichte Davids: Neue Einsichten und Anfragen* (OBO 176; Freiburg (Switzerland) and Göttingen: Universitätsverlag and Vandenhoeck & Ruprecht, 2000), pp. 70–93. According to Van Seters 2 Sam. 7* was originally situated at the end of David's life. The divine oracle was originally followed by Solomon's uncontested succession (2 Kgs 2.1–4, 10–12*, Solomon was already mentioned in 2 Sam. 5.14).

46.   For 2 Sam. 11–12 as later interpolation see McKenzie, S.L., 'The So-called Succession Narrative in the Deuteronomistic History', in A. de Pury and T. Römer (eds), *Die sogenannte Thronfolgegeschichte*, pp. 123–35. Other scholars argue that the story of David's adultery in 2 Sam. 11–12 was part of an eighth- or seventh-century edition of the SN, written in order to counter the suspicion that the historical Solomon was not the son of David (see for instance: Knauf, E.A., 'Le roi est mort, Vive le roi! A Biblical Argument for the Historicity of Solomon', in L.K. Handy [ed.], *The Age of Solomon: Scholarship at the Turn of the Millennium* [Studies in the

aim of this succession narrative would have been to introduce Solomon as David's successor. The fact that this succession was quite troublesome is perhaps a problem for a modern reader's conception of pro-monarchic history-writing. But compared to what Assyrian sources report about the succession of Sennacherib (and the role of the mother of the later king) or of Esarhaddon who favoured the younger son against his 'normal' successor, a Judean audience of the seventh century would have been little shocked by certain events related to David's succession.

The collection of material which appears as a likely candidate for a Josianic setting is the 'History of David's Rise' (HDR). Although Deuteronomistic language is sparse in 1 Sam. 16–2 Sam. 5*, the HDR has nevertheless undergone a Deuteronomistic edition, which is apparent, for instance, in the regnal formula of 2 Sam. 2.4; 3.2–5; 5.4–5. The extremely positive depiction of David in the HDR can easily be understood as a piece of Josianic propaganda. In the HDR, David is always successful, since he benefits from the support of the national god, Yahweh. One of the recurring themes in the HDR is the statement that 'Yahweh was with David' (1 Sam. 16.18; 17.37; 18.12, 14, 28; 20.13; 2 Sam. 5.10), and the divine presence necessarily makes David irresistible. The accession of the Judean David to the throne not only of Judah (2 Sam. 2.4), but also of 'all Israel' (2 Sam. 5.3) is therefore presented as being a consequence of the divine will. Besides, David does not even have to fight against the Northern territories in order to establish his reign over Israel, but all the Israelite tribes, according to the HDR (5.1–2), come of themselves to David in order to anoint him as king over Israel (5.3). One can see immediately how such a narrative would concur with the ambitions of the nationalistic party at Josiah's court. Josiah, who was described by the royal scribes as a 'David *redivivus*', a 'new David', appears as the natural heir elected by Yahweh in order to restore the former glory of the Israelite state. His policy of national expansion is presented as a restoration of

History and Culture of the Ancient Near East 11; Leiden, New York and Cologne: Brill, 1997], pp. 81–95). This idea remains nevertheless highly speculative. For a seventh-century Succession Narrative without 2 Sam. 15–17* and 19* see Fischer, A.A., *Von Hebron nach Jerusalem: Eine redaktionsgeschichtliche Studie zur Erzählung von König David in II Sam 1–5* (BZAW 355; Berlin and New York: de Gruyter, 2004), esp. p. 317. Fischer rejects the idea of an independent Court History and an independent story about David's rise. According to him, a seventh-century Judean 'David redaction' created the first edition of Samuel.

the 'Golden Age' of the Davidic empire – a restoration, which only Josiah can operate.

In this light, the HDR appears as a direct call to political submission to Judah addressed to the Northern provinces, and especially to Benjamin. In effect, the authors of the HDR present David from Judah as the natural heir to the Benjaminite Saul; he is even recognized as such by Saul's own children, in particular by Jonathan, Saul's legitimate successor, who is immediately ready to swear loyalty to David, and to become his vassal (1 Sam. 18.1–3; 20.8; 23.16–18)![47] In a general way, the recurrence of the verb *ăhab* ('to love') in the HDR has often been noted (1 Sam. 16.18; 18.1, 3, 16, 20, 22, 28; 20.17; 2 Sam. 1.26). Here, this verb has a clear political meaning, as in Assyrian treaties, and refers to the loyalty of a vassal vis-à-vis his suzerain. By making explicit that all of Saul's house (except Saul himself) paid tribute to David and recognized him as the legitimate king of Judah and Israel, the HDR clearly affirms the legitimacy of the pretensions of the Davidic house on the Northern territories at the time of Josiah's reign.[48] It is quite clear that this presupposes already the integration and negative transformation of the older Saul material into the so-called HDR. And it is therefore doubtful whether an HDR could ever have existed without the stories about Saul since his (now negative) character is necessary to legitimate David's rise to power. The end of Saul in his battle against the Philistines (1 Sam. 31) may reflect in a certain way the Assyrian campaign, which ended with the collapse of Israel. The occupation of Israelite towns on both sides of the Jordan can easily be related to the Assyrian occupation policy.[49]

47.   There are also some erotic undertones in the relationship between Jonathan and David, which is reminiscent of that between Gilgamesh and Enkidu. *The Epic of Gilgamesh* was very poular in the Assyrian period.

48.   One may also note that the story of David's victory against Goliath, which contains a few Deuteronomistic elements, would suit well the nationalistic propaganda of Josiah's court. The description of Goliath's equipment (17.5–7) probably corresponds to the typical equipment of a Greek mercenary in Egypt in the seventh century. Goliath's defeat against David, in spite of his heavy equipment and military superiority, thus suggests that Judah has nothing to fear of the powerful Egyptian neighbour as long as it benefits from Yahweh's protection (cf. in particular 17.36, 45) – a certitude, however, contradicted by Josiah's death at the hand of Pharaoh in 2 Kgs 23.29...

49.   See on this, Fischer, *Hebron*, pp. 283–84.

The Josianic version of the HDR may have been transmitted, originally, with a first version of the promise of 2 Sam. 7*. It is unlikely, in effect, that the hope of an everlasting dynasty would be a pure creation of the Deuteronomistic school at the Babylonian or Persian period, and this theme would have comforted the Davidic ideology enhanced by the Josianic administration. However, it is difficult, if not impossible, to recover the extent of the original document behind the present text of 2 Sam. 7.1–17, which presupposes the bringing of the ark to Jerusalem (2 Sam. 6*) and a redactional link with the book of Judges (v. 11) and which is now primarily concerned with the temple in Jerusalem.

Summing up: After the collapse of the Northern kingdom in 722 BCE, the scribes in Jerusalem transformed the traditions about its first king Saul into an introduction for the story about the rise of David, the 'real' chosen king of Israel. This greater HDR (which contained parts of the following: 1 Sam 1; 9.1–10.16; 11.1–15; 13–14; 16–27; 29; 31; 2 Sam. 2–5) was conceived as propaganda and legitimization for the reign of Josiah, the 'new David'. It operated also as the opening for the story of the monarchy, which is to be found in the books of Kings.

4.3. The Books of Kings

Select Bibliography

McKenzie, S.L., 'The Books of Kings in the Deuteronomistic History', in S.L. McKenzie and M.P. Graham (eds), *The History of Israel's Tradition: The Heritage of Martin Noth* (JSOTSup 182; Sheffield: Sheffield Academic Press, 1994), pp. 281–307.

McKenzie, S.L., *The Trouble with Kings: The Composition of the Book of Kings in the Deuteronomistic History* (SVT 42; Leiden: Brill, 1991).

Na'aman, N., 'Sources and Composition in the History of Solomon', in L.K. Handy (ed.), *The Age of Solomon: Scholarship at the Turn of the Millennium* (Studies in the History and Culture of the Ancient Near East 11; Leiden: Brill, 1997), pp. 57–80.

Provan, I.W., *Hezekiah and the Books of Kings: A Contribution to the Debate about the Composition of the Deuteronomistic History* (BZAW 172; Berlin: de Gruyter, 1988).

Although they are closely related in the Greek traditions (1–4 Kingdoms), the books of Samuel and Kings belong to very different literary genres.

The basic structure of Kings is constituted by a continuous chronology of the Judean and Israelite kings, from David to Zedekiah, Judah's last king. On the whole, the books of Kings are clearly divided into three parts: Solomon's reign (1 Kgs 1–11), the history of Israel and Judah up to the fall of the Northern kingdom (1 Kgs 12–2 Kgs 17), and the history of Judah down to the exile and the end of the Southern monarchy (2 Kgs 18–25). The description of Solomon's reign is much more explicit than the reign of other kings; this may be explained in particular by the account of the construction and inauguration of Jerusalem's temple during Solomon's reign (1 Kgs 5–8). As a matter of fact, the temple occupies a central role throughout the books of Kings.[50] Jeroboam, the first king of the Northern kingdom after its separation from Judah, is described as the founder of two sanctuaries in Dan and Bethel, which appear in the books of Kings as illegitimate concurrence with the temple of Jerusalem (1 Kgs 12). Consequently, all subsequent Northern kings will be systematically blamed for what is designated as 'Jeroboam's sin'. The Southern kings will be compared to their 'father' David (1 Kgs 15.3; 11; 2 Kgs 14.3; 16.2; 18.3; 22.2) and be evaluated, for their part, on their loyalty to the Jerusalem temple and their condemnation of the other cultic places (so-called 'high places', *bāmôt*). Significantly, several narratives describe various attempts by Southern kings to reform the Jerusalem temple (2 Kgs 12: Joash; 18: Hezekiah; 23: Josiah), which are generally followed by a return to the previous idolatry (2 Kgs 16.10–18: Ahaz; 21: Manasseh). But only Josiah's reform corresponds to a full restoration of the temple of Jerusalem (2 Kgs 23), thus establishing an implicit parallel between Josiah, the reformer king, and Solomon, the founder of the temple. It is striking to observe, furthermore, that in the case of these two kings the major achievement of their kingship is related to the temple. Finally, the temple is also at the centre of the report on the capture of Jerusalem by the Neo-Babylonian army (2 Kgs 25), and there is an obvious parallel between the destruction of the temple at the end of Kings and the *construction* at the beginning. This parallel is even made explicit by the mention, in 2 Kgs 24–25, of the Neo-Babylonian army deporting several of Solomon's vessels (2 Kgs 24.13; 25.13–17).

50.   The story of Elijah and Elisha, which has no relationship to the problem of the temple and the cult centralization, forms a discrete unit within Kings (1 Kgs 17–2 Kgs 13*), which probably belongs to a quite late stage of editing within the books of Kings, as is the case for most of the prophetic material.

The fact that the building and inauguration of Solomon's temple find a double conclusion – in the history of the reformation of the temple in 2 Kgs 23 and of its destruction in 25 – is a further indication of the presence of at least two conflicting redactions in Kings, a seventh-century (Josianic) and an exilic one. It confirms the common idea that the story of Josiah's reform in 2 Kgs 23 was originally the conclusion of the first edition of the books of Kings. It remains now to see what can be attributed to this edition for each of the main sections of Kings.

Although there are still some attempts to reconstruct a history of Solomon dating from the tenth century and reflecting the supposedly historical king, this approach should definitely be abandoned. It is very clear now that the idea of a 'Solomonic empire' is a complete fiction, and that 1 Kgs 3–11* projects realities from the Neo-Assyrian empire in order to construct a glorious past for 'Israel'. Solomon's relationship to the Phoenicians, who furnish the wood necessary for the building works of Solomon, is comparable to the situation that prevailed in Neo-Assyrian times. The representation of Solomon as the wise king, friend and protector of the arts, takes up elements from common royal ideology in Egypt and Mesopotamia but may also more specifically be related to the representation of several Neo-Assyrian suzerains, such as Sennacherib, Esarhaddon and Assurbanipal. The description of forced labour imposed by Solomon upon Israel (1 Kgs 5.27–32*) may well be inspired by the Assyrian infliction of forced labour upon Judah in the seventh century BCE.[51] Several stages in the building account of Solomon's temple (1 Kgs 6–8) can also be found in the Mesopotamian literature, but the story 'is particularly similar to Assyrian building accounts'.[52] This is true, in particular, for the

---

51.   Cf. Knauf, E.A., 'King Solomon's Copper Supply', in E. Lipínski (ed.), *Phoenicia and the Bible* (OLA 44 [Studia Phoenicia 11]; Leuven: Departement Oriëntalistiek and Peeters, 1991), pp. 167–86; p. 175. A later redactor found this parallel between Solomon and the Assyrian kings quite scandalous and tried in 9.22 to exempt the Israelites from the corvée.

52.   Hurowitz, V.A., *I Have Built You an Exalted House: Temple Building in the Bible in Light of Mesopotamian and Northwest Semitic Writings* (JSOTSup 115; Sheffield: Sheffield Academic Press, 1992), quotation p. 313; for details see pp. 130–310. For parallels between 1 Kgs 6–8 and the temple-building records of Sennacherib see also McCormick, C.M., *Palace and Temple: A Study of Architectural and Verbal Icons* (BZAW 313; Berlin and New York: de Gruyter, 2002), who understands 1 Kgs 6–8 'as a verbal icon that is related to the architectural icon of Sennacherib's palace' (p. 194).

following steps: decision to build (1 Kgs 5.15–19), acquisition of building materials (5.20–26), description of the labour force (5.27–32), description of the temple and its furnishings (1 Kgs 6–7), dedication of the sanctuary (1 Kgs 8).

Such parallels suggest the existence of a first version of the Solomon story in the Neo-Assyrian period. The detailed reconstruction of this story, however, proves to be difficult. In 1 Kgs 1–11 as in the rest of 1–2 Kgs, the presence of redactions concerned with the explanation of the exile and leading the reader to the catastrophe of Jerusalem's final fall is pervasive. It should not necessarily be assumed that later redactors, when revising older documents, always accurately preserved their original sources. In addition to this, the reconstruction of the original account on Solomon is made all the more complicated by the fact that the oldest Greek text of 1 Kgs 1–11 probably reflects a different Hebrew original, which may preserve a more ancient version of these chapters than the Masoretic tradition. Roughly, the Neo-Assyrian edition of 1 Kgs 1–11 may have encompassed the following:[53] 1 Kgs 3.1a, 4*, 5, 6aα ('Solomon said'), 7*, 8a, 9a, 11*, 12aβ ('I will give you a wise heart'), 13, 15*; 4.1–6 (7–19?); 5.9–16*, 19*, 20, 22–32*; 6.1–36*; 7.15–51*; 8.1–6*, 12–21*, 62, 63b; 9.15–19, 23; (10.1–13*?[54]); 10.14–29*; 11.41–43*.

Thus, the first version of 1 Kgs 3–11* would have begun with Solomon's dream at the sanctuary of Gibeon, Yahweh appearing to him, and the divinity granting him a 'wise heart'.[55] 1 Kgs 3.4–15 therefore functions as the opening to the entire Solomon story, which

53.   For a similar, although not identical, reconstruction see Wälchli, S., *Der weise König Salomo: Eine Studie zu den Erzählungen von der Weisheit Salomos in ihrem alttestamentlichen und altorientalischen Kontext* (BWANT 141; Stuttgart, Berlin and Cologne: Kohlhammer, 1999).

54.   The story about the Queen of Sheba looks like a tale from 'Thousand and One Nights'. The 'kingdom of Sheba' came to existence about 730 BCE, but the best setting for the biblical story is probably the Persian period. The same might be true for the 'judgement of Solomon' in 3.16–28. Even if this story, which origi-nally did not deal with Solomon (the name of the king is never mentioned), is sometimes located in the seventh century, it probably was inserted in 1 Kgs 3–11 at the same time as the story about the Queen of Sheba (for both texts see also Knauf, 'Copper Supply', pp. 174–75, note 26).

55.   Some scholars have suggested that 1 Kgs 3 has replaced an original account in which Yahweh commanded Solomon to build a temple (see for instance Kapelrud, A.S., 'Temple Building: A Task for Gods and Kings', *Or* 32 [1963], pp. 56–62). But there are no clear indications to support this interesting idea.

is placed under the heading of the 'wise king', a classical motif in ancient Near Eastern royal ideology. It is followed by a brief report listing Solomon's functionaries and detailing the organization of the kingdom in ch. 4. The account of Solomon's reputation for wisdom in 5.9–14, which confirms the accomplishment of the divine promise in 3.4–15, serves as an introduction to the building report in 1 Kgs 5–8, the very centre of the Solomon story. The construction of the Jerusalem sanctuary implies an international collaboration with the Phoenician king Hiram, who supplies the wood necessary for the construction (5.15–32*). The building account itself takes place in chs 6–7*; it is immediately followed by the report on carrying the ark inside the sanctuary (8.1–13*[56]) and a prayer of Solomon (vv. 14–21*), which posits an indissoluble bond between the Davidic dynasty and the temple of Jerusalem. The emphasis placed upon Yahweh's choice operated 'among the tribes' clearly recalls the formulation of Deut. 12.14, which belongs to the Josianic layer of Deut. 12. The account concludes with sacrifices for the dedication of the temple (8.62, 63b). The oldest text in chs 9 and 10 takes up the description of Solomon's royal activities. Finally, the original account of Solomon concludes with a final notice specifying the total length of Solomon's reign (11.42–43). The reference in v. 41 to a 'Book of the Acts of Solomon' may stem from the exilic edition of the Deuteronomistic History. It would designate the original story of Solomon dating from the reign of Josiah and partly integrated into 1 Kgs 3–11.

Apart from administrative lists and reports in 1 Kgs 4; 9 and 10, the original story of Solomon's reign concentrates on the presentation of the king as a temple builder (chs 5–8). All the kings from the Neo-Assyrian and Neo-Babylonian period are also presented as temple and palace builders or restorers.[57] Hence, this original account typically

---

56.   We cannot discuss here the problem raised by vv. 12–13, which state that Yahweh desires to dwell in the darkness. The Greek version quotes this poem at another place, after 8.53. So we might have here a fragment from an older text. The mention of darkness probably alludes to the clouds in which the weather-god Yahweh hides himself.

57.   It has been observed that the building activities in 1 Kgs 5–7 resemble more a restoration than a new construction (Rupprecht, K., *Der Tempel von Jerusalem: Gründung Salomos oder jebusitisches Erbe?* [BZAW 144; Berlin: de Gruyter, 1977]). This might be a reflection either of historical realities or of the fact that Assyrian kings are often depicted as temple restorers more than as temple builders.

reflects the ideology of the royal scribes of the seventh century, who use the Neo-Assyrian royal literature in order to present Solomon as the founder king. It may be surprising that it is Solomon, and not David – the founder of the dynasty – who is presented, in the original version of 1 Kgs 3–11*, as the ideal king according to Neo-Assyrian criteria, and one whose reign is described as a reign of peace, prosperity and renown for his kingdom. Apparently, there were more existing traditions about David in the seventh century than about Solomon, who could manifestly be much more easily constructed on the Neo-Assyrian model. According to the Josianic scribes, the greatness of the 'Israelite' kingdom in the Solomonic period is clearly presented as a result of the building of the temple. This ideology may also be found in the account of Josiah's reign, where the renovation of the temple in 2 Kgs 23 is presented as the prelude to the recovery of the former greatness of the Davidic monarchy.

The reconstruction of the original form of the subsequent history of the two kingdoms of Israel and Judah from Solomon's death to Josiah is still more complicated. The important textual divergences between the oldest Greek text of 1 Kgs 12 (= 3 Kgdms 12.24a–z) and the Masoretic tradition make the recovering of the original text in this chapter a complicated matter, which cannot be discussed here.[58] In any case, the original account must have included a first version of Jeroboam's rebellion against Rehoboam, Solomon's son, which led to the secession of the Northern tribes and the creation of the Northern kingdom. It must also have contained an account of the creation of the two Northern sanctuaries of Dan and Bethel (and the introduction of the two bovine statues) by Jeroboam (see 1 Kgs 12.26–33), since this motif (designated as 'Jeroboam's sin') continuously serves for the subsequent evaluation and criticism of the Northern kings after Jeroboam. This motif comes to an end in 2 Kgs 23.15, when Josiah destroys the altar in Bethel, thus putting an end (according to the biblical ideology) to Jeroboam's cultic innovation.

---

58.   For details see Schenker, A., 'Jeroboam and the Division of the Kingdom in the Ancient Septuagint: LXX 3 Kingdoms 12.24 a–z, MT 1 Kings 11–12; 14 and the Deuteronomistic History', in A. de Pury, T. Römer and J.-D. Macchi (eds), *Israel Constructs its History: Deuteronomistic Historiography in Recent Research* (JSOTSup 306; Sheffield: Sheffield Academic Press, 2000), pp. 214–57, and McKenzie, *Trouble*, pp. 22–40, who is rather sceptical about the reconstruction of an older source from 3 Kgdms 12.24 a–z.

The whole history of the two kingdoms has been thoroughly rewritten and considerably expanded by the adjunction of numerous stories, especially those introducing prophetic material such as the Elijah and Elisha narratives. Most of the original account must have consisted of a list of notices on the successive Northern and Southern kings, giving information such as the name of the king, the date of accession to the throne and the reign's length, and establishing a relative chronology between the Northern and Southern kings. There are differences of detail between the pattern of the notices on the Northern and the Southern kings, which may indicate that the Judean scribes had more information about the Judean than the Northern kings.

Judean Kings	*Israelite Kings*
Introductory synchronism	Introductory synchronism
The king's age at his enthronement	–
Length of reign	Length of reign
Name of his mother	–
Ideological judgement	Ideological judgement
Final reference to the Chronicles of the kings of Judah	Final reference to the Chronicles of the kings of Israel
Death of the king	Death of the king
Burial	–
Name of the successor	Name of the successor

The Josianic scribes apparently had at their disposal royal chronicles from the Northern and Southern kingdoms, to which they refer as the 'Book of the Annals of the kings of Judah/Israel'. The Annals of the kings of Israel must have come to Jerusalem after the fall of Samaria in 722. Their use in the books of Kings clearly reflects, however, a Southern perspective on the Northern kingdom, whose kings are systematically blamed for pursuing 'Jeroboam's sin' and not respecting the Jerusalem temple. The Southern kings, for their part, are judged according to their conformity to the Davidic model, the founder of the Jerusalem dynasty. Although the evaluation of these kings varies, none of them conforms to the Davidic standard except Hezekiah (2 Kgs 18.3–6) and Josiah (2 Kgs 22.2). In this way, the royal notices already prepare the climax of the seventh-century edition of Kings, with the reign of Josiah in 2 Kgs 22–23*. In addition to the regnal notices, the original edition of Kings should also have included a report on Samaria's destruction and deportation in 2 Kgs 17.1–6, and the comment in 17.21–23, which points back to the beginning of the Northern Kingdom in 1 Kgs 12 and reiterates the sins of Jeroboam as explanation for the collapse of Samaria.

Finally, the conclusion of the first edition of the books of Kings in the Neo-Assyrian period closed with the account of Josiah's reform,[59] which ended with the following statement on Josiah: 'Before him, there was no king like him, who turned to Yahweh with all his heart, with all his soul and all his might' (2 Kgs 23.25aα), which offers a fitting conclusion to the Josianic edition of Kings. Since this statement is a literal parallel of Deut. 6.5, which was part of the original opening of the first (Josianic) edition of the Deuteronomic Code in Deut. 6.4–5, Josiah is obviously portrayed as the one and only king who enacted the divine instructions promulgated in this code. More precisely, even, the account of Josiah's reform in 2 Kgs 23 constitutes with Deut. 12 and 1 Kgs 5–8* the last of the three pillars of the Deuteronomistic ideology of centralization in the Neo-Assyrian period. While Deut. 12.13–18 lays down the requirement of cult centralization in Jerusalem, Solomon accomplishes the first step of this programme when building the temple, while Josiah imposes the Jerusalem temple as the central sanctuary of Judah (on Hezekiah as precursor of Josiah's reform, see IV.1 above). The original reform account in 2 Kgs 22–23* may have comprised the following verses: 22.1–7*, 9, 13aα; 23.1, 3–15*, 25aα. In any case, the original conclusion of 2 Kgs 23* provides a compelling argument that the Neo-Assyrian edition of the books of Kings, exactly like that of Deuteronomy, Joshua and Samuel, was composed by the scribes of the royal court in Jerusalem and was intended to support the politics of administrative, economic and religious centralization of the court under the reign of Josiah.

5. Summary: The Origins of the Deuteronomistic Library in the Neo-Assyrian Period

Summing up the above enquiry it is quite obvious that the origins of the Deuteronomistic literary productions should be located in the Jerusalem court, during the seventh century BCE. The first Deuteronomists were high officials, most of them probably scribes. An

59.   For the oldest version of 2 Kgs 22–23 see above, III.2.

important number of literary forms, which occur in the books of Deuteronomy to Kings, are imitation of Assyrian literary conventions. The case is especially clear for Deuteronomy and Joshua. The rhetoric of the Deuteronomic Code is taken over from Assyrian vassal treaties (the clearest parallel comes from Esarhaddon's loyalty oath, of which a copy probably existed in Jerusalem). The conquest stories in Josh. 5–12* are also inspired by Assyrian military propaganda, as Van Seters and others have shown. The first scrolls of Deuteronomy and Joshua were therefore composed as the Judean answer to Neo-Assyrian rhetoric of power and propaganda. These books claim for the Judean national god Yahweh the functions and the sovereignty of the Assyrian king and deities. According to Mann the Assyrian ideology is militaristic and nationalistic,[60] and the same terms apply to the relation of Yahweh and his people in Deuteronomy and Joshua. The books of Samuel and Kings also reveal parallels to Assyrian literary conventions. The description of Solomon as temple builder or restorer and wise and wealthy king (1 Kgs 3–11*) depends on Assyro-Babylonian royal propaganda, and the framework running from 1 Kgs 12 through 2 Kgs 23 is similar to royal chronicles from Assyria and Babylon. The story of Saul's decline and David's rise (1 Sam. 9–2 Kgs 2*) reveals less influence from Assyria; this fact may point to older traditions, which were reworked here. Nevertheless the insistence on a stable Davidic dynasty could be understood as polemic against the Assyrian difficulties which arose always after the death of a king. Were the stories of David, Solomon and the chronicles of the following kings until Josiah already put together in one scroll, or did they still exist independently as a loose collection? It is quite tempting to assume that there was already a first edition of one scroll comprising David's rise, Solomon's temple building, the *translatio imperii* from the North to the South and the presentation of Josiah as a new David and a new Solomon. The aim of this scroll, as well as of the scrolls of Deuteronomy and Joshua, would be to give an ideological support for the politics of centralization and for the claim that the kingdom of Judah was the 'real Israel'. The ideology of centralization did affect the political, economic and religious domain. After 722 Jerusalem had become a 'real capital' generating a concentration of political and

---

60.   Mann, M., *The Sources of Social Power*. I. *A History of Power from the Beginning to A.D. 1760* (Cambridge: Cambridge University Press, 1986, reprinted 1997), pp. 231–37.

economic power. This new situation is reflected in the ideology of cult centralization and in the attempt of the Josianic Deuteronomists to promote on the level of the state religion a monolatrous veneration of Yahweh.

The Deuteronomistic propaganda was confronted by a first crisis in 609 BCE when the Egyptian Pharaoh whose vassal he had become meanwhile killed Josiah. But the real drama happened in 597 and 587 when Jerusalem was destroyed by the Babylonians and the royal family and the court were deported to Babylon.

Chapter 5

THE CONSTITUTION OF THE DEUTERONOMISTIC
HISTORY IN THE NEO-BABYLONIAN PERIOD

1. Setting the So-called 'Exilic Period'

Select Bibliography

Albertz, R., *Israel in Exile: The History and Literature of the Sixth Century* BCE (Studies in Biblical Literature 3; Atlanta, GA: Society of Biblical Literature, 2003).

Barstad, H.M., *The Myth of the Empty Land: A Study in the History and Archaeology of Judah during the 'Exilic' Period* (Symbolae Osloenses; Oslo: Scandinavian University Press, 1996).

Grabbe, L.L. (ed.), *Leading Captivity Captive: 'The Exile' as History and Ideology* (JSOTSup 278; Sheffield: Sheffield Academic Press, 1998).

Lipschits, O. and J. Blenkinsopp (eds), *Judah and the Judeans in the Neo-Babylonian Period* (Winona Lake, IN: Eisenbrauns, 2003).

1.1. From Josiah to Exile

After the death of Josiah, who was killed by Pharaoh Neco in 609 for some obscure reasons,[1] Judah became for a short time vassal of Egypt. Neco countered the plans of the rural aristocracy, which had tried to put on the throne a younger son of Josiah. He appointed Josiah's eldest son Eliakim and, according to the book of Kings, changed his name to Jehoiakim (interestingly it is the Egyptian king who recognizes by this new name that the national God of Judah was Yahweh [= Jeho]). But very soon (from 605) the Babylonians under Nebuchadnezzar took control of the Levant. Egypt defeated, Jehoiakim had no other choice

---

1. He had probably already submitted to Egypt after the decline of Assyrian power and was thought to have betrayed his allegiance.

than to switch his allegiance and pay tribute to the Babylonian king. But in 601, the Babylonians failed to invade Egypt and were defeated and driven back. The Egyptians controlled again for a short time the south of the Levant. The withdrawal of the Babylonian army provoked a regaining of nationalism and Jehoiakim apparently joined an Egypt-led coalition against Babylonia. This led to a new Babylonian campaign in Syria-Palestine and the siege of Jerusalem. During the siege Jehoiakim died (was he murdered by a Babylonian partisan?) and was succeeded by his son Jehoiachin, who surrendered and probably avoided the destruction of Jerusalem. According to 2 Kgs 24 and Jer. 52 the Babylonians deported the royal family, the court and the upper classes of the society. Jehoiachin is mentioned in Babylonian inscriptions as a prisoner along with other kings from the Levant; he apparently retained his title as king of Judah. This means that the new 'king' in Judah appointed by the Babylonians, Zedekiah, a son of Josiah, was in fact a governor, confronted with a reduced administrative apparatus and the absence of a strong army. In 595 a rebellion broke out in Babylonia and this may have inspired the vassal states in the west to gather into an anti-Babylonian coalition, which turned again to Egypt for support. As a matter of fact the Pharaoh Psammetich and his son Hophra increased Egyptian influence on the Levantine coast. Zedekiah and his advisers became therefore openly pro-Egyptian and broke the allegiance to Babylonia. In 589, the Babylonian army again invaded Palestine and besieged Jerusalem; the city was taken in 587 or 586 and this time heavily destroyed as were most of the Judean fortresses and fortified places. The temple and palace of Jerusalem were burned down and the remaining treasures were taken to Babylonia. Apparently a second deportation was organized. Gedaliah, a member of the Shaphan family, was appointed governor in Mizpah, but some years later was murdered by the anti-Babylonian resistance. This probably led to a new punitive action of the Babylonians, maybe to a new deportation and to an important Judean emigration to Egypt (Jer. 43). We do not know what happened after these events; probably Mizpah remained the administrative centre, from where a Babylonian commander governed the Judeans who had remained in the land.

Most specialists consider that the figure of the population deported by the Babylonians did not exceed a total of 5–10 per cent of the *entire* population of Jerusalem and Judah. If one estimates the Judean population at the beginning of the sixth century BCE at about 80,000 to 100,000 this percentage can be corroborated by the indications in Jer.

52.28–30 which give a total of 4,600 for three deportations. R. Albertz has recently argued that this number is much too small. His guess is that about 25 per cent of the Judean population went into exile; this percentage would be comparable to the 18,000 people mentioned in 2 Kgs 24.14 and 16.[2] E. Stern has pointed out that during the Babylonian period the sites excavated in the Judean territory outside Jerusalem 'attest to a complete destruction and gap in the history of the vast majority of the settlements'[3] in contrast to the region of Benjamin. This does not necessarily imply a very high number of deportees – the Babylonian Chronicle relating the capture of Jerusalem in 597 does not specify any deportations, but only mentions an important booty – it suggests a population movement away from the destroyed areas especially to Benjamin. This view concords with 2 Kgs 25.22–23 and Jer. 40.1–6; both texts relate that the Benjaminite town of Mizpah became the administrative centre of Judah during the Babylonian occupation. What is more important than the exact amount of Judean deportees is the fact that the Babylonians apparently deported the intellectual and economic elites. The peasants and underdogs remained in the land and probably were put in charge by the Babylonians of farming the fields of the deportees (Jer. 39.10). But the latter were skilled in writing and producing ideology; they invented the 'myth of the empty land' and the idea that Yahweh had left Judah to accompany them into exile. Consequently they considered themselves to be the 'true Israel', contrary to those who remained in Judah-Benjamin. This way, the 'exile' became a foundation myth for Judaism arising in the Persian period.

1.2. The Invention of the 'Exilic Period'

When Noth created the 'Deuteronomistic History', there was no question for him that the entire work was above all a reflection on Jerusalem's defeat and the 'exile'. Since then, the exile has always played a central role in the interpretation of the Deuteronomistic History, especially in German scholarship. The finale in 2 Kgs 25.27–30, relating the improvement of King Jehoiachin's situation at

2. Albertz, *Exile*, pp. 81–90.
3. Stern, E., 'The Babylonian Gap: The Archaeological Reality', *JSOT* 28 (2004), pp. 273–77; and see Lipschitz, O., 'Demographic Changes in Judah between the Seventh and the Fifth Centuries B.C.E.', in Lipschitz–Bleukinsopp, *Judah and the Judeans*, pp. 323–76.

the Neo-Babylonian court, implied for Noth that the Deuteronomist wrote shortly after these events, about 560 BCE. So the 'exilic period' was born to designate the historical context of the Deuteronomistic History. Nevertheless this concept is rather misleading from a social-historical perspective, since it is mostly an ideological construction. Historically, the so-called 'exilic period', to which is generally assigned the time span between 597 (the first deportation of the Jerusalem court and elite) and 539 (Cyrus' rise to power), does not correspond to the Neo-Babylonian period (626–539), nor to the fact that an important part of the deportees or emigrants stayed in Babylonia and Egypt after 539 notwithstanding the possibility of return to Judah. The creation of an 'exilic period' produces also the false impression that the deportation was an event specific to the Judean history, whereas quantities of deportations took place under the Neo-Assyrian and Neo-Babylonian dominations, including in Samaria and Judah. Finally, the notion of an 'exilic period' suggests that the entire population of Judah would have been deported to Babylon, which corresponds to the ideology of the Deuteronomistic scribes (see for instance 2 Kgs 25.21) but definitely not to the historical reality.

Historically, it is more appropriate to speak of the 'Neo-Babylonian period' for the period down to 539 BCE, and to interpret the Babylonian deportations in Judah in the larger context of the Neo-Babylonian domination in the East in the first part of the sixth century. It remains perfectly true, of course, that the Babylonian exile is a central issue in the Deuteronomistic History. But this does not necessarily imply, as Noth and many others after him have believed, that the Deuteronomistic reflection on the exile only corresponds to the so-called 'exilic period'. For Judaism, the exile remained a decisive issue during the following centuries, and, in a sense at least, until today. The exile became part of the construction of Jewish identity. It is clear that the events of 597 and 587 constituted a major crisis for the Judean elite, and especially for the Deuteronomistic school. This crisis led the Deuteronomists, who had experienced the fall of the Judean monarchy, to modify significantly their views of the origins of Israel and the Judean monarchy and to re-edit entirely the previous literary works of their predecessors from the Neo-Assyrian time.

1.3. The Exilic Edition of the Deuteronomistic History: The Concept of Crisis Literature

There is no doubt that the events of 597 and 587/586 produced a major crisis for the collective Judean identity and, given the important destructions and population movements, one cannot argue that this crisis is a pure invention of modern biblical scholarship. Nevertheless, it is true that the destruction of Jerusalem affected the deported elites more than the rural and the poor. The elites (especially the royal officials[4]) had been separated from their sources of power. More generally speaking, after 597/587, the traditional pillars which supported the ideological and political coherence of a monarchic state in the ancient Near East had fallen into ruin. The king was deported, the temple destroyed and the geographical unity of Judah had come to an end because of deportations and voluntary emigrations. It was quite logical to explain this situation by the defeat of the national deity Yahweh by the more powerful Babylonian gods.

Among the upper class, different groups tried to overcome this crisis, producing ideologies meant to give meaning to the collapse of Judah. We may present these ideologies following a theory of A. Steil. This sociologist, influenced by Max Weber's approach, has analysed the semantics of crises related to the French revolution.[5] In my view his model applies also to the reactions to the fall of Judah that are to be found in the Hebrew Bible. Steil distinguishes three types of attitudes to a crisis: as from the prophet, the priest and the mandarin.[6] The *prophetic attitude* considers the crisis as the beginning of a new era. The representatives of this view are people who stand in the margins of society, but who nevertheless are able to communicate their views. The position of the conservative representatives of the collapsed social structures can be summed up as the *priestly attitude*. Here, the only way to overcome the crisis is to return to the sacral God-given origins of society and to ignore the new reality. The so-called '*mandarin*

---

4.   Interestingly 2 Kgs 24.14, 16 does not explicitly mention priests among the deportees. According to 2 Kgs 25.18–20 two important priests were killed after the destruction of Jerusalem: it is possible that members of the priestly class remained in Judah, and that some sacrificial cult did continue (cf. Jer. 41.5).

5.   Steil, A., *Krisensemantik: Wissenssoziologische Untersuchungen zu einem Topos moderner Zeiterfahrung* (Opladen: Leske & Budrich, 1993).

6.   The expression denotes a high-ranking official or bureaucrat, bent generally on a conservative attitude.

position' sums up the attitude of high officials, who try to understand the new situation and to make do with it in order to maintain their former privileges. The mandarins try to objectivize the crisis by the construction of a history, which provides the reasons for the breakdown of the former societal structures.

One may summarize the three attitudes as follows.

	Prophet	*Priest*	*Mandarin*
Situation	Marginal	Representative of the former power	Belonging to the high officials
Legitimization	'Personal knowledge'	Tradition	Intellectual instruction
Semantic of crisis	Hope for a better future	Return to mythical origins	Construction of a history
Reference	Utopia	Myth	'History'

Applied to the Hebrew Bible and the interpretations of the destruction of Jerusalem, these three attitudes can be easily recovered. The so-called 'Second Isaiah', the anonymous prophet or prophetic group, whose oracles are collected in the second part of the book of Isaiah (chs 40–55), considers the exile as a necessary transition to a new order and a recreation of Israel by Yahweh: 'Do not remember the former things, or consider the things of old. I am about to do a new thing; now it springs forth, do you not perceive it? I will make a way in the wilderness and rivers in the desert ... to give drink to my chosen people, the people whom I formed for myself so that they might declare my praise' (Isa. 43.18–21). These oracles were probably written when the Persian king Cyrus was about to defeat the Babylonian empire. Second Isaiah can be understood in some ways as a propagandist of Cyrus whose arrival is presented as the beginning of a new era; he is even called the messiah of Yahweh (45.1–7). As for Yahweh, he is promoted to be the only 'real God'; the other deities are criticized as human artefacts. In the Hebrew Bible Second Isaiah is therefore the inventor of monotheism. The monotheistic ideology is used in Isa. 40–55 to demonstrate that the destruction of Jerusalem and the deportation were not due to the weakness of Yahweh, but part of his 'pedagogical project' to create a new Israel.

The priestly attitude to the end of the monarchy and the destruction of the temple can be detected in the so-called priestly document in the

Pentateuch. According to recent research, the original priestly document comprised only Gen. 1–Exod. 40* (or Gen. 1–Lev.9*).[7] It contained stories and genealogies presenting the origins of the world and of mankind, stories about Israel's ancestors, Israel's sojourn in Egypt, the demonstration of Yahweh's power to Pharaoh, the exodus out of Egypt, the arrival on Yahweh's mountain and the construction of a mobile sanctuary in the wilderness. The priestly authors set all the important institutions for the rising Judaism in the mythical origins of mankind and the people. The Shabbat is founded with the creation of the world, alimentary laws are given after the Flood, circumcision is as old as Abraham, the Passover is linked to the exodus and the sacrificial cult was already founded in the wilderness. There is no more need for the monarchy and the state; therefore the priestly class could easily accept the loss of political autonomy, as long as the new lords conceded some autonomy to the local cults, as the Persians certainly did.[8] For the priestly conception, the stability of the world is guaranteed by the mythical foundations, therefore the collapse of the Judean monarchy does not really affect the veneration of Yahweh through cult and rituals.

The biblical candidate for the 'mandarin attitude' to crisis is the Deuteronomistic school. Contrary to the priestly milieu, the Deuteronomists of the Babylonian period who are the descendants of the scribes and other officials of the Judean court are obsessed with the end of the monarchy and the deportation of the Judean elites. How to reconcile these events with the nationalistic ideology of the first Deuteronomistic writings from the end of the seventh century BCE? For the Deuteronomists, the exile had to be explained. And this explanation will be given by the construction of a history, which spans from the beginnings under Moses until the destruction of Jerusalem and the deportation of the high classes (Deut. 1–2 Kgs 25*). In doing so, the Deuteronomists rework older scrolls from Assyrian times. They

---

7.   See especially Pola, T., *Die ursprüngliche Priesterschrift: Beobachtungen zur Literarkritik und Traditionsgeschichte von Pg* (WMANT 70; Neukirchen–Vluyn: Neukirchener Verlag, 1995). According to the traditional critical view, the priestly document ended either in Deut. 34* or in Josh. 18–19*. But even if one accepts one of the traditional views, this does not alter the fact that the priestly writers are mostly interested in Israel's mythical origins.

8.   We have no clear indication of the Babylonian attitude. According to the book of Ezekiel it seems that the deportees could gather for cultic celebrations. Jer. 37–43 may indicate that Yahwistic worship continued in Palestine.

establish a coherent history, which they divide into different periods (Moses, conquest, Judges, the rise of monarchy, the two kingdoms, the history of Judah from after the fall of Samaria until the fall of Jerusalem). This history aims to present all the negative events – the split-up of the Davidic dynasty or the Assyrian and Babylonian invasions – as 'logical' consequences of the non-obedience of the people and its leaders to Yahweh's will. And Yahweh's will is expressed in the book of Deuteronomy, which recalls the original 'covenant'[9] or treaty between Yahweh and Israel. Yahweh himself did provoke the invasion of the Babylonians (2 Kgs 24.3 and 20) in order to punish Judah for its veneration of other deities. As Second Isaiah, the Deuteronomists try to counter the idea that Marduk and the other Babylonian deities had defeated Yahweh. But in contrast to Second Isaiah, the exilic writings of the Deuteronomistic school do not reveal a clear monotheistic ideology. Their concern is not the non-existence of other deities but the superiority of Yahweh in spite of the evidence.

The work of the Deuteronomists in the Babylonian time is therefore the first attempt to create a comprehensive history of Israel and Judah. There are other examples in antiquity, which show a link between a situation of crisis and history writing. Thucydides writes in the fifth century BCE the *History of the Peloponnesian War*, for 'those inquirers who desire an exact knowledge of the past as an aid to the interpretation of the future' (1.22). Similarly, Herodotus composes his *History* in order to explain the reasons for and the troubles of the Persian wars (see the foreword to the First Book). In the third century BCE the Babylonian priest Berossos constructs a historical narrative of the Babylonian civilization as an answer to the cultural crisis generated by the spreading of Hellenism. As for the Deuteronomistic History, one may doubt if one should call this work a 'historiography', but this is very much a matter of definition.[10] Of course, the Deuteronomistic History is not historiography or history in the modern sense of Ranke's definition: 'how it actually happened'.[11] And Marc Brettler is right to emphasize that 'any understanding of history which depends on

---

9.   The Hebrew word *bᵉrît* is normally translated 'covenant'. In fact it covers the same semantic field as the Assyrian *adê*.

10.   See for details under I.3.4.1.

11.   Even if this famous statement should better be translated as 'how it essentially was', see Evans, R.J., *In Defence of History* (London: Granta Books, 1997), p. 17.

historicity cannot be profitably applied to the biblical corpus'.[12] The exilic edition of the Deuteronomists remains nevertheless an attempt to construct a comprehensive past in order to explain the present.

2. The Structure and Ideology of the Deuteronomistic History's Exilic Edition

There is still some debate about the geographical location of the sixth-century BCE Deuteronomists. Noth was thinking of Mizpah, the administrative capital of Judah under Babylonian occupation, and this view is still widely shared. But in contrast to Jer. 40–41 where Mizpah is frequently mentioned, the Deuteronomistic report in 2 Kgs 25 does not lay stress on it.[13] The governor Gedaliah was obviously a member of the Shaphan family, and there are strong reasons to think that members of this family were key figures in the Deuteronomistic school since the days of King Josiah.[14] But this does not necessarily mean that all Shaphanides were Deuteronomists, or that they all remained in Mizpah. If one analyses 2 Kgs 24–25 and Jer. 39–41, one may easily observe two conflicting views about life in Judah after the Babylonian invasion. The Jeremiah texts, which should not be ascribed to a Deuteronomistic redaction, express hope for ongoing life in Judah after the destruction of Jerusalem. According to Jer. 39.14 and 40.2–6, the prophet Jeremiah, who is not mentioned in the books of Kings (!), chooses to remain with the non-exiled population in the land. These texts legitimate the idea that Yahweh is on the side of the remnant community in Judah (see also Jer. 32.1–15). The same view is also emphasized by the welfare that the government of Gedaliah produces in the account of Jeremiah: 'they harvested an abundance of wine and summer fruits' (40.12). Interestingly this statement is missing in the parallel account in 2 Kgs 25.22–26, which, as Seitz rightly observes, seems to 'downplay the potential rule of Gedaliah'.[15] The presentation of Jer. 40 stands in

---

12.   Brettler, M.Z., *The Creation of History in Ancient Israel* (London and New York: Routledge, 1995), p. 11.

13.   In the Deuteronomistic History, Mizpah plays an important role in relation to Samuel: in 1 Sam. 7 Samuel is judging and gathering Israel in Mizpah, as in 1 Sam. 10.17.

14.   See III.1.

15.   Seitz, C.R., *Theology in Conflict: Reactions to the Exile in the Book of Jeremiah* (BZAW 176; Berlin and New York: de Gruyter, 1989), p. 217.

opposition to the conclusion of the Deuteronomistic History: 'So Judah was deported away from her land' (2 Kgs 25.21). This view reflects clearly an exilic perspective. The same can be said of Solomon's prayer (1 Kgs 8), which presents the temple as a *kiblah*, the point toward which the deported community should pray (vv. 48–50). The call of 1 Kgs 8.47 to return to Yahweh is parallel with Deut. 30.1–10, which also clearly addresses a group in exile. It seems therefore plausible to locate the group who produced the exilic edition of the Deuteronomistic History among the intelligentsia in Babylon.[16] We do not possess much information about the social and economic condition of the deportees, but one can reasonably argue that high court officials were well treated and even involved in the Babylonian administration of the exiles. 'Perhaps Judah's scribes found employment within the palace and temple as Babylonian scribes, continuing their same life of work but for a new employer'.[17] Those former officials from the Judean court could easily have brought with them scrolls, which they re-edited during the Babylonian time. The fact that the final chapters of the Deuteronomistic History do not contain any negative statements about the Babylonian king and his army (see for the opposite attitude Isa. 13–14) who are presented as executors of Yahweh's anger fits well with the location of the exilic Deuteronomists in Babylonia.

In a way, the whole Deuteronomistic History maintains the assertion that the end of the monarchy, the destruction of Jerusalem and the loss of the land result from Yahweh's anger. The theme of the land is in the very centre of this History: the book of Deuteronomy constantly repeats Yahweh's promise to give the land; the book of Joshua relates the total conquest of the land, and the final chapters of Kings the loss of the land, which is announced in the Deuteronomistic speeches that structure the whole history. Those speeches, as already observed by Noth, are the pillars that organize the Deuteronomistic History into different periods. The most important discourses are

16.   For a Babylonian location of the Deuteronomists see also Albertz, *Exile*, pp. 282–85; Person Jr, R.F., *The Deuteronomic School: History, Social Setting, and Literature* (Studies in Biblical Literature 2; Atlanta, GA: Society of Biblical Literature, 2002), pp. 28–29.

17.   Berquist, J.L., *Judaism in Persia's Shadow: A Social and Historical Approach* (Minneapolis, MN: Fortress Press, 1995), p. 16; for more details see pp. 15–17.

Deut. 1–30*; Josh. 1.1–9*; Josh. 23*; Judg. 2.6–3.6*; 1 Sam. 12.1–15*; 1 Kgs 8* and 2 Kgs 17*. All these texts underwent later redactional editing,[18] but it seems quite clear that they were composed in their original form in order to organize the exilic edition of the Deuteronomistic History.

The construction of Deuteronomy as Moses' final discourse provides the model for the following speeches, especially the testaments of Joshua and Samuel. The Deuteronomic laws, especially the insistence on cult centralization and exclusive worship of Yahweh, function now as criteria which enable the addressees to understand the following history from the conquest to the loss of the land. The first period after the Mosaic foundations is introduced by a speech of Yahweh to Joshua in Josh. 1.1–2, 5–6(7)[19] in which he confirms the total conquest of the land. The accomplishment of the conquest is emphasized in Joshua's final discourse in ch. 23, which takes up the statement in Josh. 21.43–45. Since the introductory speech, as well as other texts in Joshua, insists on a total conquest, one may conclude that the primitive form of the farewell speech in Josh. 23 reflected the same ideology, and that the text was reworked later in order to modify this ideology. The original text can be reconstructed from Josh. 23.1–3, 9, 11, 14–16a; it contains the following elements: review of the foregoing history (vv. 3 and 9), exhortations (v. 11), blessing and curses (vv. 14–16). The original speech in Josh. 23 imitates the structure of Deuteronomy (chs 1–3: historical review; 5–26: exhortations and laws; 28: blessings and curses). By this device, Joshua appears clearly as Moses' successor. And as Moses' curses end in Deuteronomy with the announcement of deportation, Josh. 23.15–16

18.   See the recent enquiry of Nentel, J., *Trägerschaft und Intentionen des deuteronomistischen Geschichtswerks: Untersuchungen zu den Reflexionsreden Jos 1; 23; 24; 1Sam 12 und 1Kön 8* (BZAW 297; Berlin and New York: de Gruyter, 2000).

19.   The description of the 'great Israel' in vv. 3–4 is clearly a later insertion, since it does not fit with the idea that the given land is limited by the river Jordan; the exhortation in v. 8 is also very late, it has a parallel in Ps. 1. Both texts were written to correlate the 'Prophets' and the 'Writings' with the Torah. Often it is argued that the original speech ended in v. 6, but v. 7 fits very well as a conclusion. It emphasizes the idea that the attitude towards the Mosaic law is crucial in any situation.

also foresees the loss of the land if the addressees do not respect Yahweh's treaty.

The introduction to the following period stands in Judg. 2.6–12, 14–16, 18–19. This discourse is delivered off-stage by the Deuteronomistic author himself, since there was no fitting figure available to introduce the anarchic time of the Judges. In the Deuteronomistic History this text followed immediately Josh. 23.16.[20] The original introduction in 2.(6–9), 10–12, 14–16, 18–19[21] enables the Deuteronomists to invent a period of wars and anarchy between the conquest and the origins of monarchy, the so-called 'period of the Judges'. Judg. 2.10–19* constructs the time of Joshua as a golden age and presents the following period in a cyclic way: the Israelites are more interested in other deities than in Yahweh. Yahweh gets angry and dispatches other peoples to oppress the Israelites. But then he delivers them by sending 'judges', in fact charismatic leaders, who repel the enemies. But after the death of the judge, the cycle starts anew, until a new deliverer is sent, and so on. The idea that Yahweh uses other people to punish the Israelites is already an allusion to the end of Judah, which is the work of the Babylonians who execute Yahweh's will. In the Deuteronomistic construction the period of Judges comes to an end with Samuel's farewell address in 1 Sam 12.1–4*, 6a, 7 (8*), 9, 10aαb, 11–15.[22] This speech is quite similar to Joshua's address in

20.   Josh. 24 and Judg. 1.1–2.5 were inserted later, as we will see, in order to split up this link. There is much dispute about the question whether the original report of Joshua's death is kept either in Josh. 24.29–31 or in Judg. 2.6–9. We do not need to decide this matter, since the narration is the same either with Josh. 23*; Josh. 24.29–32; Judg. 2.10–19* or with Josh. 23; Judg. 2.6–19*.

21.   Verse 13, which interrupts the link between vv. 12 and 14, is a later attempt to define the identity of the 'other gods' of v. 12. Verse 17 contradicts the presentation of the period of the Judges in vv. 15–16, 18–19. The verse was added later in order to emphasize the stubbornness of the people. In contrast to 2.6–19*, 2.20–3.6 reflects the idea that the conquest was not totally fulfilled. The same idea appears in the additions to Josh. 23; it probably reflects the territorial conflicts of the Persian period.

22.   In recent publications Samuel's final discourse appears more and more as a 'late Deuteronomistic text' (see the summary of research in Nentel, *Trägerschaft*, pp. 140–65). The reasons for this classification depend mainly on vv. 6–8, which mention Jacob, as well as Moses and Aaron together. It may be plausible to assume that these verses result from a reworking of an older text, which mentioned only the exodus and the installation in the land. Verse 8, as it stands now, attributes interestingly the gift of the land to Moses and Aaron,

Josh. 23*. Both texts begin by mentioning the high age of the speaker, they contain a recapitulation of the foregoing history (in Josh. 23 centred on the conquest, in 1 Sam. 12 on the Judges and installation of the king), both speeches end with the alternative of blessing or curses. 1 Sam. 12.9–11 provides an inclusion with Judg. 2.10–19* and summarizes the stories in Judg. 4–11, whereas 12.12–13 alludes to the rising of monarchy, as reported in chs 8–11. 1 Sam. 12.13–15 introduces the following history of the monarchy reflecting already on a negative ending. The next period, which is the history of the 'United Monarchy', is delimited by Solomon's prayer during the inauguration of the Jerusalemite temple (1 Kgs 8). The exilic redactors build upon the earlier text from the Josianic edition of Kings (vv. 14–20*) and add, with a new introduction, a long prayer (vv. 22–51*) and a final blessing (vv. 54–56). Like Josh. 23 and 1 Sam. 12, the first part of the speech is a summary of former events, which underlines that all divine promises (here those made to David) have been fulfilled (v. 20). Verses 14–21 refer to the dynastic promise of 2 Sam. 7. As 1 Sam. 12.6–8*, 1 Kgs 8.16 and 21 present the exodus out of Egypt as the very beginning of the relationship between Israel and Yahweh. The following prayer switches to the future. The first part of this long sequence (vv. 22–26) offers a transition. There is still mention of the 'father David', who will not occur later in this speech, but now v. 25 makes the promise of an eternal dynasty conditional, a result of the reflection about the situation after 587 BCE. The same situation appears in the introduction to the seven occasions for prayer (vv. [27]28–30[23]). Here Solomon states that Yahweh does not really dwell in the temple, but in heaven; the temple is the place where he puts his name. The same ideology may be found in the exilic redaction of Deut. 12 (vv. 8–12). In contrast to the importance given to the building of the temple in the foregoing story, these verses highlight that Yahweh is not constrained to his sanctuary; he might therefore be worshipped outside the temple. The occasions for

whereas Joshua is not mentioned at all. This is perhaps a later correction, which may be compared to the last verses of the Pentateuch, Deut. 34.10–12, in which Moses is presented as incomparable to any other of Israel's heroes.

23.   Verse 27 is often considered as a later addition, it interrupts the link between vv. 26 and 28 and speaks of 'God' in the third person.

prayer, which are presented in vv. 31–51*,[24] reinforce the same ideology. Every description of these occasions contains the same basic elements: the situation of prayer, the localization of the person praying, the appeal to Yahweh that he should listen from heaven, and the divine intervention as required. In contrast to the appeal to Yahweh, which remains identical, there is an interesting evolution as to the place of prayer. In the first case mentioned, the place is clearly located in the temple, before the altar (v. 31). Then (v. 35) prayer goes in the direction of the sanctuary. And finally, at the end, the praying individuals are set in another country and they address their request towards the land of the fathers, the city and the temple (vv. 46–51). During the inauguration of the temple, its function is already defined as fitting for a group which is outside the land! Interestingly, the occasions for prayer in vv. 33–40 and 46–51 correspond to the curses of Deut. 28:[25] defeat (1 Kgs 8.33; Deut. 28.25), no rain (1 Kgs 8.35; Deut. 28.25), famine, pestilence, blight, mildew, locust or caterpillar, enemies (1 Kgs 8.37; Deut. 28.21–22, 38, 25), deportation and exile (1 Kgs 8.46; Deut. 28.64–65). These parallels also establish a clear compositional and thematic link between the book of Deuteronomy and the books of Kings, and underline the importance of 'exile' in the composition of the Deuteronomistic History during the Babylonian period. 1 Kgs 8* concludes the period of the 'United Kingdom', an idea which may well be a Deuteronomistic invention. After this speech, ch. 9 introduces the decline of Solomon's reign, which prepares the next period: the parallel

24.   The literary unity of this passage is debated. It is often argued that vv. 44–51 constitute a later insertion since there are some stylistic differences from vv. 33–41. But these are not really important, so that it is still possible to consider the whole sequence as the work of one author (Nentel, *Trägerschaft*, pp. 228–29). Nevertheless, there is some plausibility to consider not vv. 44–51, but vv. 41–45 as an interpolation. In contrast to the other cases, these verses have no parallels with Deut. 28 (see in the following); the idea of a foreigner (the word *nokrî* is seldom encountered in the Deuteronomistic History, it appears only in Deut. 14.21; 15.3; 17.15; 23.21; 29.21; Judg. 19.21; 2 Sam. 15.19; 1 Kgs 11.1, 8; all these texts use the term with a negative connotation, with the possible exception of the late text Deut. 29.21) coming from far away to worship Yahweh (v. 41) is not a Deuteronomistic idea, but fits better into the Hellenistic period, when proselytism did develop. The mention of war is not very logical after v. 33 where Israel is already defeated.

25.   Burney, C.F., *Notes on the Hebrew Text of the Book of Kings* (Oxford: Clarendon, 1920), pp. 112–15.

history of the kingdoms of Judah and Israel. This period ends in 2 Kgs 17 with the fall of Samaria and a Deuteronomistic comment on it. 2 Kgs 17.7–20 is the last structuring discourse in the Deuteronomistic History. Since no other speaker was available, it is an anonymous comment of the Deuteronomistic author, which was inserted in the original form of this passage between vv. 1–6 and 21–23.[26] This last speech, which has numerous parallels with Josh. 1; 23; Judg. 2.6–3.6; 1 Sam 12 and 1 Kgs 8, is a summary of the whole Deuteronomistic History. The summary starts with a reminder of the exodus which, as already mentioned, is for the Deuteronomists the foundation myth of Israel. The identification of Yahweh as the god who led the Israelites out of Egypt and the warning against other gods are two main themes of Deuteronomy, and 2 Kgs 17 contains many other thematic and semantic links with the first book of the Deuteronomistic History.[27] The mention of the driving out of the nations (v. 8) alludes to the conquest stories in Joshua. The list of infractions in vv. 9–11 has a very close parallel in 1 Kgs 14.23–24, which deals with religious practices under Rehoboam, the first king of Judah (!). The forsaking of Yahweh (v. 16) refers back to the time of the Judges (Judg. 2.12–13). The theme of the continuous sending of the prophets (vv. 13–14) probably starts with Samuel the last judge and first prophet, and continues with the different prophets mentioned in Kings.[28] The statement of v. 15: 'They followed the nations that were around them' probably alludes to the wish for a king in 1 Sam. 8 (see vv. 5 and 20). The cast images (v. 16), as well as the sins of Jeroboam in the older text 2 Kgs 17.21–22, are a clear reference to 1 Kgs 12. The passing of children through fire (v. 17) covers the time from Ahaz (2 Kgs 16.3) to Manasseh (2 Kgs 21.6). Finally, the comparison of Judah with Israel (vv. 19–20) alludes to the end of Judah in 2 Kgs 24–25. 2 Kgs 17.7–20 (21–23) summarizes the whole Deuteronomistic History. In fact, the last period (2 Kgs 18–25) is already included in this summary, because there is, intriguingly, no concluding discourse after the collapse of the

26. See also Aurelius, E., *Zukunft jenseits des Gerichts: Eine redaktionsgeschichtliche Studie zum Enneateuch* (BZAW 319; Berlin and New York: de Gruyter, 2003), pp. 71–95. It is not excluded that some parts of this sequence may stem from later redactors.

27. Aurelius, *Zukunft*, p. 2, n. 1, provides a very useful listing.

28. These verses may be an addition, since they betray late language and most of the prophetic stories in Kings were inserted at a later stage than the Babylonian edition of the Deuteronomistic History.

Southern kingdom. Marc Brettler has argued that 2 Kgs 17.7–12 is 'a misplaced fragment of a speech which justified the exile of Judah'.[29] This is nicely speculated but not a necessary assumption. The Deuteronomistic scribes in the Babylonian period opted for an 'open end' of their history for the following reasons: first, it was difficult to provide a detailed explanation for the end of the Judean kingdom so shortly after the positive account of Josiah's reform; and, second, they probably were not sure how to evaluate the chances for the restoration of the Davidic dynasty and how to look at the future. There were perhaps even conflicting views about the future of the monarch. And finally, by ending the story with 2 Kgs 25.21: 'and all Judah was deported away from her land', they made out of the exile the matrix of an identity for the 'true Israel'.

We may summarize the structure of the Deuteronomistic History through the above discourses in a diagram.

Deut. 1–30:	*Moses' farewell speech:*	ORIGINS
	criteria to evaluate the following	
	history.	
	Ch. 28 (and elsewhere):	
	<u>announcement of the exile</u>	
Josh. 1:	Yahweh's speech to Joshua:	
	<u>announcement of the conquest</u>	
		CONQUEST
Josh. 23:	*Joshua's farewell speech:*	
	accomplishment of the conquest;	
	<u>announcement of the exile</u>	
Judg. 2.6–3.6:	discourse	
	introducing the time of the Judges	
		THE TIME OF JUDGES
1 Sam. 12:	*Samuel's farewell speech:*	
	summary of the foregoing history,	
	<u>announcement of divine sanction</u>	
		THE UNITED MONARCHY

---

29.   Brettler, *Creation*, p. 122.

1 Kgs 8:	Solomon's inauguration speech:
	fulfilment of promises to David,
	<u>announcement of exile</u>
	THE TWO KINGDOMS
2 Kgs 17:	discourse: comment on the
	collapse of Israel;
	summary of the foregoing history,
	<u>announcement of Judah's exile</u>
	THE LAST DAYS OF JUDAH
2 Kgs 25	(open end): exile

It is obvious that the exile, the deportation out of the land, is the comprehensive theme that binds together the different traditions and periods as organized in the Babylonian edition of the Deuteronomistic History. This exilic perspective also contributes to create the myth of the empty land as expressed in 2 Kgs 25.21. Consequently, those who remained in Palestine do not really belong to Judah, and will be considered by some of the so-called Golah (the exiles) as the unclean 'people of the land', which has no right to claim the possession of the land. This territorial conflict will become an important issue during the Persian period; it is prepared by the ideology of exile in the Deuteronomistic History. But let us now consider some important points of the exilic edition of this History.

3. The Exilic Edition of the Deuteronomistic History

3.1. The Book of Deuteronomy: The Reader's Guide to the History

Mainly concerned with the ideology of centralization and of absolute loyalty to Yahweh in its Assyrian edition (Deut. 6.4–5; 12–26*; 28*), the book of Deuteronomy operates in its exilic edition as overture to the story from conquest to the loss of the land, as depicted in Joshua, Judges, Samuel and Kings.

3.1.1. The Literary Fiction of Deuteronomy

The literary fiction of Deuteronomy as Moses' last speech reflects the situation after 597 and 587 BCE. By directly addressing their audience, the Deuteronomists in a way made them contemporaries with Moses, and this fiction corresponds to the actual situation of the group in Babylonia to which the Deuteronomists address their history: as at the time of Moses, they find themselves outside the land and wait for instructions about the possibility of entering this land. Since the monarchy failed, the Deuteronomists locate all important institutions in the period of 'origins', making Moses the mediator between Yahweh and Israel. Traditionally, it is the king who represents the deity and transmits the law; these functions are now taken over by Moses. In fact, in the Deuteronomistic presentation, no new divine law is revealed after Moses. All the following heroes as well as the kings have to conform their acts to the law of Moses, which works as criterion for the comprehension of the following history.

3.1.2. The Construction of Israel's Origins in Deut. 1–3

The opening chapters Deut. 1–3 (the original account probably contained 1.1*, 6–7a*, 8*, 19–30, 32–45; 2.1–3, 4–9*, 25–30a*, 31–35; 3.1–7, 10a, 12a, 23–28)[30] present themselves as a recapitulation of former events in the wilderness since the exodus from Egypt. These stories have parallels in the book of Numbers (Deut. 1.19–45

---

30.   Almost everyone agrees that ch. 4, which presents a monotheistic ideology coming close to Second Isaiah, is an addition from the Persian period. The formation of chs 1–3 seems a very complex one (see the different proposals of Rose, M., *5. Mose* [Zürcher Bibelkommentare: AT 5; Zürich: Theologischer Verlag, 1994], pp. 371–416 and 471–88, as well as of Otto, E., *Das Deuteronomium im Pentateuch und Hexateuch: Studien zur Literaturgeschichte von Pentateuch und Hexateuch im Lichte des Deuteronomiumsrahmen* [FAT 30; Tübingen: Mohr Siebeck, 2000], pp. 12–109 and 129–38). The most important observations, which lead to the reconstruction as suggested above, are the following: 1.9–18 interrupts the order to conquer the land (1.6–8*) and the story about the refusal of the conquest (1.19–45). 2.10–24 repeats the story of 2.1–9* and adds numerous geographical details (also in 3.8–9, 10b–11, 12b–16), which are not typical for the Deuteronomistic style. 3.18–22 anticipates the announcement of Joshua's installation in v. 28.

and Num. 13–14: refusal of the conquest and divine sanction; Deut. 2.1–23 and Num. 20.10–21; 21.10–20: crossing through Edom and Moab; Deut. 2.25–3.11 and Num. 21.21–35: conquest of Transjordan territories; Deut. 3.21–29 and Num. 27: divine order for the installation of Joshua), and scholars have often regarded the accounts in Numbers as the 'older sources' on which the Deuteronomists relied. But this view is not convincing and has been challenged in several recent works.[31] If the Deuteronomists really wanted to recapitulate the stories from Numbers, why should they quote so few of these accounts? And if they depended on the text from Numbers, it is difficult to believe that they dropped out such important scenes as for instance Moses' intercession in Num. 14 which convinces Yahweh not to destroy the whole people. If the Deuteronomists had known Num. 14.12, where Yahweh makes a sharp distinction between Moses and the people, how would they have been able to write Moses' statement in Deut. 1.37: 'Even with me, Yahweh was angry on your account' (see also 3.26)? Deut. 1–3 contains therefore older accounts on which the authors of Numbers relied.[32] In Num. 13–14, the so-called 'spy story' is the centre of a huge cycle of rebellions (Num. 11–20), whereas in Deuteronomy this story appears as a prologue to the conquest of Transjordan. It is placed at the very beginning of Moses' historical 'recapitulation' and provides a paradigm of the themes of conquest and loss of the land, which run from Joshua to Kings: each revolt against Yahweh and Moses may imply the loss of the land and the constraint to live and to die outside the land. The conquest stories in Deut. 2–3 further reflect a 'moderate' view as to territorial claims: the Edomite, Moabite and Ammonite territories are excluded from the land given to Israel by Yahweh. This recognition of borders should probably be understood as an appeal to accept the territorial organization of the Levant under Babylonian occupation.[33]

---

31.   See especially Van Seters, J., *The Pentateuch: A Social Science Commentary* (Trajectories; Sheffield: Sheffield Academic Press, 1999), pp. 148–51.

32.   It seems quite obvious that the Deuteronomists did not simply make up these accounts. But it is impossible to reconstruct and to locate these older traditions.

33.   The kings Sihon and Og are mythical figures, and their land not clearly delimited. Their defeat by Israel serves as a paradigm for a successful conquest in case Israel conforms to the law (here especially to Deut. 20).

These chapters create a 'collective memory';[34] they situate the origins of the group, they address the myth of the exodus and the promise and conquest of the land.

3.1.3. The References to the 'Fathers' and the Exodic Origin Myth

This construction of the past is reinforced by the numerous references to the 'fathers' or 'ancestors' (*ābôt*) which play an extremely important role for the understanding of Deuteronomy's ideology.[35] They often appear within stereotyped expressions. The most important of these formulas relates the fathers to an oath of Yahweh, which concerns mainly the gift of the land sworn to the fathers (1.8, 35; 6.1, 18 etc.), but also the 'covenant' (7.12; 8.18 etc.). Quite frequent also is the use of the title by which Yahweh is referred to as the 'god of the fathers'. Another expression is about the 'not knowing' of the fathers often related to 'other gods', whom the fathers did not know (13.7; 28.64 etc.). Who are those fathers? It is generally assumed that they refer to the Patriarchs Abraham, Isaac and Jacob. Indeed certain texts, for instance Deut. 1.8 and 34.4, explicitly identify the fathers with the Patriarchs; but this identification is very probably due to very late redactors. If one analyses carefully the different contexts in which the fathers appear, one has to conclude that for the Deuteronomistic school the fathers mentioned in Deuteronomy are not the Patriarchs, but refer in most cases to Egypt or designate the ancestors in general. Let us consider the following example in Deut. 6.18–19. These verses contain a motivation for the necessity to conform to Yahweh's laws: 'so that it may go well with you, and so that you may go in and take possession of the good land which Yahweh swore to give to your fathers by thrusting out all your enemies before you, as Yahweh has said'. The semantic field of this assertion is a military one; the phrase 'to go and take possession' refers to the tradition of the wars of Yahweh. This military context contradicts the pacifist attitude of the Patriarchal

---

34.   See on this Halbwachs, M., *On Collective Memory* (trans. L.A. Coser; The Heritage of Sociology; Chicago, IL: Chicago University Press, 1992).

35.   For more details and all references see Römer, T., 'Deuteronomy in Search of Origins', in G.N. Knoppers and J.G. McConville (eds), *Reconsidering Israel and Judah: Recent Studies on the Deuteronomistic History* (SBTS 8; Winona Lake, IN: Eisenbrauns, 2000), pp. 112–38.

narratives. Furthermore, the use of the adjective 'good' to describe the land does not occur in the stories of Abraham, Isaac and Jacob. The parallels in Exod. 3.8 and Num. 14.7 refer to the Exodus tradition. This is the context in which the fathers must be located. For the Deuteronomists the land was promised to the fathers in Egypt (the same idea is attested in Ezek. 20). If the Deuteronomistic fathers refer to Egypt, does this mean that the Deuteronomists were unaware of the Patriarchal tradition? This is not the case, but apparently they were hostile to the origin myth of the Patriarchs. The conclusion of the law in Deut. 26 contains a prayer, which starts with the following words: 'A wandering Aramean was my father; and he went down to Egypt'. If this text is meant to allude to Jacob, he appears in an unfavourable light: he is a stranger and he is about to perish. For the Deuteronomistic school, Egypt is the beginning of Israel's history; the ancestors before were 'Arameans'. This rejection of the Patriarchal tradition reflects ideological conflicts during the Babylonian and Persian period. Ezek. 33.24 shows that the population who remained in Judah during the Babylonian occupation claimed the possession of the land, arguing that they were the descendants of Abraham who already inhabited the land. It seems therefore that during the sixth and fifth century BCE, two origin myths competed: an autochthonous, genealogical myth and an exodic, 'vocational' myth, according to which the identity of a group is not defined by descent but by the acceptance of an original 'constitution' or a treaty between the deity and the group.

3.1.4. Deut. 5 and the Organization of the Law

The Deuteronomistic school was advocating the latter concept which is detailed in ch. 5; this chapter followed in the exilic edition directly after Deut. 1–3*. Deut. 5*[36] (with 6.1–3) was placed before the Josianic introduction in 6.4 in order to give a clear location for the origin of the law and to legitimate Moses as the only mediator between Yahweh and the people. According to this text the original treaty is located on the mountain of Yahweh, at Horeb. One should not look for Horeb on a map; the name is a literary construct from a Hebrew

---

36.   The introduction in 5.1a*, which mentions Moses in the third person, was introduced after the insertion of ch. 4. The original introduction in 5.1 was 'Hear Israel', a parallel to 6.4.

root meaning dry, waste or desert. The importance of the treaty is stressed by the following assertion: 'Not with our fathers did Yahweh establish this treaty, but with us, who are all of us here alive today' (5.3). The reality of this treaty (the Deuteronomic laws) is emphasized for the exilic community, which had become 'contemporary' with Moses. Interestingly, the Deuteronomists create a summary of a sort of this covenant, which is the 'Decalogue',[37] the 'ten commandments'[38] that Yahweh communicates to the people gathered at his mountain.

The Decalogue in 5.6–31* corresponds to Deuteronomistic ideology, especially the emphasis on the Exodus, the appeal for exclusive veneration of Yahweh and the polemics against 'popular religion' (images, magic). The 'social laws' in vv. 17–21 are common to ancient Near Eastern law and occur also in the last part of the Deuteronomic code. It has often been observed[39] that the organization of the Decalogue corresponds roughly to the arrangement of laws in Deut. 12–26:

Deut. 5.6–11	*Deut. 12–13; 14.21–29*[40]
Exclusive veneration of Yahweh, no other gods, no illegitimate use of Yahweh's name	Centralization of the Yahweh worship, laws about apostasy
Deut. 5.12–15	*Deut. 15–16*
Shabbat, seventh day	Laws for the seventh year; festivals
Deut. 5.16	*Deut. 17–18*
Parents	Authorities
Deut. 5.17–21	*Deut. 19–25*
Life in society	Life in society

37.   We cannot enter here into the endless discussion about the two versions of the Decalogue in Exod. 20 and Deut. 5. It is difficult to decide which of the two versions is the older one. In the present state of the text, however, it is quite clear that Exod. 20 is linked with Priestly concerns (see the reference to Gen. 1.1–2.3 in order to legitimate the Shabbat), whereas Deut. 5 corresponds to the Deuteronomistic ideology (it refers to Egypt in the Shabbat prescription). We also leave aside the question if there existed once an older, shorter Decalogue.

38.   In fact, neither in Exod. 20 nor in Deut. 5 are these commandments counted. The expression 'ten words' only occurs in Exod. 34.2; Deut. 4.13 and 10.4. All these texts are probably later than the exilic edition of Deuteronomy.

39.   See for instance Kaufmann, S.A., 'The Structure of the Deuteronomic Law', *Maarav* 1 (1979), pp. 105–58.

The Decalogue pattern of the Deuteronomic Law code should therefore be considered as a result of the exilic edition of Deuteronomy; the Decalogue is therefore not an independent summary of old and genuine Israelite ethics, but rather a table of content of the law code in Deut. 12–26.

Four of the Decalogue's commandments are expressly motivated. This means that they were new principles, which were (in contrast to vv. 17–21) not widely accepted. They reflect ideological changes in the Yahwistic religion, which the intelligentsia created during the sixth century BCE. The first one, which would become very important for Judaism, is the prohibition of statues and images of Yahweh[41] in 5.8a, 9b–10, which was later applied to a more general prohibition of visual representations (vv. 8b–9a). The defence of a 'wrongful use' of Yahweh's name alludes to a magic conception of the deity's name. The prohibition was later understood as a general interdiction to pronounce the name of Yahweh.[42] The long explanation in 5.13–16 shows the novelty of the understanding of the Shabbat as the seventh day of the week, which arose probably during the exilic period; the name is often considered as of Babylonian origin designating originally a festival of the new moon (see Amos 8.5). Its transformation is perhaps linked to the invention of a 'sacred time' instead of the 'sacred space' (the temple), which was not available in exile.[43] The commandment to honour the (living) parents should be understood as a transformation of the veneration of the dead ancestors to which the Deuteronomists were strongly opposed

40.   Deut. 14.1–20 is a postexilic, probably Priestly, addition, see Mayes, A.D.H., 'Deuteronomy 14 and the Deuteronomic World View', in F. García Martínez *et al.* (eds), *Studies in Deuteronomy* (Festschrift C.J. Labuschagne; SVT 53; Leiden, New York and Cologne: Brill, 1994), pp. 165–81.

41.   In monarchic times there was probably a statue of Yahweh in the Jerusalemite temple, which was probably destroyed or deported by the Babylonians, see for more details Uehlinger, C., 'Anthropomorphic Cult Statuary in Iron Age Palestine and the Search for Yahweh's Cult Images', in K. van der Toorn (ed.), *The Image and the Book: Iconic Cults, Aniconism, and the Rise of the Book Religion in Israel and the Ancient Near East* (CBET 21; Leuven: Peeters, 1997), pp. 97–156.

42.   This practice is clearly attested in the thrid century BCE since the Greek translators of the Pentateuch replace Yahweh by *kurios* (the Lord).

43.   The transformation of the Shabbat may also be linked with the introduction of a solar calendar, in place of the lunar one

(Deut. 18.11; 26.14). One may also underline the new importance of the family structures after the breaking down of the other institutions. In a way, we may find in these new prescriptions the origin of important markers of Jewish identity from the Persian period until today: a religion without images, a non-sacrificial Shabbat worship, and the importance of family as 'religious agent'.

The story in 5.23–31 legitimates Moses' role as mediator between Yahweh and Israel. The Decalogue was addressed directly to the people who could not endure the immediate presence of Yahweh and therefore charged Moses to become their go-between. Telling this story, the Deuteronomists transfer the traditional functions of the king to Moses.

The exhortations, which in the exilic edition were built around Deut. 6.4–5 (6.1–3; 6.6–7*, 10–25*), and which take up the language of the Decalogue, are mainly concerned with the exclusive veneration of Yahweh and his bestowing of the land as well as the conditions linked to this gift. The theme of the land becomes dominant in 8.7–20*; 9.1, 4–6*:[44] in Deut. 8* it is opposed to the wilderness, which is described as a space of death and danger where Israel could only survive with Yahweh's help. Interestingly, there is no allusion to the continuous rebellion of the people as in the book of Numbers. Deut. 8.14–16 stands much closer to Jer. 2.4–9 than to the ideology of Numbers. The very negative view of the sojourn in the desert expressed in Numbers should therefore be later than the exilic edition of Deuteronomy. After the retrospect of Deut. 8*, Deut. 9.3–6* presents an outlook of the conquest of the land preparing on the narrative level the book of Joshua and providing for the addressees hope for a 'new conquest'. 10.12–13 takes up again the basic exhortation of 6.4–5 and concludes the exilic introduction to the law code in Deut. 12–26.[45]

---

44.   The intolerant discourse about strict separation from the other people in ch. 7 belongs probably to a new edition of the Deuteronomistic History in the Persian period as we will see. The same redactors probably added 8.1–5 as a new transition after the insertion of ch. 7.

45.   The other texts in 9–11* were added later. The 'historical summary' in 9.7–10.11, which relates the story of the golden calf as a representation of Yahweh, is traced back to Israel's revolt against Yahweh at the very beginning of his revelation and belongs probably to the Persian edition of the Deuteronomistic History (see for a similar view, Rose, *5. Mose*, pp. 505–14). 10.14–22 seems to presuppose the Priestly edition of Genesis and show the same style and ideology as Deut. 4.

As we have already seen, the original law in Deut. 12 was revised by the addition of vv. 8–12, which reinterprets the ideology of centralization in the context of an exilic situation. Deut. 13.1–10* was supplemented by vv. 12–19*. Introducing the theme of the *ḥērem* (the devotion/destruction of the booty in honour of the deity), these verses prepare the accounts in Josh. 6 and 7. Their style and ideology come close to the laws of warfare (Deut. 20), which probably were also added in the exilic edition of Deuteronomy as a 'legal' introduction to the conquest stories and not as concrete instructions for war (which were totally useless during the Babylonian and Persian periods). The main additions to the laws concerning the authorities introduce prescriptions about the king (17.14–20) and the prophets (18.9–22).[46] We will discuss the law about the king in our analysis of the Deuteronomistic ideology of kingship during the Babylonian period. The statements about the prophets make Moses the first of Israel's prophets. 18.9–22 reveals the Deuteronomistic attempt to control the prophetic milieu and to forbid the methods of popular religion to communicate with the deity: magic, divination, necromancy and so on. The 'true' prophet becomes a successor to Moses, whereas all 'false' prophets are threatened with death. The Deuteronomists invent a very easy way to distinguish the true from the false prophets: 'if a prophet speaks in the name of Yahweh but the word does not become reality, it is a word that Yahweh has not spoken. The prophet has spoken it presumptuously' (v. 22). This *post hoc* criterion tends to legitimate the prophets of doom who had announced the collapse of Israel and Judah. For the Deuteronomistic school, which started during the Babylonian exile the editing of the scrolls of Amos, Hosea, Micah, Zephaniah and also parts of Jeremiah,[47] only those prophets had divine legitimacy. Such a conception also betrays a conflict among the Judean intelligentsia during the Babylonian and Persian periods. The Deuteronomists, as well as their Priestly colleagues, were hostile to prophetic charismatic groups, which announced a new paradisaical era where prophecy would be given to the whole people and no more scribal or priestly mediation needed (see Joel 3). For the Deuteronomists, only a dead prophet is a good prophet; that means

---

46. For a discussion about the diachrony of these chapters see above, IV/.2.2.

47. Albertz, R., 'Exile as Purification: Reconstructing the "Book of the Four"', in P.L. Reddit and A. Schart (eds), *Thematic Threads of the Book of Twelve* (BZAW 325; Berlin and New York: de Gruyter, 2003), pp. 232–51.

only written prophecies under scribal control are acceptable. This will become the dominant view in latter Judaism; the Talmud states that after the exile Yahweh's spirit was taken away from the prophets and given to the 'wise men' (*Baba Bathra* 12a). By making Moses the first of all prophets, all the prophetic figures of the Deuteronomistic History[48] appear as preachers or interpreters of the Mosaic law.

The exilic redactors revised slightly the social laws in ch. 21–25*[49] and more thoroughly the conclusion in ch. 26 by adding the historical summary in vv. 5–9, a confession of cultic purity in vv. 12–15 and a formula for the conclusion of the treaty between Yahweh and Israel in vv. 16–19. The historical summary reinforces the exodic origin myth, the prayer in v. 15 has a close parallel in Solomon's prayer in 1 Kgs 8.34; this parallel makes clear that the place chosen by Yahweh can only be the Jerusalemite temple. The conclusion of the covenant links back to Deut. 5.1–3 (see also the parallels between 26.16 and 6.4–5). Since the treaty is not (only) concluded with the 'fathers' but with the present generation, the formula in 26.16–19* intends to actualize the original treaty for the exilic addressees.[50] This new conclusion of the treaty was immediately followed by the updated blessings and curses in ch. 28, which now included clear allusions to the exile, as 28.58–68 which concluded Moses' speech. The exilic edition of Deuteronomy ended with the installation of Joshua as Moses' successor in 31.1–8 and with the report of Moses' death outside the promised land in 34.1*, 4*, 5–6. The fact that Moses dies outside the land is highly significant for an exilic audience. Traditionally dying outside one's homeland is considered as one of the worst curses (see for instance Isa. 22.16–18; Amos 10.17). The death of Moses in the fields of Moab therefore provides a possibility of

48.   Most of the prophetic legends (especially the stories about Elijah and Elisha) were added to the Deuteronomistic History in a new edition at the end of the Babylonian or the beginning of the Persian period, but already in the exilic edition prophetic figures appear: Samuel, Nathan, Ahijah and so on.

49.   They probably also added the strange law in 25.17–19, according to which all Amalekites must be exterminated. On the compositional levels this text explains Yahweh's rejection of Saul in 1 Sam. 15

50.   Deut. 27 is a later, possibly post-Deuteronomistic, addition; see Na'aman, N., 'The Law of the Altar in Deuteronomy and the Cultic Site Near Shechem', in S.L. McKenzie and T. Römer (eds), *Rethinking the Foundations: Historiography in the Ancient World and in the Bible* (Festschrift J. Van Seters; BZAW 294; Berlin and New York: de Gruyter, 2000), pp. 141–61.

identification for the deportees, who were probably afraid to pass away in an 'unclean' land. According to 34.6, Yahweh himself buries Moses so that his grave remains unknown 'until today'. The insistence that nobody knows the place of Moses' tomb may well be explained by the Deuteronomistic hostility toward the popular cult of the dead (see Deut. 18.11 and 26.14). One may even guess that there existed a veneration of a tomb attributed to Moses and that the Deuteronomists were eager to eradicate such a cult. In the exilic edition of the Deuteronomistic History, Deut. 34.1–6* concludes the era of Moses. The next age (the conquest) opens in Josh. 1.1 ('After the death of Moses, the servant of Yahweh, Yahweh spoke to Joshua...'), an opening that fits well after Deut. 34.6.

3.2. From the Conquest of the Land to the Conquest of the Law: Reinterpreting Joshua

The exilic edition opened the conquest account by a programmatic speech of Yahweh to Joshua in 1.1–2, 5–7,[51] which depicts Joshua as Moses' successor but not as his equal. Even after Moses' death, Joshua remains his 'assistant' (*m^{e}šāret*)[52] who has to act according to all that Moses had commanded (v. 7[53]). The initial discourse operates a transition: the installation of Joshua as a military leader ends with an appeal to observe the prescriptions of Deuteronomy. This strategy reveals a reinterpretation of the conquest accounts in the exilic period. They are no more primarily an ideological support for the integration of 'Benjamin' into Judah (as it was the case in the Assyrian time); the revised and enlarged edition of these accounts puts forth the idea that the 'Israelites' are the legitimate owners of the land since Yahweh has handed it over to them by driving out the other people; but according to the Deuteronomists, Israel can only remain in the land if it conforms

51. For this speech see above V/.2.
52. Josh. 1.1–2 creates a difference between Moses, servant *('ebed)* of Yahweh and Joshua, assistant (*m^{e}šāret*) of Moses. The honorific title *'ebed*, which alludes to the function of a 'Prime Minister', is in the Deuteronomistic History mainly used for Moses and David. Joshua is only once called *'ebed* of Yahweh: at the moment of his death in Judg. 2.8 (=Josh. 24.29).
53. The original text of v. 7 as represented by the Greek version does not speak of Moses' law, but of everything he commanded. This is of course an allusion to the Deuteronomic 'law'.

to Yahweh's will as expressed in Deuteronomy. The land becomes more and more an ideological concern, especially with the addition of the crossing of the Jordan in Josh. 3–4*. This story followed immediately after Joshua's speech to the people and its call to follow him in the same way they followed Moses (1.10–18). The announcement of 1.11 that the Israelites will cross the Jordan in three days is taken up in 3.2 ('at the end of three days ...'). The Rahab-story in Josh. 2, which interrupts this chronology, is therefore a later non-Deuteronomistic addition.[54] The story of the Jordan crossing is based upon the ideology that this river constitutes the eastern border of the Promised Land. This contradicts the historical reality since the kingdom of Israel comprised territories located on the eastern side of the Jordan. In order to accommodate to that reality, the Deuteronomists made the Transjordanian tribes cross with the other tribes, before they are allowed to return to their possessions (see 22.1–6). The conception of the Jordan as a border of Israel's land probably arose after 733 when the eastern parts of the Israelite kingdom were transformed into Assyrian provinces. The Deuteronomistic fiction should therefore be understood as an accommodation to the territorial repartition of the Levant under the Babylonians. The crossing of a river and its more or less miraculous drying out are also common literary topics of conquest stories (see for instance Assurbanipal's crossing the Idide river,[55] Kroisos' crossing the Halys in Herodotus' *Histories* 1.75 and Xerxes' crossing of the Lysos in 7.108–109). The exilic Deuteronomistic account of the Jordan crossing approximately comprised the following verses: 3.2, 3–4*, 6–7, 14–16; 4.10–14*.[56] This story highlights Joshua as Moses' successor who does everything according to the orders of Moses. 4.14 provides a fitting conclusion: 'On that day Yahweh exalted Joshua in the eyes of all Israel, and they feared him as they had feared Moses, all the days of his life.' The time of Moses and Joshua appears therefore as a 'golden age', when everything went well since the people respected Yahweh's and Moses' commandments and could therefore occupy the land. These commandments are 'materialized' in the 'ark of the

54.   As we will see later, this story was inserted during the Persian period to counter the Deuteronomistic ideology of segregation.

55.   See Van Seters, J., 'Joshua's Campaign of Canaan and Near Eastern Historiography', SJOT 2 (1990), pp. 1–12; p. 7.

56.   See, for a quite similar reconstruction, Van Seters, 'Campaign', p. 10.

covenant',[57] which represents Yahweh's presence during the crossing and during the conquest. The theme of the ark is also a comprehensive leitmotif of the Deuteronomistic History since it reappears especially at the beginning of Samuel and 1 Kgs 6–8. The conquest story moved in the exilic edition from 4.14 to 5.13–15 and 6*; this story was the opening of the first edition of Joshua. The Deuteronomists added to the former Jericho account[58] especially vv. 1, 6a, 7, 10*, 12, 16*, 17, 20a, 24a, 26. These additions insist on the fact that it is not Israel's military power that leads to victory but Yahweh's miraculous intervention through his presence in the ark (v. 17). The new introduction in v. 1, stating that Jericho was totally shut up, establishes a link with the law about warfare in Deut. 20.11 (a town that opens its gates must not be destroyed), providing a new reason for the destruction of Jericho. The concluding remark in v. 26 where Joshua curses anyone who would rebuild Jericho provides an editorial link to different periods. It is an application of Deut. 13.17 and a preparation for 1 Kgs 16.34 where the attempt to rebuild Jericho has a catastrophic outcome. The Deuteronomistic editors of the Babylonian period also provide in 7.2–6, 8–9 a new introduction to the conquest of Ai in Josh. 8*, which they complete by adding vv. 3–9, 22, 24, 28. The wrong report of the spies and the defeat of the people in 7.2–6 remind of Deut. 1. By adding this story, the redactors create a scheme, which they also use to organize the book of Judges: fault of the people (7.1–4) – divine sanction: defeat (7.5–6) – lament (7.8–9) – positive divine intervention (8.1–29*). This new edition modifies the ideology of the older account by introducing (as in Deut. 1) an account of failure; the possession of the land is only possible for those who act according to Yahweh's commandments (8.8). Whereas the Josianic account was mainly concerned with the territory of Benjamin, 10.28–43* enlarges the

57.   The original function of this ark is not very clear. Some scholars argue for a military symbol representing the deity's presence in war, others think of a footstool of the invisibly enthroned deity; for more details see Seow, C.L., 'Ark of the Covenant', *ABD* 1 (1992), pp. 386–93.

58.   See above IV.3.3. The Greek version of Josh. 6 offers a quite different organization of the story, which we cannot discuss here. There are many chapters in Joshua, where the Greek text differs remarkably from the Hebrew text; see on this Auld, A.G., *Joshua Retold: Synoptic Perspectives* (Old Testament Studies; Edinburgh: T. & T. Clark, 1998) and van der Meer, M.N., *Formation and Reformulation: The Redaction of the Book of Joshua in the Light of the Oldest Textual Witnesses* (SVT 102; Leiden: Brill, 2004).

conquest to the south and 11.1–15 to the north. The extension of this 'conquest' from Hazor to Hebron corresponds roughly to the extension of the kingdoms of Israel and Judah, which the exilic Deuteronomists claimed to be the land that Yahweh had allotted to Israel. According to 10.36–37, Hebron was taken by Joshua and 'all Israel'. This contradicts the tradition of Caleb as conqueror of Hebron (see Josh. 15.13–14), which did not fit with the Deuteronomistic ideology of the conquest of the whole land by Joshua and 'all Israel'.[59] Since the different lists of territories, borders and towns do not reveal Deuteronomistic concerns[60] (they are often considered as stemming from a Priestly milieu), the Deuteronomistic edition of Joshua possibly enlarged the concluding remark in Josh. 11.23 by adding 21.43–45. After the return of the Transjordanian tribes in 22.1–6 the conquest ended with Joshua's final discourse in 23.1–3, 9, 11, 14–16a, which insists on the total conquest of the land, but announces already the exile.[61] In the exilic edition of the Deuteronomistic History the books of Deuteronomy and Joshua are closely tied together. They appear as a golden age, where Yahweh has established his treaty and law through Moses and has given the land through Joshua. For the exilic Deuteronomists conquest and law are related. To possess the land one must obey the Law, mediated by Moses and the Deuteronomists.

3.3. The Invention of a Period of Judges (Judg. 2.6–19*–1 Sam. 12*)

Even if many handbooks of the Hebrew Bible present the period of the Judges as a historical reality, this period is nothing other than a literary invention of the Deuteronomistic school. The Judean scribes probably inherited an Israelite scroll,[62] which contained several stories of

---

59.   There was apparently a debate about the conquest of Hebron since 11.21–22 (a later interpolation) reaffirms that the conqueror was Joshua, contrary to the non-Deuteronomistic texts in Josh 15.13–14 and Judg. 1.12–15. The spy story in Num. 13–14 looks like a compromise since Joshua and Caleb act together.

60.   Except Josh. 15* and 18*; the origin of these texts may be the seventh century. See above IV/.3.1 and for Josh. 15 de Vos, J.C., *Das Los Judas: über Entstehung und Ziele der Landbeschreibung in Josua 15* (SVT 95; Leiden: Brill, 2003). He admits a seventh-century origin for Josh. 15, but thinks that the text was inserted much later into the book of Joshua.

61.   For details see above V/.2.

62.   This may have happened after 722 BCE, or under Josiah if the scroll was conserved at the sanctuary of Bethel.

saviours (Judg. 3.12– 9.55* or even 3.12–12.7*).[63] With the exception of Othniel (3.7–11, the story is clearly a Judean addition) these heroes are all of Northern origin and that observation favours the existence of a Northern document; during the Babylonian period this scroll was interpolated by the Deuteronomists in order to create an inter-mediate period between the origins (Deuteronomy–Joshua) and the history of the monarchy (Samuel–Kings).

3.3.1. The Deuteronomistic Editing of Judges

As already mentioned the Deuteronomists created the introduction in Judg. 2.6–12, 14–16, 18–19. With this prelude they transformed the ideology of the older collection, which celebrated the feats of Northern legendary heroes by introducing a new, overwhelming topic: the Israelites' veneration of other deities,[64] which provokes Yahweh's anger. The military problems that some tribes encounter with their neighbours are transformed into Yahweh's punishments; the saviours become 'Judges' sent by Yahweh after Israel had returned to him. All the stories are now presented as a repeated cycle of apostasy and return to Yahweh. In the Deuteronomistic perspective this period

---

63.   Since our aim is to present the Deuteronomistic editing of the book of Judges, we will not discuss the pre-Deuteronomistic origins of the saviour stories. According to Noth the Deuteronomist had at his disposal two kinds of material: stories and a list of 'minor Judges'. Since Jephthah appeared in the list as well as in a story, the Deuteronomist split the list and inserted in its midst the Jephthah story (10.1–5; 12.6–15). According to W. Richter, the original saviour book ended in 9.55; for a summary of his position see Mayes, A.D.H., *Judges* (OT Guides; Sheffield: Sheffield Academic Press, 1989).

64.   One should notice that these other deities are in Judges often called the Baals and the Asherahs, and rarely 'other gods' (*ʾelōhîm ʾaḥērîm*), which is the standard appellation in Deuteronomy and Kings. This may be an indication that the different scrolls were edited and revised by different Deuteronomists who nevertheless belonged to the same group. Such a hypothesis allows also explaining the different profile of Judges compared to other Deuteronomistic scrolls. It has often been pointed out that the Deuteronomistic texts in Judges are not concerned with cult centralization, but above all with the exclusive veneration of Yahweh. This does not necessarily mean that the Deuteronomistic redaction of Judges is necessarily later than those of Deuteronomy or Kings. Since the scroll of Judges originated in saviour stories from different Northern tribes it was difficult to introduce the theme of cult centralization.

foreshadows the story of the monarchy, which is presented as an alternation of acceptable and unacceptable kings.

Apart from the introduction in Judg. 2.6–19*, the exilic Deuteronomists added the story of Othniel (3.7–11), which is a strict application of the scheme presented in the introduction. They reworked the older stories especially in 3.12–15; 4.1–3; 6.1–2a, 11–24*; 8.33–35; 10.6–10a*, 17–18*.[65] In the exilic edition of Judges the twelfth Judge is not Samson but Samuel (see 1 Sam. 7.15–17). This means that Judg. 12 was once followed by the birth story of Samuel in 1 Sam. 1 (Judg. 12.15 and 1 Sam. 1.1 are geographically linked through the mention of Ephraim). The burlesque Samson stories in Judg. 13–16, which probably reveal Hellenistic influences,[66] as well as Judg. 17–18 and 19–21, should be considered as post-Deuteronomistic pieces that were added in order to create an independent book of Judges (without the Samuel stories).

The Deuteronomistic story of Samuel (1 Sam 1;[67] 2.18–21; 3*; 7.5–17) reveals him as a figure of transition. He is the last Judge and fights successfully against the Philistines; but he also brings this time to an end as he tries to transform the charismatic office of the Judge into a hereditary one by appointing his sons as successors (8.1–3). For the Deuteronomists, Samuel is also the second great prophet after Moses; as such he plays an important role in the institution of the monarchy, which occupies the last chapters of the Deuteronomistic period of Judges in 1 Sam. 8–12. The question of the monarchy is treated already in Deut. 17.14–20 and appears then in Judg. 6–9 in a narrative context. After the deportation of the royal family to Babylon,

---

65.   Judg. 6.7–10 is missing in a manuscript from Qumran and should therefore be considered as a much later addition. 10.11–16 is probably also younger than the exilic edition of Judges.

66.   See Nauerth, C., 'Simsons Taten. Motivgeschichtliche Überlegungen', *DBAT* 21 (1985), pp. 94–120. There are other texts in Judges that betray Hellenistic influence; they are probably late interpolations: the so-called fable of Jotham in Judg. 9.8–15 has a stunning parallel in a fable attributed to Aesop (see Briffard, C., 'Gammes sur l'acte de traduire', *Foi & Vie* 101, *Cahier Biblique* 41 [2002], pp. 12–18) and the sacrifice of Jephthah's daughter in 11.30–31, 34–40 might be inspired by the fate of Iphigenia as related by Euripides (see Römer, T.C., 'Why Would the Deuteronomists Tell about the Sacrifice of Jephthah's Daughter?', *JSOT* 77 [1998], pp. 27–38).

67.   As we have seen above (IV.4.2), 1 Sam. 1* was perhaps originally the birth story of Saul. But for the Deuteronomists it introduces the story of Samuel.

the 'eternal' Davidic dynasty seemed to have come to an end. It is not astonishing that the question of the monarchy became an issue of debate amongst the Judean intellectuals during the Babylonian and Persian periods.

3.3.2. The Deuteronomistic Attitude to Monarchy (Deut. 17.14–20 and 1 Sam. 8–12)

The so-called 'law of the king' in Deut. 17* is not meant to prescribe how to choose the best king. It is much more a summary of a sort that resumes the ambiguous Deuteronomistic attitude towards the royal institution. Deut. 17.14–20 also constitutes a table of contents of the accounts about monarchy in Judges, Samuel and Kings.

Deut. 17.14: 'When you have entered the land that Yahweh your god is giving to you … and you say, "I will set a king over me, like all the nations that are around me"', foreshadows the first story about the installation of the monarchy in 1 Sam. 8, where the elders address Samuel: 'Set a king over us to judge (!) us like all the nations' (v. 5).

Deut. 17.15 is concerned with the divine election of the king: 'The king whom you will set over you must be a king chosen by Yahweh your god.' The divine election of the legitimate king is a common topic in the ancient Near East. In the context of the Deuteronomistic History, this verse alludes to the divine election of Saul according to 1 Sam. 10.24 where Samuel asks the people: 'Have you seen the one whom Yahweh has chosen?' But the theme of divine election is also used the other way round. 1 Sam. 16–2 Sam. 5 legitimates David's (the Southern) election by recounting Saul's (the Northern) rejection (see 2 Sam. 6.21).

The prohibition of a foreign king in Deut. 17.15 alludes to the foreign (Phoenician) influences in the Northern kingdom, which, according to the Deuteronomists, hastened the fall of Samaria.

Deut. 17.16 contains a quite curious prescription: 'He must not acquire many horses for himself, or return the people to Egypt in order to acquire more horses, since Yahweh has said to you: "You will never return that way again".' Horses are a symbol of royal power and 1 Kgs 10.26 reports an impressive possession of horses and chariots by Solomon. According to Deuteronomistic ideology the ideal king should not have too much power and personal property (see v. 17b). This might reflect the reign of Josiah who was apparently controlled by the

Deuteronomistic scribes and counsellors. The link between horses and Egypt probably refers to the different attempts of Israelite and Judean kings to ally with Egypt (see for instance 2 Kgs 17.4). The 'quoted' word of Yahweh concerning the return to Egypt is not attested elsewhere; it is a Deuteronomistic invention. The worst curse in Deut. 28.68 announces such a return and according to 2 Kgs 25.26 'all the people, high and low ... set out and went to Egypt for they were afraid of the Chaldeans'.[68] Deut. 17.16 contains already a hint of the end of Israel's and Judah's history, arguing that bad kings (according to Deuteronomistic criteria) will provoke a catastrophe. Deut. 17.17, 'and he must not possess many wives for himself, or else his heart will turn away', is a clear allusion to the Deuteronomistic comment on Solomon: 'King Solomon loved many foreign women ... and his wives turned away his heart' (1 Kgs 11.1–3). Whereas in the Josianic version Solomon appeared entirely as a positive king, in the exilic edition of 1 Kgs 1–11 he is Janus-faced of a kind. Until ch. 8, Solomon is mainly the wise king, builder of the temple. But after the warning in 1 Kgs 9.1-9, the stories in 9.10–24* and 11 introduce negative behaviours that will explain the breakdown of the 'United Kingdom', which is related in 1 Kgs 12.

The conclusion in Deut. 17.18–20* contains the quintessence of the Deuteronomistic view about law and kingship: 'When he has taken the throne of his kingdom he shall write[69] a copy of this law[70] ... It shall remain with him and he shall read in it all days of his life ...' As we have noted the king is traditionally the mediator between the deity and the law. In the view of Deut. 17 the king is less the mediator than the addressee of the law (as is Joshua in Josh. 1.7). This means that the king depends on the transmitters of the law, 'Moses' and the Deuteronomistic scribes. Deut. 17.18–20 also indicates that the history of the monarchy will be evaluated according to the Deuteronomistic law, especially according to the ideology of cultic centralization and the exclusive veneration of Yahweh.

---

68.   The exilic edition of the Deuteronomistic History probably ended first with 2 Kgs 25.21: 'So Judah was exiled out of its land.' It was probably soon updated to 2 Kgs 25.26.

69.   The expression 'he shall write', means 'he shall have written' (as 'the king builds the temple' means 'he has the temple built'). Only few kings did know how to write and to read.

70.   'In presence of the levitical priests' is an interpolation from the time of the Chronicles (end of the Persian period or beginning of the Hellenistic era).

Deut. 17.14–20 reveals an ambiguous attitude to monarchy; this attitude concords with the stories about the rise of the monarchy, which the Deuteronomists locate during the period of the Judges. The idea of kingship arises for the first time after Gideon's exploits against the Midianites, when the Israelites ask him to establish a dynasty of governors: 'Rule over us,[71] you and your son and your grandson.' But Gideon declines the offer: 'I will not rule over you and my son will not rule over you; Yahweh will rule over you' (8.22–23). The argument that Yahweh is Israel's real sovereign reappears in 1 Sam. 8; it can be understood as an attempt to accept the Babylonian and Persian kings ruling over Judah and to consider them as Yahweh's tools. Gideon's son Abimelech[72] does not conform to his father's statement; he proclaims himself Israel's sovereign in Shechem and rules for three years. This experience ends in a bloodbath and Abimelech is killed by a woman. The location of the story in Shechem is an allusion to the Northern kingdom, which from the very beginning appears under very negative auspices.

After the Gideon–Abimelech prelude,[73] 1 Sam. 8–12 presents a large collection of competing stories about the origin of the Israelite monarchy. According to 1 Sam. 8 the reason for the desire to establish the monarchy is provoked in a certain way by Samuel himself; he designs that his sons should succeed him, but they behave very badly and so the Israelites ask for a king. In this story, human kingship is seen very negatively; it is a rejection of Yahweh's kingship (v. 8). Samuel gives a very critical description of the king's right who will take what he wants from the people (vv. 11–18), but finally Yahweh accepts the idea of a king over Israel (v. 22). According to the next fairytale-like story (9.1–10.16), which existed in a shorter form already in a Josianic edition, the initiative for a king comes from Yahweh himself. He orders Samuel to anoint Saul as a ruler over Israel (9.16*). In 10.17–26 the perspective changes anew. Here Saul is elected king either by

---

71.   In this story the root 'to be king' (*mālak*) is avoided; the verb used here is *māšal* (to rule).

72.   Originally, Abimelech was the son of Jerubbaal. Judg. 6.32 identifies Gideon and Jerubbaal.

73.   Judg. 17–21 contains the following refrain: 'In those days there was no king in Israel; all the people did what was right in their own eyes.' This refrain is due to post-Deuteronomistic redactors who wanted to conclude the period of Judges in Judg. 21.25.

drawing of lots (v. 21) or because of his tallness (vv. 22–23). The story opens with a negative statement of Samuel, quite similar to 1 Sam. 8: 'Today you have rejected your god, who saves you from all your calamities ... and you have said: "No! But set a king over us!"' (v. 19). Nevertheless the narrative continues with a more positive attitude since Saul is explicitly said to be chosen by Yahweh (v. 24), and those who despise him are labelled 'sons of Belial' (wicked persons).[74] The next story (1 Sam. 11*), which also belonged already to the Josianic edition, explains Saul's rise to kingship in an entirely positive way by his victory against the Ammonite king. Here Samuel takes the initiative to make Saul king over Israel (vv. 14–15).[75] But the recapitulation of this story in Samuel's final discourse (1 Sam. 12) conflicts with the positive view of ch. 11: 'But when you saw that King Nahash of the Ammonites came against you, you said to me: "No, but a king shall reign over us", though Yahweh, your god, is your king' (12.12). This view is quite similar to 1 Sam. 8; at the end of Samuel's discourse, however, kingship seems to be accepted, under the condition that the king and the people behave as faithful servants of Yahweh and respect his law. At the conclusion of his speech Samuel predicts nevertheless the destruction of the people and the king: 'if you still do wickedly, you shall be swept away, you and your king' (v. 25). At the term of the period of Judges[76] and at the beginning of the monarchic era the end of kingship is already alluded to.

How to explain the competing views about kingship in 1 Sam. 8–12? Some scholars (especially from the so-called Göttingen school[77]) argue that we should distinguish during the exilic period two or even more different Deuteronomistic attitudes towards the monarchy: the older positive accounts about the rise of Saul in 8.1–5, 22b; 9.1–10, 16*; 10.17, 18aα, 20–27*; 11 were taken over and reworked by the exilic 'DtrH', who had a positive attitude towards the monarchy, whereas 8.6–22a; 10.18aß.b–19 and 12* are ascribed to an (exilic or early postexilic) 'DtrN' who betrays a negative attitude towards the

---

74.	The etymology of 'belial' is uncertain. Some scholars explain it as 'underworld', but the signification 'unworthy' seems more plausible.

75.	In order to harmonize this account with the foregoing stories the present text speaks of a 'renewal' of Saul's kingship.

76.	For 1 Sam. 12 as conclusion of the time of Judges see above V/.2.

77.	See the history of research, II/.3.2.

monarchy.[78] In my view, this solution is odd. First of all, the positive accounts about the origins of kingship, legitimated by Yahweh, better fit in the monarchic period than the sixth century BCE. Second, one should pay attention to the result of mixing together positive and negative accounts about the origins of monarchy. A look at the arrangement of 1 Sam. 8–12 reveals a clear structure:

1 Sam. 8	1 Sam 9.1–10.16	1 Sam. 10.17–27	1 Sam. 11	1 Sam. 12
–	+	–/+	+	–

The older positive stories about Saul's rise to monarchy are framed by negative considerations about kingship. In the middle stands a story, which contains both negative and positive statements. The present arrangement of 1 Sam. 8–12 reveals an ambiguous attitude to the institution of monarchy, which corresponds to the 'mandarin' attitude of the exilic Deuteronomists. The same attitude can be found in the books of Kings where (more or less) 'good' kings alternate with 'bad' kings. The Deuteronomists of the Babylonian time were therefore not nationalistic, unconditional supporters of the Judean monarchy; as a matter of fact they had no clear position as to the future of monarchy. They wanted to leave different options open; they probably would have accepted working under a Judean king, but also in the Babylonian and Persian administration. It is often argued that the account about King Jehoiachin's release from his Babylonian prison in 2 Kgs 25.27–30 expresses hope for the restoration of the Davidic dynasty. But this story was probably added later; the exilic edition of the Deuteronomistic History ended in 2 Kgs 25.21 or 25.26; and, as we shall see, 2 Kgs 25.27–30 deals much less with the renewal of monarchy than with the birth of Diaspora.

---

78.   See for instance Dietrich, W., 'History and Law: Deuteronomistic Historiography and Deuteronomic Law Exemplified in the Passage from the Period of the Judges to the Monarchical Period', in A. de Pury, T. Römer and J.-D. Macchi (eds), *Israel Constructs its History: Deuteronomistic Historiography in Recent Research* (JSOTSup 306; Sheffield: Sheffield Academic Press, 2000), pp. 315–42. 'DtrN' is often considered as a symbol, which covers different redactional layers.

3.3.3. The Ark Narrative in 1 Sam. 4–6 (and 2 Sam. 6)

The periplus of the ark in 1 Sam. 4.1b–7.1 interrupts the story about Samuel and the origins of monarchy. It is possible that the Deuteronomists interpolated here an older Northern tradition,[79] reading it in the exilic context as a story about Yahweh leaving his land[80] (the Assyrians and the Babylonians frequently practised deportations of statues and symbols of deities from the conquered peoples). In any case the ark narrative does not contain any obvious Deuteronomistic language. The Deuteronomists would then have taken over an older text without any notable editing. An alternative solution would be to consider 1 Sam. 4–6 as a post-Deuteronomistic addition, since this narrative does not really concord with the Deuteronomistic ideology. In 6.3 the Philistine priests and magicians know exactly what to do with the ark, whereas in Deuteronomistic texts magicians are sharply condemned (Deut. 18.10; 2 Kgs 17.17). A late date for the ark narrative is also suggested by the observation that 1 Sam. 4.8–9; 5.12; 6.6 contain (ironic) allusions to the Exodus and plague story (Exod. 1–15), apparently to its Deuteronomistic and Priestly layers.[81] Finally the mockery about the statue of Dagon falling down before Yahweh's ark recalls the polemics against divine statues in Second Isaiah. The redactor who inserted 1 Sam. 4–6 would express a critical attitude towards Deuteronomistic ideology: he criticizes the ideology of the 'holy war' (despite the presence of Yahweh's ark, Israel loses the battle against the Philistines) and also the ideology of segregation (the Philistines recognize Yahweh's power). If one wants to follow the hypothesis of a post-Deuteronomistic interpolation of 1 Sam. 4–6, one should postulate for the exilic edition of the Deuteronomistic History a story about David's transfer of the ark from Shiloh (1 Sam. 3.3) to Jerusalem (2 Sam. 6.1, 15–23[82]). This story fits well with Deuteronomistic ideology: the founder of the Davidic dynasty brings the symbol of Yahweh's presence to Jerusalem in accordance with the idea of cult centralization. The story also legitimates David's kingship (v. 21) and denies any future to Saul's

---

79.   Most scholars advocate for the ark narrative a quite early date, even if some think of an exilic origin as for instance Ahlström, G.W., 'The Travels of the Ark: A Religio-Political Composition', *JNES* 43 (1984), pp. 141–49.

80.   See above IV/.4.2.

81.   Compare 6.6 with Exod. 7.14 (D) and 5.12 with Exod. 2.23 (P).

82.   Verses 2–14 create the link with the ark narrative in 1 Sam. 4–6.

family, since, at the end of the story, Saul's daughter (and eventually David's wife) remains childless until her death (v. 23).

3.4. The Foundation of the Dynasty and the Foundation of the Temple (1 Sam. 12–1 Kgs 8)

In the exilic edition of the Deuteronomistic History the stories of Saul's reign,[83] mostly war-stories, are conceived as a prelude to David's rise. 1 Sam. 13–14 was probably already linked to David's rise in the seventh century,[84] whereas 1 Sam. 15* is (at the earliest) an exilic Deuteronomistic creation, which shows that Saul's rejection by Yahweh is a consequence of his unwillingness to conform to the divine law.[85] Saul has not respected the law about the *ḥērem* (the total destruction

---

83.   Even if these stories may preserve some historical information it is impossible to claim that they were written already in the tenth century BCE. For more details see Edelman, D.V., 'The Deuteronomist's Story of King Saul: Narrative Art or Editorial Product?', in C. Brekelmans and J. Lust (eds), *Pentateuchal and Deuteronomistic Studies: Papers Read at the XIIIth IOSOT Congress, Leuven 1989* (BETL 94; Leuven: Peeters and University Press, 1990), pp. 207–20.

84.   These narratives create an opposition between Saul and Jonathan; Saul is depreciated whereas Jonathan is depicted positively. This prepares Jonathan's recognition of David's divine election, which contrasts with Saul's stubbornness. Diana Edelman has argued that the conflict between Saul and David resurged in the Persian period as a struggle between Jerusalem and Gibeon for political supremacy in Yehud and that the books of Samuel were consequently written during the Persian period (Edelman, D.V., 'Did Saulide–Davidic Rivalry Resurface in Early Persian Yehud?', in J.A. Dearman and M.P. Graham [eds], *The Land that I Will Show You: Essays on the History and Archaeology of the Ancient Near East in Honour of J. Maxwell Miller* [JSOTSup 343; Sheffield: Sheffield Academic Press, 2001], pp. 69–91). But it is not really certain that there existed an ongoing Saulide dynasty down to the Persian period. Edelman can be followed in her observation that the conflict between 'David' and 'Saul' reflected tensions between the 'Northeners' and the 'Southerners' in the Persian period. But that is probably due to reworking of older traditions.

85.   For 1 Sam. 15 as a Deuteronomistic text see Foresti, F., *The Rejection of Saul in the Perspective of the Deuteronomistic School: A Study of 1 Sm 15 and Related Texts* (Studia Theologica – Teresianum 5; Rome: Edizioni del Teresianum, 1984).The original story was revised by later redactors. Foresti distinguishes two Deuteronomistic layers; vv. 20–23a, 24–26, 29, 32–33 are certainly later additions.

of enemies and booty, Deut. 13.17–19, see Josh. 6), and more precisely the 'law' about the Amalekites[86] in Deut. 25.17–19, who became for the Deuteronomists Israel's enemies par excellence.[87] The seventh-century propaganda piece about David's rise was taken over with some additions, especially 1 Sam. 23.16–18; 24.19–21;[88] 26.17–25; 2 Sam. 3.17–19 (these additions make Saul, his son Jonathan and general Abner recognize that Yahweh has chosen David and his dynasty to reign over 'all Israel'); 2 Sam. 3.28–29 and 2 Sam. 5.11–12 (the note about Hiram of Tyre furnishing wood for David makes David a forerunner of the temple-builder Solomon). For the exilic Deuteronomists, the Davidic monarchy remains the only legitimate dynasty. Therefore they underline the fact that David is the chosen king. After the events of 597 and 587 the promise of an eternal Davidic dynasty (2 Sam. 7, the seventh-century text may have contained vv. 4, 5a, 8aß.b, 9, 11b, 12, 16) is maintained but also reworked. First of all, the promise is combined with a new topic. David wanted to build a house for Yahweh, but Yahweh tells him (through the prophet Nathan) that not he, but his son will build the temple (vv. 1–3, 5b, 13–15). These additions try to answer the puzzling question why the founder of a dynasty did not build the temple for his god as any 'normal king' in the ancient East is supposed to do. During the Babylonian and Persian period this question was apparently debated as shown by 2 Sam. 24 and the books of Chronicles.[89] One may even speculate whether the destruction of the temple in 587 was not understood by parts of the Judean population as a manifestation of Yahweh's wrath against a sanctuary which was not rightfully built (this idea is well attested in Neo-Babylonian

---

86.   In 1 Sam. 15 the Amalekites do not designate a precise group, but are a symbol for Israel's worst enemy. Originally the Amalekites were Bedouin-like tribes in the Negev. They were often involved in military conflicts with the Judeans (see 1 Sam. 30). Their importance declined under Assyrian domination.

87.   Or a code-name for the Edomites? According to Gen. 36.12 and 17, Amalek is the offspring of Esau/Edom.

88.   According to Vermeylen the whole ch. 24 should be considered as an exilic Deuteronomistic interpolation (Vermeylen, J., *La loi du plus fort: Histoire de la rédaction des récits davidiques de 1 Samuel 8 à 1 Rois 2* [BETL 154; Leuven: University Press and Peeters, 2000], pp. 145–48 and 643–44).

89.   In 2 Sam. 24 (which was inserted with chs 21–23 when a separate scroll of Samuel was created) David acquires the site where the temple will be built; in the book of Chronicles he becomes the architect of the temple and Solomon only executes his father's plans.

documents[90]). If this were the case, the Deuteronomists would have countered such speculations with a demonstration of the whole building of the temple according to Yahweh's will. Interestingly they maintain in 2 Sam. 7 the idea of an eternal Davidic dynasty without making it a conditional promise, which would have been quite easy to do. They only introduce the idea of a divine punishment for Solomon (v. 14b) probably in order to prepare the negative accounts about his reign. But this does not really affect the emphasis on the everlasting dynasty (vv. 15–16). This may be understood as a hint that during the Babylonian occupation the Deuteronomists discreetly favoured the re-establishment of a Davidic descendant to kingship (perhaps they even considered deportees such as Shesbazzar or Zerubbabel from whom we hear at the very beginning of the Persian period as legitimate successors from Davidic lineage to the throne[91]); but as we have seen they remained very cautious about the future of the Judean monarchy.

During the sixth century the story of David's rise (1 Sam. 1*; 2.12–26*; 3*; 7.5–13*; 8–12*; 13–14*; 16–18*; 19.1–17*; 20–27; 29–31*; 2 Sam. 1–5*; 6.15–23*; 7.1–17*; 8*)[92] was probably supplemented by a first draft of the court narrative (probably without 2 Sam. 11–12 and most parts of 15–17 and 19).[93] The quite intriguing story of Solomon's ascent to the throne (1 Kgs 1–2) prepares the audience for a Solomon narrative, which has become more ambiguous than in the seventh-century edition. In contrast to Solomon, David is depicted in his final discourse, 2.1–4 (a Deuteronomistic creation combining elements from 2 Sam. 7.14–15 and 1 Kgs 8.25), as the exemplary king who speaks like Moses and refers to his Law. Significantly, the promise

90.   Nabonidus affirms that the Shamash temple in Sippar broke down because it had been built without divine permission, see Hurowitz, V.A., *I Have Built You an Exalted House: Temple Building in the Bible in the Light of Mesopotamian and North West Semitic Writings* (JSOTSup 115; Sheffield: Sheffield Academic Press, 1992), pp. 160–62.

91.   See also Edelman, 'Rivalry', pp. 73–77.

92.   For the ark narrative see our comments above. The story of David's rise was supplemented in the Persian era, especially with 1 Sam. 19.18–24; 28 (these texts reveal an interest for Saul in the Persian period, see also Nihan, C., '1 Samuel 28 and the Condemnation of Necromancy in Persian Yehud', in T. Klutz [ed.], *Magic in the Biblical World: From the Rod of Aaron to the Ring of Solomon* [JSNTSup 245; London and New York: T. & T. Clark International and Continuum, 2003], pp. 23–54) and David's prayer in 2 Sam. 7.18–29.

93.   For details see above IV/.4.2.

of an eternal dynasty becomes more conditional than in 2 Sam. 7: 'Yahweh will accomplish his word that he spoke to me: "*If* your descendants take heed to their way, to walk before me in loyalty with all their heart and all their being, then there shall not fail a successor on the throne of Israel"' (1 Kgs 2.4). David's final words present him as the exemplary king against whom his successors will be measured in the books of Kings; the condition expressed in v. 4 introduces the leitmotif of the Deuteronomistic presentation of the monarchy: all kings will be judged according to Mosaic Law, especially to cult centralization and exclusive veneration of Yahweh.

In the exilic edition the Solomon narrative is clearly divided into two parts: the positive beginnings until the building and dedication of the temple (1 Kgs 3–8) and the quite decadent ending of his reign (1 Kgs 9–12). As we have already seen, Solomon's prayer and discourse for the inauguration of Yahweh's sanctuary close the story about the foundation of the Judean monarchy (1 Sam. 13–1 Kgs 8). The second part of Solomon's reign (1 Kgs 9–11) initiates the story about the 'divided' monarchy.

In 1 Kgs 3–8 the exilic redactors revised the older account in reworking especially 3.1–15 and ch. 8. By adding 3.1b–3, the Deuteronomists introduce the theme of the 'high places' (*bāmôt*) where Solomon and the people sacrifice.[94] After the construction of the temple, Judean kings will be criticized because of the ongoing sacrifices at the high places (1 Kgs 15.14; 22.44; 2 Kgs 12.4; 14.4; 15.4, 35; 16.4; 21.3), which were, according to the Deuteronomists, destroyed by the 'good kings' Hezekiah (2 Kgs 18.4) and Josiah (2 Kgs 23.5–20).[95] The *bāmôt* were local (open air?) sanctuaries where Yahweh was venerated probably in association with his 'wife' Asherah. The Deuteronomistic opposition to these cult places started already in the seventh century BCE when the court and the temple tried to control all cultic and economic activities in Judah. In the exilic edition of the Deuteronomistic History, which can be labelled as 'crisis literature', the

94.   It is often argued that v. 2 was added later than v. 3, because it constitutes a doublet, which extends cultic activities from Solomon to the people.

95.   For the Northern kingdom only Jeroboam is directly accused of the *bāmôt* cult (1 Kgs 12.31–32). In 2 Kgs 17.9, 11 the collapse of Samaria is attributed to the *bāmôt*, which may in fact refer to the Judean high places. For more details on the high places see Barrick, W.B., 'High Place', *ABD* 3 (1992), pp. 196–200.

theme of the high places allows the explanation of why even quite acceptable kings contributed finally to the fall of Judah. The polemic against high places was probably also directed against cultic activities that went on in Judah during the Babylonian occupation (see Ezek. 6.3). The exilic version of the positive part of the Solomonic reign in 1 Kgs 3–8[96] comes to an end with his prayer in 8.14–51*; here, as we have seen, the temple is transformed into the place towards which the exiles should turn in prayer.

In 1 Sam. 13–1 Kgs 8 the Deuteronomists draw the picture of three archetypal kings: Saul, who represents the Northern kingdom rejected by Yahweh; David, who symbolizes the ideal Judean king who is promised to reign over 'all Israel', and Solomon, who foreshadows most of the Judean kings. He builds the temple and reigns over the place that Yahweh has chosen; but he does not conform totally to Deuteronomistic ideology of centralization and monolatry. Therefore, after his reign, the 'united kingdom' established by David breaks up.

3.5 The Story of the Two Kingdoms (1 Kgs 9–2 Kgs 17)

3.5.1. Solomon and the Crisis of Monarchy

After the positive portrait of Solomon, which culminates in his temple building, the exilic redactors create a jar in 1 Kgs 9. In a divine speech (vv. 1–9), which echoes 1 Kgs 3, Yahweh announces that all may be lost if the king and the people will not conform to Yahweh's will: Israel will be exiled (v. 7) and the temple will become a heap of ruins (v. 8).[97] This prediction of a catastrophe, which for the audience has already become reality, introduces the story of the split kingdoms Israel and Judah. At the end of this story the kingdom of Israel is destroyed (2 Kgs 17) and its population deported; and these events already foreshadow the fate of Judah and Jerusalem (2 Kgs 24–25). According to the Deuteronomists, the beginning of the end was Solomon's misbehaviour

---

96. Other important exilic additions are 1 Kgs 3.6, 9b, 14; 5.17–18 (to explain why David was unable to build the temple); 6.11–13 (even the temple building is related to the obedience to Yahweh's law); 7.1–12 (the construction of the king's palace).

97. According to the Old Syriac and Old Latin versions. The Masoretic text reads 'exalted' and is either a scribal error or a dogmatic correction.

after the temple building. The divine speech in 9.1–9 concludes with the reasons for Yahweh's wrath against his people: 'Because they have forsaken Yahweh, their god, who brought their fathers out of the land of Egypt, and embraced other gods, worshipping them and serving them; therefore Yahweh has brought this disaster upon them.' According to this text, the main failure of Israel is the cult of other gods, which Yahweh does not tolerate; he alone is the god of the Israelites since he led them out of Egypt. After this statement, the mention of the Egyptian king's daughter in 9.24,[98] who moves to the house Solomon built for her, prepares the negative comment on Solomon in ch. 11. Whereas the Deuteronomistic Yahweh is the god who separates Israel from Egypt, Solomon allies himself to Egypt. In the exilic edition of the Deuteronomistic History, the Egyptian connections of Israelite and Judean kings always produce a negative result (see especially 2 Kgs 17.4; 23.29). The marriage of Solomon to an Egyptian princess also introduces his presentation as a womanizer in ch. 11, where Pharaoh's daughter is mentioned again in v. 1, together with Moabite, Ammonite, Edomite, Sidonian[99] and Hittite women. In the original version of 11.1–13, which roughly consisted of vv. 1* (without 'many foreign women'), 3a, 4, 5–7*, 9–13*, 'the issue is the number of seductresses, consistent with Deut. 17:17a's admonition that a king should "not multiply wives for himself, lest his heart turn away"'.[100] In a later edition this account was reworked and the focus shifted to Solomon's interest in foreign wives. In this new edition, the focus had shifted to mixed marriages, the prohibition of which became a main concern of the Deuteronomistic school in the Persian period (see Deut. 7; 9.1–6; 12.2–7; Ezra 9–10; see also the mention of Solomon in Neh. 13.26). The older Babylonian edition is more concerned with the veneration of

---

98.   This verse takes up 1 Kgs 3.1. Whether the historical Solomon was married to an Egyptian princess, as is often assumed, lies beyond plausibility. The Greek version of the Solomon story mentions Pharaoh's daughter quite differently; there are also important differences between the Greek and the Hebrew text of 1 Kgs 11. In several cases the Greek version seems to be based on a Hebrew text older than the Masoretic version. For more details see Barrick, W.B., 'Loving Too Well: The Negative Portrayal of Solomon and the Composition of the Kings History', *Estudios Bíblicos* 59 (2001), pp. 419–49.

99.   The Sidonians in v. 1 are lacking in the Greek version and may be a later addition. But the Greek text mentions them in v. 5 and v. 7.

100.   Barrick, 'Loving', p. 435; see also pp. 432–35 for the reconstruction of the earliest version of 1 Kgs 11.

other gods; therefore the *bāmôt*, where, according to 3.4, Yahweh was worshipped, are transformed by the exilic redactors into cultic places for Moabite, Ammonite and other deities (vv. 5–7). On the compositional level, 11.5–7 prepares for 2 Kgs 23.13 where it is said that Josiah 'defiled the high places … which king Solomon of Israel had built for Astarte the abomination of the Sidonians, for Chemosh the abomination of Moab, and for Milcom the abomination of the Ammonites'.

In 1 Kgs 11.9–13 Yahweh declares his anger and his punishment: his kingdom will be given to someone else except one tribe (Judah); because of David this will only happen after Solomon's death. The next and only time this anger formula reappears is at the end of the story about the two kingdoms in 2 Kgs 17.18 where it is combined with the statement that 'none was left but the tribe of Judah alone'. This statement points back to the secession of Israel related in 1 Kgs 12.20, which 'left none remaining, except the only tribe of Judah'. 'Just as 1 Kings 11 delineates the political transition from the united kingdom to the divided monarchy, 2 Kings 17 marks the transition from the divided monarchy to a new era':[101] the last days of Judah.

1 Kgs 11.1–13* clearly reveals that in the exilic edition of the Deuteronomistic History only two kings are totally positive figures: David and Josiah. Solomon, who was in the seventh-century BCE story an Assyrian-like, wealthy and temple-building king, is now an ambiguous monarch; he introduces the series of kings who sponsor other deities and other cult places than the temple of Jerusalem.[102] Therefore, the Deuteronomists inserted the episode of the beginnings of Jeroboam, the first king of 'Northern' Israel, before the final notices about Solomon (11.41–43) in vv. 26–40*.[103] The story of the prophet Ahijah of Shiloh and the torn garment is a Deuteronomistic creation, which reminds of Saul's tearing of Samuel's robe in 1 Sam. 15.27–28.

---

101. Knoppers, G.N., *Two Nations Under God: The Deuteronomistic History of Solomon and the Dual Monarchies.* (HSM 52; 2 vols.; Atlanta, GA: Scholars Press, 1993), I, p. 168.

102. In the exilic edition of Kings even Hezekiah is depicted less positively. His removal of the high places was not definitive and the visit of a Babylonian embassy ends with an oracle of deportation (2 Kgs 20.12–19). In a later edition of Kings, Solomon is transformed by non-Deuteronomistic editors into a thousand-and-one-nights-type king (see 1 Kgs 10.1–13 and probably also 3.16–28).

103. Verses 11.14–25 are commonly considered as a later addition, which breaks the link between v. 13 and v. 26. There is no doubt that 11.26–40 is a composite text; vv. 32–35 and 39 are most likely expansions of the original text.

The presentation of Ahijah as a Shilonite also creates a parallel with Samuel (see 1 Sam. 3). Ahijah appears thus as a new Samuel who partially applies the theme of Saul's rejection to the Davidic line. In contrast to the Josianic edition, not only the North is blamed for the secession but also and foremost Solomon. In an exilic perspective the account about the split of the Davidic kingdom already alludes to the end of Israel and Judah. The idea that Yahweh offered a stable dynasty also to Jeroboam (11.38) is certainly an exilic invention, which relativizes in a certain way the promise of an eternal Davidic dynasty. But how could a Northern king respect Yahweh's law about Jerusalem as the only place to worship him? Therefore Yahweh's 'offer' to Jeroboam has also a somewhat ironic undertone. Be that as it may, the Deuteronomists under Babylonian and also Persian rule modified the triumphalist perspective of the Josianic edition of Kings. In the exilic edition, kingship is in crisis since the time of Solomon, and this crisis probably also reflects the identity crisis of the exiled generation of the high royal officers.

3.5.2. Prophets and Kings

Ahijah of Shiloh is the first of a long series of prophets who appear in the books of Kings. His activity frames Jeroboam's reign. In 1 Kgs 11 he declares that Yahweh has established Jeroboam king over the Northern tribes, in 1 Kgs 14 he announces to the king's wife Yahweh's judgement and the death of his son. In the present books of Kings, almost half of the text is devoted to the appearance of prophets. Besides Ahijah we find an anonymous prophet proclaiming the destruction of Bethel (1 Kgs 13), Jehu (1 Kgs 16.1–7), Elijah (1 Kgs 17–19; 21; 2 Kgs 1–2), another anonymous prophet (1 Kgs 20), Micaiah (1 Kgs 22), Elisha (2 Kgs 2–9; 13.14–21), Jonah (2 Kgs 14.25), Isaiah (2 Kgs 19–20) and the prophetess Huldah (2 Kgs 22.14–20). In these stories we may distinguish two types of prophetic activities. Some prophets pronounce divine oracles (mostly oracles of punishment) and their fulfilment is expressly stated. Ahijah's oracle against Jeroboam's house is fulfilled in Baasha's revolt (1 Kgs 15.27–29), and Jehu's oracle against Baasha is accomplished in Zimri's insurrection (1 Kgs 16.11–12). Elijah's oracle against Ahab is fulfilled in Jehu's slaughter of the Omride dynasty (2 Kgs 9.25–26) and Huldah's announcement of Judah's fall is accomplished in 2 Kgs 24–25 (see especially 24.2–3a).[104] These texts conform to the Deuteronomistic ideology of prophetism. According to Deut. 18.18, Moses inaugurates Yahweh's sending of prophets who are the mediators of the divine word which never fails (Deut. 18.22). For the Deuteronomists, prophets have a legitimating function: their oracles, which always get fulfilled, demonstrate that Yahweh directed the whole history of Israel and Judah, and that he also provoked the disastrous end of the two states. The above-cited texts fit well in the exilic edition; they may be related to the first edition of the prophetic books of Jeremiah, Hosea, Amos, Micah and perhaps Zephaniah, which was very probably undertaken at the end of the sixth century BCE by the same Deuteronomistic school.[105]

On the other hand, the books of Kings contain prophetic stories that come close to anecdotes: the prophets appear as miracle-doers, healers, magicians and visionaries. Those stories often interrupt unexpectedly the Deuterononomistic reports and appear sometimes in the Greek version at different places; therefore one should consider them as post-Deuteronomistic additions.[106] This is obvious for the story of the man of God from Judah proclaiming the destruction of Bethel in 1 Kgs 12.33–13.33. That this story was interpolated is made evident by the technique of resumptive repetition in 12.32–33 and 13.33 and by the late, non-Deuteronomistic vocabulary.[107] The same observations apply to the Elijah and Elisha stories, with the possible exception of Elijah's confrontation with Ahab in 1 Kgs 21 and Elisha's

104. Huldah's oracle on Josiah is a bit strange: she declares that he will be buried in peace (2 Kgs 22.20); nevertheless his death is quite violent since he is killed by Pharaoh (23.29). Therefore it is often claimed that this oracle has been written down during Josiah's lifetime. But a better explanation would be that this text tries to explain Josiah's death positively. He was buried in his tomb and did not experience the destruction of Jerusalem and the temple.

105. See above and Albertz, *Exile*, pp. 204–11; 302–45.

106. See especially McKenzie, S.L., *The Trouble with Kings: The Composition of the Books of Kings in the Deuteronomistic History* (SVT 42; Leiden: Brill, 1991), pp. 81–100.

107. See Rofé, A., 'Classes in the Prophetical Stories: Didactic Legenda and Parable', in G.W. Anderson *et al.* (eds), *Studies on Prophecy* (SVT 26; Leiden: Brill, 1974), pp. 143–64; pp. 158–63 and Van Seters, J., 'The Deuteronomistic History: Can It Avoid Death by Redaction?', in T. Römer (ed.), *The Future of the Deuteronomistic History* (BETL 147; Leuven: University Press and Peeters, 2000), pp. 213–22.

implication in Jehu's revolt.[108] The Elijah and Elisha cycles, as well as 1 Kgs 20 and 22*, were added to the books of Kings during the Persian period.[109]

In the Babylonian edition of the Deuteronomistic History the time from the Omride dynasty to Jehu's revolt was covered roughly by the following texts: 1 Kgs 16.23–34; 21*; 22.39–54; 2 Kgs 1.1–2a, 17*, 18; 3.1–3; 8.16–29; 9.1–10.27*, 28–36. In these texts the Deuteronomists depict a very negative portrait of the Omride dynasty, which is judged as negatively as the founder of the Northern kingdom. But before addressing this issue, we should briefly deal with the Isaiah stories, even if they appear in the last part of the Deuteronomistic History. The stories about the prophet Isaiah and King Hezekiah in 2 Kgs 18.13–20.19 also appear, with some differences, in the book of Isaiah (36–39). The debate often focuses on the alternative whether these accounts were originally written for the books of Kings or for the book of Isaiah. But the matter seems more complicated. 2 Kgs 18–20 contains very different stories, which can hardly be attributed to one author. 2 Kgs 18.13–19.7 and 35–37* relate the siege of Jerusalem, which the Assyrians suddenly give up. Here Isaiah intervenes in a typical Deuteronomistic way proclaiming a divine oracle: Yahweh will force the Assyrian king to return unsuccessfully to his land (19.6–7); this oracle is immediately fulfilled (19.35–37*). The second story about the siege in 19.8–34 is a doublet of the first one; its ideology and language fit better the book of Isaiah, especially its second part, which contains monotheistic statements and polemics against the gods of the nations (see especially 2 Kgs 19.15–18, 25, 30–31). The story about Isaiah as a healer (2 Kgs 20.1–12) and the sign

---

108. According to Rofé 1 Kgs 21 should also be considered as an addition from the Persian period. In his view the story expresses the same ideology as the books of Ezra and Nehemiah which are opposed to marriages with foreign women, see Rofé, A., 'The Vineyard of Naboth: The Origin and the Message of the Story', *VT* 38 (1988), pp. 89–104.

109. This is now argued by many scholars, see for instance McKenzie, *Trouble*, and Otto, S., 'The Composition of the Elijah–Elisha Stories and the Deuteronomistic History', *JSOT* 27 (2003), pp. 487–508. According to Otto the Elijah and Elisha stories were composed about 750 in the Northern kingdom. This is quite possible for Elisha, the stories about Elijah do not reveal many pre-Deuteronomistic features: 1 Kgs 17–18 are close to the ideology of Deutero-Isaiah, and 1 Kgs 19 which criticize the ideology of the foregoing chapters must even be later.

Hezekiah asks for fits also better into the context of Isaiah, where it counters the refusal of a sign by Ahaz in Isa. 7.10–12. These stories were therefore composed as a transition between the first and the second part of Isaiah.[110] They were probably introduced into the books of Kings at a late stage, when the Deuteronomistic History was dissolved and the books of Joshua to Kings became the first part of the 'Prophets'. Through the insertion of those Isaiah stories at the end of Kings the redactors underlined the close relation between the Former Prophets, whose last book is Kings, and the Later Prophets, whose first book is Isaiah. It is quite possible that most of the other prophetic stories were also inserted at this stage in order to strengthen the 'prophetic character' of Kings.

3.5.3. The Northern Kings

The exilic redactors of Kings took over the evaluation of the Northern kings that figured already in the Josianic edition. As we have already seen, no king from the North is judged positively since they all worship Yahweh outside Jerusalem, especially at Bethel. Behaving that way, all kings of the North pursue 'the sins of Jeroboam'. Nevertheless, there is an interesting change in the evaluative formulas. The first kings after Jeroboam from Nadab to Joram, the last king of the Omride dynasty, are basically appreciated in the same way: they walk in Jeroboam's way and/or his sins, and so doing they provoke Yahweh. From Jehu on until Pekah, the same formula occurs for each king: 'he did what was evil in the eyes of Yahweh[111] ... he did not depart from the sins of

110.   The story about the Babylonian embassy in 20.12–20 is more difficult to locate. Since King Merodach-baladan (*Marduk-apal.idinna*) ruled independently in Babylon from 720 to 709, vv. 12a and 13, which establish a parallel between the wealth of Hezekiah and the wealth of Solomon, may belong to the Josianic edition of Kings. 20.14–19 presupposes the destruction of the temple; it fits well in the exilic edition of the Deuteronomistic History and may have been composed at the same time as 18.13–19.7, 35–37*; but it also provides a transition to Isa. 40–55, which presupposes the destruction of Jerusalem and the exile.

111.   This first statement is not made for Jehu (2 Kgs 10.29), who is for the Deuteronomists the most appreciated Northern king, because of his putsch against the Omride dynasty. The only king who gets no evaluation is Shallum, since his 'reign' lasted only one month (2 Kgs 15.13–15).

Jeroboam, son of Nebat which he made Israel to sin'. The last king Hoshea 'did what was evil in the eyes of Yahweh yet not as the kings of Israel who were before him' (2 Kgs 17.2). These changes indicate that the Deuteronomists wanted to differentiate between the first nine kings and the next nine ones. The first kings, and especially the Omrides, are the worst; in the Deuteronomistic History most of them are targets of oracles of annihilation; the series that starts with Jehu (Jehoahaz, Jehoash, Jeroboam, Zechariah, [Shallum], Menahem, Pekaiah, Pekah) is somewhat better, probably because of Jehu's annihilation of the Omride dynasty. The last king Hoshea is not explicitly blamed for pursuing the sins of Jeroboam; in the final comment on Israel's end, all Israelites are said to have 'continued in all the sins that Jeroboam committed; they did not depart from them' (2 Kgs 17.22). This is a way to underline that Israel's demise is not provoked by its last king (maybe the Deuteronomists had even some sympathies for his anti-Assyrian revolt), it is the result of a long history of bad kings who did commit themselves and the people with other gods and illegitimate yahwistic sanctuaries. Evidently the Deuteronomists are not interested in economic and political achievements of the kings; they are mainly preoccupied with underlining the faults that provoked in their view Yahweh's anger and the fall of Israel (and Judah). Omri, who was certainly one of the most important Northern kings, since the Assyrians often refer to Israel as 'house of Omri' even after the end of the Omrides, is presented very briefly in 1 Kgs 16.23–27: he is said to be worse than the kings before him, probably because of his foundation of Samaria, Israel's capital, which in fact overshadowed Jerusalem. Ahab is undoubtedly the worst king in the Deuteronomistic eyes (1 Kgs 21.5) since he introduced the Phoenician Baal as well as Asherah into the official cult and married the Phoenician princess Jezebel (1 Kgs 16.29–33; 21*). In the exilic edition the Ahab story was probably enlarged. Since he had a peaceful death, and the Omride dynasty did last until Yoram, the Deuteronomists invented a short story about Ahab's repentance (21.27–29) in order to explain why Yahweh's judgement on the house of Omri was postponed. In the concluding comment on Israel's end in 2 Kgs 17 (see above) it becomes quite clear that the two main reasons for the collapse of the Northern kingdom are the calves of Jeroboam as well as the worship of Baal and Asherah (see especially v. 16). In contrast to the Josianic edition, the exilic edition of Kings could not focus any more on Israel as a contrast to Judah's 'reformation' under Josiah. Therefore the end of Israel was presented as foreshadowing the end of Judah (see above the remarks on 2 Kgs 17).

3.5.4. The Southern Kings (from Rehoboam to Ahaz)

The story of the Judean kingdom until the end of Israel offers an alternation of kings who are judged almost positively and those who are considered as bad as their colleagues from the North. The (almost) good kings Asa, Jehoshaphat, Jehoash, Amaziah, Azariah and Jotham are all appreciated in the same way: 'he did what was right in the eyes of Yahweh[112] ... yet the high places were not taken away', whereas the bad kings (Rehoboam, Abijam,[113] Jehoram, Ahaziah, Ahaz) commit, like the kings of Israel, 'the evil in the eyes of Yahweh'. One may distinguish three periods in the story of the Judean kings. The first period is characterized by an opposition between the two bad kings Rehoboam (1 Kgs 14.21–31) and Abijam (1 Kgs 15.1–3, 7–8) under whose reign the high places proliferate and Asherah is worshipped as Yahweh's spouse (the mention of male prostitutes is probably related to the cult of Asherah). They are followed by two 'reforming' kings, Asa (15.9–24) and Jehoshaphat (22.41–51*), who eradicate the veneration of Asherah. One should not take this information as historical, it seems more likely that the Deuteronomists were interested to create (partial) forerunners of Josiah's reform. The next period is marked by Athaliah who in fact did reign over Judah; for the Deuteronomists she cannot be considered as a queen: she is half-Israelite, half-Phoenician, and her reign interrupts in fact the Davidic dynasty. The troubles start with Jehoram who marries Athaliah and acts like the Northern kings (2 Kgs 8.16–24). His son Ahaziah (8.25–29; 9.14–29*) behaves in the same way (the formula 'walk in the way of the kings of Israel' also alludes to the fact that these kings were in fact vassals of Israel) and is killed by Jehu during his revolt against the king of Israel. After his death Athaliah reigns at least for six years (11.3), but the Deuteronomists try hard not to present her as queen: she is a usurper who must be killed (11.1–6a, 8, 11–14, 16–18*, 19b*, 20*). The killing of Athaliah, the destruction

---

112.   The first part of the formula differs for Jehoshaphat: he walked in the way of his father.

113.   Abijam walks in the sin of his father.

of the statues of Baal and his priests also foreshadow some of Josiah's cultic reforms. Four (almost) positive kings follow Athaliah. The restoration of the temple under Jehoash (12.1–14*, 18–22*[114]) parallels and prepares for Josiah's restoration in 22.4–7, 9b. One may wonder why the three following kings, Amaziah (14.1–22*), Azariah (15.1–7) and Jotham (15.32–38), obtain the same evaluation as Jehoash.[115] The Deuteronomists probably presented them quite positively in order to strengthen the contrast with Ahaz (16*), who reigned when Israel collapsed, and who is presented as walking in the way of the kings of Israel (v. 3). He is accused especially of human sacrifices (v. 3), submission to the Assyrians (v. 8: he uses the temple treasure to pay the Assyrian king) and introducing Assyrian practices into the temple (v. 15).[116] Through this presentation of Ahaz, the Deuteronomists strengthen the parallels between Israel and Judah and induce the idea that Judah was in danger being incorporated into the Assyrian empire as Israel had been in 2 Kgs 17. The end of Judah is only postponed because of the two exceptional kings (in the Deuteronomists' eyes) Hezekiah and Josiah, whose reigns are the highlights of the last period of the Deuteronomistic History.

3.6. Cultic Reforms and the End of Judah (2 Kgs 18–25)

Between the reigns of Hezekiah and Josiah the Deuteronomists paint two very bad kings, Manasseh and Amon (2 Kgs 21*). After Josiah four equally bad kings follow under whose reign Judah finally collapses.

The exilic Deuteronomists took over the positive presentation of Hezekiah from the Josianic edition of Kings. He is the first king to have eradicated the high places; he is also said to have abolished the veneration of Asherah and to have destroyed a bronze serpent, which is probably

---

114. The Deuteronomistic report was later reworked by priestly redactors (see especially v. 17).

115. According to 14.6 Amaziah did not kill the sons of his father's murderers out of respect for Deut. 24.6, but this verse may be a later addition.

116. Ahaz builds a new altar for the sacrifices according to a Damascene model; the former (yahwistic) altar is now used 'to inquire by', which means to practise divination by the consultation of entrails, a typical Assyrian usage.

linked to the veneration of this goddess (18.3–6).[117] Hezekiah's reign forms a sharp contrast with the time of Ahaz who introduced Assyrian symbols into Jerusalem. In the Josianic edition this contrast was probably even sharper than in the exilic reworking of the Hezekiah story. According to 18.6 Hezekiah 'rebelled against the king of Assyria and would not serve him', but 18.14–16 (which probably belongs to the exilic revision[118]) states that Hezekiah submitted to the Assyrian king, promising that he would be a loyal vassal. The exilic redaction 'displays an interest in Hezekiah's actions as a partial cause for the Babylonian exile'.[119] The events under his reign are related with the fall of Samaria and the story of the Babylonian embassy alludes ultimately to the Babylonian exile. Of course, Hezekiah remains a very positive, reforming king and Yahweh delivers him and Jerusalem from an Assyrian siege. But even in his reign the exilic Deuteronomists inserted hints of the end of Judah.

The following king, Manasseh, belongs to the Deuteronomistic top list of the worst kings. Although he reigned for about 55 years, the Deuteronomists are only interested in his cultic counter reform, which annihilate the measures of Hezekiah. Manasseh, who is explicitly compared to the Northern king Ahab, reintroduces Assyrian practices into the temple as well as the veneration of Asherah (probably as Yahweh's companion). The long enumeration of Manasseh's cultic failures in 21.1–3, 5–9*, 16–18[120] prepares of course for Josiah's tremendous reform, it shows also that Manasseh contravened all the important laws of Deuteronomy:

---

117.   See Olyan, S.M., *Asherah and the Cult of Yahweh in Israel* (SBLMS 34; Atlanta, GA: Scholars Press, 1988), pp. 70–71. On the other hand Swanson, K.A., 'A Reassessment of Hezekiah's Reform in Light of Jar Handels and Iconographic Evidence', *CBQ* 64 (2002), pp. 460–69 has argued that the serpent is better understood as an Egyptian symbol, which Hezekiah removed as a sign of his submission to the Assyrians. Interestingly the account associates this statue with Moses, and this can hardly be a Deuteronomistic invention. Num. 21.1–9 is a late midrash, which tries to explain the origin of this statue.

118.   This is also argued by Campbell, A.F. and M. O'Brien, *Unfolding the Deuteronomistic History: Origins, Upgrades, Present Text* (Minneapolis, MN: Fortress Press, 2000), pp. 447–48. For a reconstruction of the Deuteronomistic account during the Babylonian period (18.1–19.7*, 35–37*; 20.12–20 [?]) see above 3.5.2.

119.   Sweeney, M.A., *King Josiah of Judah: The Lost Messiah of Israel* (Oxford: Oxford University Press, 2001), p. 68.

120.   Verses 10–15 are probably an interpolation by a redactor, who wanted to make Manasseh the main if not the only king responsible for Judah's fall.

v. 2: Manasseh 'followed the abominable practices of the nations that Yahweh drove out before the Israelites.	Deut. 18.9: 'You must not learn to imitate the abominable practices of those nations.'
vv. 3 and 7: Manasseh made a statue of Asherah.	Deut. 16.21: 'You shall not plant a tree as (symbol of) Asherah.'
vv. 3 and 5: He worshipped and built altars for the host of heaven.	Deut. 17.3: 'If someone goes to serve and worship other gods, the sun or the moon or the host of heaven, I forbid it.'
v. 6: 'He made his sons pass through fire; he practised soothsaying and augury, and dealt with necromancers and with wizards.'	Deut. 18.10–11: 'No one shall be found among you who makes a son or a daughter pass through fire, or who practises divination, or is a soothsayer, or an augur, or a sorcerer, ... or a necromancer ...'
v. 16: 'Manasseh shed very much innocent blood.'	Deut. 19.10: 'the blood of an innocent person may not be shed.' (See also 21.8–9.)

One may reasonably guess that during Manasseh's long reign some important events took place and that his reign was quite a peaceful time for Judah. But the Deuteronomists are not interested in these aspects; they construct Manasseh in order to prepare for Josiah's 'restoration' of the Deuteronomic law and also to bring forward another important reason for Yahweh's destruction of Judah.

Not much is made out of Manasseh's short-reigning successor Amon, who is described as being as evil as his father Manasseh (21.19–26). The statement that 'he abandoned Yahweh, the god of his fathers' has a parallel in Judg. 2.12 (no other text occurs where Yahweh is designated in this way between Judg. 2 and 2 Kgs 21). The whole period from the time of the Judges until the reign of Josiah thus appears as a period of permanent crisis,[121] which was only (temporarily) brought to an end by Josiah.

---

121. The same idea occurs in 23.22: 'No such Passover has been kept since the day of the judges who judged Israel, even during all the days of the kings of Israel and the kings of Judah.'

In contrast to Hezekiah no negative aspects are added to the presentation of Josiah (2 Kgs 23*) who remains the exemplary king. Even his quite dishonouring death (he is killed by Pharaoh) is not explained by any fault he would have committed; on the contrary through the mouth of the prophetess Huldah (see above) the Deuteronomists characterize this death as 'peaceful', since it saved him from the experience of Jerusalem's destruction. Besides the addition of 23.25b–26a,[122] 27–30 the exilic redactors reworked the former seventh-century text especially interpolating the prophetic oracles about the destruction of Jerusalem and the fate of Josiah. They probably also added the celebration of a Passover in order to integrate the time of the Judges[123] into the Deuteronomistic chronology, and they also underlined the defilement of the Bethel sanctuary, which during the exilic period possibly was a serious rival to the (partially) destroyed temple of Jerusalem.[124] The Babylonian version of Josiah's reform would then have comprised: 22.1–7*, 9, 13aα, 14–16a, 17–19aαb, 20; 23.1, 3–15*,[125] 19, 21a, 22–23, 25–26a, 27–31. As we have already seen, the story of the book-finding belongs to the last revision of this account, which was made during the Persian period, in order to present the 'Book' as a substitute for the temple (see above III/.2). The exilic version of 2 Kgs 22–23 focused on two slightly contradictory points. First, Josiah appears as the perfect king on all points. He represents the Deuteronomistic ideal of kingship. Monarchy could have had a future if kings behaved like Josiah and conformed to the Mosaic (Deuteronomistic) Law. Second, and despite Josiah's achievements, destruction and exile must be announced. But because of his exceptional behaviour and unlike the foregoing kings, Josiah is totally exempted from any responsibility for Judah's end.

The last four kings (Jehoahaz, Jehoiakim, Jehoiachin, Zedekiah) stand again in a jarring contrast to Josiah. They are all judged by the same formula: 'and he did what was evil in the eyes of Yahweh, according to

---

122. Verse 26b, which makes Manasseh the only monarch responsible for Jerusalem's fall, was probably added by the same redactor who inserted 21.10–15.

123. Interestingly the parallel account in Chronicles states that 'no passover like it had been kept in Israel since the days of the prophet Samuel' (2 Chron. 35.18).

124. Blenkinsopp, J., 'The Judaean Priesthood during the Neo-Babylonian and Achaemenid Period', *CBQ* 60 (1998), pp. 25–43.

125. Verses 16–19 take up the story of 1 Kgs 13 and were added simultaneously with the prophetic legend.

all that his father(s) had done' (2 Kgs 23.32, 37; 24.9; 24.19[126]). The Deuteronomists do not offer any details about the religious faults of these kings. They adopt a critical attitude towards Jehoiakim and Zedekiah's revolts against the Babylonians (24.1; 24.20), which provoked the destructions and deportations of 597 and 587. In contrast to Hezekiah who resisted the Assyrian assault with Yahweh's help, there is no possibility to escape from the Babylonian attack, because Yahweh himself sent the Babylonian army (24.2 and 20a) in order to annihilate Judah and Jerusalem. Although the Deuteronomistic History sympathizes with kings who are engaged in anti-Assyrian politics, it does not display an anti-Babylonian ideology. Two reasons explain this different attitude. The Deuteronomists were eager to show that Jerusalem's fall did not mean that the Babylonian gods had vanquished Judah's national god. Therefore the events of 597 and 587 could only be explained by making Yahweh or his anger the agent of Judah's collapse. The second reason was more materialistic. Since the Deuteronomists probably belonged to the deported elite, they were not interested in expressing anti-Babylonian statements in Babylonia and it is quite possible that they were even inclined to collaborate with the Babylonian administration.

Where did the exilic edition of the Deuteronomistic History end? Quite often it is assumed that it concluded with the last account of the books of Kings, the release of Jehoiachin from his Babylonian prison (2 Kgs 25.27–30). But as we will see, this short note fits better into the Persian period. As already noted, the statement of 2 Kgs 25.21: 'So Judah was exiled out of his land', offers a good conclusion to a 'history of crisis', which focuses on the explanation of exile[127] and which gives the impression that the 'true Israel' was deported to Babylonia. The last chapters of the exilic edition then probably comprised: 23.31–24.3,[128] 5–20*; 25,1–15*,[129] 18–21*. These chapters were probably written

126. For the last king, Zedekiah, we have 'Jehoiakim' instead of 'his father(s)'. This is quite logical since Zedekiah was the uncle of his predecessor. Interestingly he is compared not to his predecessor Jehoiachin, but to Jehoiakim. This could be a scribal error, or more likely an alteration due to the addition of the positive account relating Jehoiachin's rehabilitation.

127. The idea of an empty land during the Babylonian time is an ideological construction, which is unfortunately taken for a fact in some class-books. Even the Deuteronomists were aware that there were people left in Palestine, see 25.12.

128. The focus on Manasseh in v. 4 was inserted later, as were 21.10–15 and 23.26 (see above).

129. The details about the temple furniture in 25.15–17 are often considered an insertion.

soon after the events of 587. When reading these reports it is quite easy to guess that the Deuteronomists belonged to the group deported in 597 (given the quite pejorative statement about the identity of the deportees of 587). After the assassination of Gedaliah in 582, the history was updated by the adding of 25.22–26. These verses conclude with the remaining people descending to Egypt (which is in a certain way the Deuteronomistic origin myth of the Egyptian Diaspora). This descent to Egypt refers to the last curse of Deut. 28 (v. 68), which announces a 'return' to Egypt. In a certain way the whole Deuteronomistic History becomes through this addition a story, which deals with a passage 'from Egypt to Egypt'.[130] The whole history between Yahweh and Israel with its foundation in the myth of the exodus seems annihilated. One has often wondered why the Deuteronomists did not provide at the end of their history of Judah a conclusive statement, as they did for Israel in 2 Kgs 17. They probably did not stand at a sufficient distance from the last events they related; this is a phenomenon which can also be observed in contemporaneous presentations of a country's history 'from the beginnings until now'. Historians usually stop looking for an exhaustive conclusion when they come to events the consequences of which cannot be evaluated at the time they write. This may well apply to the Deuteronomistic History which has no definitive conclusion. We have argued that the exilic edition is a crisis literature, which seeks to present the causes for the collapse of Judah. At this stage there is no real interest to explore the future, all efforts are concentrated on explaining the present by describing or constructing the past.

4. Summary: The Exilic Edition of the Deuteronomistic History

Even if the origins of the Deuteronomistic school should be situated during the decline of the Assyrian empire, the chronological construction of a history from the origins to the end of the monarchy (Deuteronomy–Kings) clearly presupposes the destruction of Jerusalem and the occupation of Judah by the Babylonians. Using Weberian categories one may describe the first Deuteronomistic History as a crisis literature. Exploring or even inventing the past provides a possibility to

---

130.   See Friedman, R.E., 'From Egypt to Egypt: Dtr[1] and Dtr[2]', in B. Halpern and J.D. Levenson (eds), *Traditions in Transformation: Turning Points in Biblical Faith* (Winona Lake, IN: Eisenbrauns, 1981), pp. 167–92.

explain a present which is not easily acceptable by the Judean elites. The whole history is conceived in an exilic perspective and it is no wonder that the 'exile' becomes during the Persian period a new foundation myth for the 'real Israel'. The importance of the exile, which does not reflect much of historical reality, also suggests that the Deuteronomists (or at least most of them) were among the deportees of 597. They probably saved older scrolls from the official library and rewrote them in Babylon in order to show that Yahweh still remains a mighty god, despite the Babylonian supremacy. One may even speculate whether the Babylonians encouraged this history, since it taught the Judeans to understand the Babylonian king and his army as acting on behalf of Yahweh's will. It is indeed quite possible that the Babylonians employed the exiled Deuteronomists as interpreters and scribes. In the exilic edition of the Deuteronomistic History there is understandably not much concern about the future. During the Persian period some speculation about the future will be added as well as other concerns related to the new situation. But in the second half of this period the Deuteronomistic History would be split into different books and virtually disappear until it was discovered by modern research.

Chapter 6

EDITING THE DEUTERONOMISTIC HISTORY DURING THE PERSIAN PERIOD

1. Social and Political Context in Judah during the Persian Period

Select Bibliography

Berquist, J.L., *Judaism in Persia's Shadow: A Social and Historical Approach* (Minneapolis, MN: Fortress Press, 1995).

Briant, P., *From Cyrus to Alexander: A History of the Persian Empire* (trans. P.T. Daniels; Winona Lake, IN: Eisenbrauns, 2002).

Carter, C.E., *The Emergence of Yehud in the Persian Period: A Social and Demographic Study* (JSOTSup 294; Sheffield: Sheffield Academic Press, 1999).

Edelman, D., *Persian Imperial Policy and the Rebuilding of Jerusalem* (London: Equinox, 2005).

Elayi, J. and J. Sapin, *Beyond the River: New Perspectives on Transeuphratene* (trans. J.E. Crowley; JSOTSup 250; Sheffield: Sheffield Academic Press, 1998).

Grabbe, L.L., *A History of the Jews and Judaism in the Second Temple Period. I. Yehud: A History of the Persian Province of Judah* (London and New York: T. & T. Clark, 2004).

Person Jr, R.F., *The Deuteronomic School: History, Social Setting, and Literature* (Studies in Biblical Literature 2; Atlanta: Society of Biblical Literature, 2002).

In most presentations of the Deuteronomistic History, the exilic period is considered to coincide with its final redaction. On this point there is a consensus between scholars who adopt the Cross model of a twofold edition, those from the Göttingen school who advocate three major exilic layers[1] and those who follow Noth's proposal of one single

---

1.   Some scholars who follow this model assign 'DtrN' to the early postexilic period; but they generally do not insist on the possible implications of such a date.

exilic Deuteronomist. This view is based on Noth's argument that the last event related in 2 Kgs 25 (Jehoiachin's rehabilitation) took place around 562 BCE. Since there are no allusions to the end of the Babylonian empire it is commonly concluded that the last (or only) Deuteronomistic redaction occurred around 560. Nevertheless, this view has been challenged with good reasons. Person insists on text-critical evidence that Deuteronomistic editing continued through the Persian period. Numerous additions made to the Masoretic text (which do not figure in the Hebrew text translated into Greek) reveal in fact Deuteronomistic language. Person considers this observation as an important argument for the ongoing redactional activity of the Deuteronomistic school during the postexilic period. Nevertheless, this argument should be handled very cautiously. It is not easy to decide when the different additions to the Hebrew text were made, and some may actually stem from the Hellenistic period. The Deuteronomistic style is indeed very easy to imitate, and can be found even in writings from the Christian era.[2] But it is true that a number of texts inside the Deuteronomistic History deal with issues that fit better in the Persian rather than earlier periods. This is especially true of texts where a strict separation of Israelites from other nations is requested; and also of those which try to substitute the 'cult of the book' for traditional temple worship. Both topics fit well into the first half of the Persian period (Persian I: 539 to c. 450 BCE[3]). Even if this time-span belongs to the most obscure era in the history of Palestine, it is the period when the transformation of the Yahwistic Judean religion into Judaism took place.

The small province of Yehud did not hold much of the Persians' attention; our information for factual history of this area comes mostly from the biblical accounts (especially in the books of Ezra, Nehemiah, Haggai and Zechariah), which reflect the ideology of the Judean elite during the Persian period.

According to the biblical presentation, Cyrus immediately after his victory over Babylon in 539 published a decree in which he allowed the Judean exiles to return to Judea and encouraged them to rebuild

---

2.   See on this matter Römer T. and J.-D. Macchi, 'Luke, Disciple of the Deuteronomistic School' in C.M. Tuckett (ed.), *Luke's Literary Achievement: Collected Essays* (JSNTSup 116; Sheffield: Sheffield Academic Press, 1995), pp. 178-87.

3.   For this division see Carter, *Emergence*, pp. 115–16.

the temple of Jerusalem. This presentation is certainly wishful thinking or an ideological construction, which tends to demonstrate how the Persians cared for the exiled Judean community. The first Persian emperors claim to have restored the local cults and the exiled populations to their homes. Even if such claims belong to royal propaganda, it appears nevertheless that the religious politics of the Persians were somewhat different from that of their predecessors. They were not eager to convert the peoples of the empire to Mazdeism. One may even speculate about a Persian syncretism of a sort that allowed for identification of local deities with manifestations of Ahura Mazda.

During the Babylonian period the provincial seat was located at Mizpah; we do not know when or why Jerusalem became again the capital of the province (*medinah*) of Yehud.[4] It is quite clear that the rebuilding of the temple and other building activities in Jerusalem under Nehemiah[5] reflect its rising importance during the first part of the Persian period. One of the first governors (*peḥa*) of Yehud was apparently Zerubbabel, a deportee, descendant of the royal Davidic line and commissioned by the Persians, who probably thought that his royal pedigree would convince the autochthonous population to collaborate with him. It is possible that his arrival in Jerusalem gave rise to hopes and attempts of restoration of the Davidic monarchy (see in this sense Hag. 2.22), but there is no clear evidence of an anti-Persian revolt as is often argued. Zerubbabel's very sudden disappearance in the biblical texts suggests nevertheless that the Persians dismissed him from office in order to prevent any messianic expectations. Some of the following governors are known through epigraphic evidence; the real power regarding internal affairs seems to be held by the priestly and lay elites gathered around the temple of Jerusalem.

4.   It has often been argued that at the beginning of the Persian period Yehud was not autonomous but part of a larger province of which Samaria would have been the capital. Yehud would have split from Samaria only under Nehemiah. This view should be given up. There is more evidence for the fact that Yehud was already an independent province during the Neo-Babylonian period.

5.   According to the biblical presentation and the traditional scholarly view the temple was rebuilt during the years 520–515. Recently, Diana Edelman (see bibliography) has argued that it makes better sense to correlate the reconstruction of the temple with the building activities of Nehemiah. This would make sense indeed, since it is widely acknowledged that important changes occurred in the province of Yehud during the reign of Artaxerxes I (465–424).

We do not have precise information about the borders and the population of Persian I Yehud. The number of 42,000 exiles who would have returned from Babylon to Judah according to Ezra 2 and Neh. 9 is clearly unrealistic. During the first part of the Persian period, there were many fewer inhabitants in Yehud and especially in Jerusalem.[6] It is well attested that the members of the Babylonian Golah were not very eager to return to Jerusalem. The Babylonian archives of the Murashu family reveal an important number of Jewish names; and the recently discovered existence of a Babylonian 'town of the Judeans' (*Al-Yâhûdu*) next to Nippur[7] also underlines the importance of the Babylonian Jewish Diaspora during the Persian period. The Jews who returned from Babylon, maybe even under Persian instigation, remained strongly connected to their former homeland. And there is no doubt at all that the economic and ideological power was in the hands of the (returned) Golah, which controlled the restored city of Jerusalem. It is often argued that Persian Yehud was constituted as a 'citizen-temple community',[8] the Jerusalem temple being the central institution. According to this theory the citizen-temple community was first limited to the Golah community which was organized in several *bêt 'abôt* ('father houses') and exempted from taxation. During the mid fifth century BCE (under Nehemiah) the religious temple-citizen community merged with the political province of Yehud. This theory is problematic since it is based on the idea that Yehud was not autonomous before Nehemiah; there is also no clear evidence and there are no parallels in the Persian period for a tax-exempt community (or a whole province!). These remarks do not affect the major role that the Jerusalem temple played in Persian Yehud. The temple was invested by priestly and lay members of the Golah and became the religious and probably also administrative centre. An important number of biblical texts from the Persian period

6.   It is very difficult to give any precise indication as long as we ignore the extension of Persian Yehud. According to Carter, *Emergence*, pp. 246–48, one should think of about 20,000 to 30,000 people living in Persian Yehud.

7.   Pearce, L.,'New Evidence for Judeans in Babylonia', in O. Lipschitz and M. Oehming (eds), *Judah and the Judeans in the Persian Period* (Winona Lake, IN: Eisenbrauns, 2005).

8.   The inventor of this theory is the Russian scholar J. Weinberg; see especially his work *The Citizen-Temple Community* (JSOTSup 151; Sheffield: JSOT Press, 1992).

establish a sharp distinction between the Golah, as elite community, and the 'people of the land', the rural population which had remained in Palestine during the Babylonian occupation. This Golah perspective can be detected in some late additions in the Deuteronomistic History as well as in certain passages in the books of Jeremiah and Ezekiel which probably also underwent, at least partially, Deuteronomistic editing. The returned elite from Babylon considered itself as the 'real Israel', which therefore excluded the entire non-exiled population. One might even imagine that some of those arrived in Jerusalem were recruited among other ethnic groups in Babylon;[9] it is clear that the theme of the exile became an ideological criterion to define those who belonged to the 'true Israel'. This topic is clearly reflected in some texts inside the Deuteronomistic History, which construct a sharp division between the insiders and the outsiders.[10] There were certainly members of the Deuteronomistic group amongst the elite that the Persians ordered back to Jerusalem for the purpose of administrative business. They brought with them the exilic edition of the Deuteronomistic History and revised it to make it fit the new challenges of the Persian period.

2. The Main Themes of the Persian Edition of the Deuteronomistic History

Select Bibliography

Albertz, R. and B. Becking (eds), *Yaswism after Exile: Perspectives on Israelite Religion in the Persian Era* (Studies in Theologie und Religion 5, Assen: Royal Van Gorcum, 2003).

Linville, J.R., *Israel in the Book of the Kings: The Past as a Project of Social Identity* (JSOTSup 272; Sheffield: Sheffield Academic Press, 1998).

MacDonald, N., *Deuteronomy and the Meaning of 'Monotheism'* (FAT II/1; Tübingen: Mohr Siebeck, 2003).

Mullen Jr, E.T., *Narrative History and Ethnic Boundaries: The Deuteronomistic Historian and the Creation of Israelite National Identity* (Semeia Studies; Atlanta: Scholars Press, 1993).

9.   See for this idea Davies, P.R., *In Search of 'Ancient Israel'* (JSOTSup 148; Sheffield: JSOT Press, 1992), pp. 75–93.

10.   Stulman, L., 'Encroachment in Deuteronomy: An Analysis of the Social World of the D Code', *JBL* 109 (1990), pp. 613–32.

The audience of this revised edition were the members of the insider group who could easily identify themselves with a 'conquest generation' as depicted in the books of Deuteronomy and Joshua and whose identity had to be constructed in opposition to the 'people of the land'.[11] Linked to this concern is the reinforcement of the Golah perspective. The Persian revision of the Deuteronomistic History also introduces texts revealing a clear monotheistic ideology.

2.1. Segregational Revision in Deuteronomy to Judges

The analysis of the threefold edition of the centralization law in Deut. 12 (see above III/.3) led to the conclusion that Deut. 12.2–7 represents the latest layer. The ideology of separation from the autochthonous people reflects the struggle between the Golah community and those who had remained in the land. The same topic appears in Deut. 7 and 9.1–6; both texts were probably added in the Persian period. Deut. 7 links the idea of Israel's 'election' to the necessity of separation from the 'other nations'. The structure of the chapter shows how the insider-group feels threatened by the others: vv. 1–5 and 15–26 which deal with the other nations surround vv. 6–14 which insist on the election of Yahweh's people. This election implies separation from the people living inside the land that the addressees are about to occupy (7.1); separation itself is described in a very aggressive way. They as well as their cultic symbols must be destroyed; no intermarriage is allowed (7.2–5). The ideological, non-realistic character of these verses appears immediately: why should one insist on the prohibition of intermarriage if all these people are to be utterly exterminated? Thus it is quite clear that the main concern of this text resides in the refusal of marriage between members of the Golah community and the 'people of land'. The closest parallel to Deut. 7.1–5 is to be found in Ezra 9 (cf. especially Deut. 7.3 and Ezra 9.12; the list of the 'nations in the land' in Deut. 7.1 comes very close to the list in Ezra 9.1). The end of Deut. 7 (especially vv. 21–26) alludes to the conquest stories in the book of Joshua, which are now primarily understood as stories of segregation. The insistence on the destruction of religious symbols confirms that the

---

11. The expression *ʿam hāʾāreṣ* which until the sixth century primarily means the rural aristocracy changes its signification into a depreciative meaning which has subsisted in modern Hebrew.

'Deuteronomistic reform' was not widely accepted, either by the rural populations in Yehud or by the Egyptian Diaspora, which during the Persian period continued to worship Yahweh along with other deities.[12] Deut. 9.1–6 betrays an ideology similar to ch. 7 and may well stem from the same redactor. This passage introduces the idea of the 'wickedness' of the nations to be conquered; such an idea does not appear in the exilic edition of the conquest stories.[13]

The idea of separation underlies also the regulations about edible animals in Deut. 14*. The list in vv. 2–21 (which was probably supplemented in vv. 12–18) has a parallel in Lev. 11 and reflects Priestly concerns. This is perhaps an indication that the Persian revision of the Deuteronomistic History paid already some attention to Priestly interest, preparing in a way the compromise that gave birth to the Torah.

Deut 23.1–9* also reflects the ideology of segregation. The exclusion of the Moabites and Ammonites is directly related to Ammonite (Neh. 13.4–9: Tobiah) and Moabite (Neh. 13.28: Sanballat) opposition to Nehemiah's rebuilding activities.[14] The friendly attitude to the Edomites certainly reflects the fact that during the first part of the Persian period Jewish villages may have coexisted with Edomite ones in the Negev around Hebron.[15] Quite a similar ideology is expressed in 25.17–19,

---

12. The Elephantine papyri attest the veneration of Yaho together with two other deities. According to Jer. 44 the cult of the 'Queen of Heaven' was also very popular during the Persian period. Ezek. 8 can also be understood as polemical against the continuation of ongoing polytheism during the sixth and fifth centuries BCE.

13. The following story in 9.7–10.11 which is another version of the molten-calf episode (Exod. 32–34) is difficult to locate. The insistence on the disobedience of the people fits quite well with the exilic edition. But it is astonishing that the emphasis is put on the fact that already at Horeb the people provoked Yahweh to wrath (9.8). The golden-calf episode also clashes somewhat with the foregoing recapitulation of the wilderness period in Deut. 8 where a positive relation between Yahweh and Israel in the wilderness is stressed (Yahweh tested Israel, but nothing is said about rebellion). One could therefore understand Deut. 9.7–10.11* (9.22–24; 9.27a; 10.6–11 are later interpolations) as an attempt to correct Deut. 8. The fact that the episode is not integrated in the historical recapitulation of Deut. 1–3 is another argument for a later interpolation. The redactor who integrated the story possibly wanted to establish a link with the Moses story preserved in parts of Exodus.

14. Neh. 13.1–3 even quotes Deut. 23.2–7; this text is generally explained as a very late interpolation.

15. Stern, E., *Archaeology of the Land of the Bible. II. The Assyrian, Babylonian, Persian Periods 732–332* BCE (ABRL; New York: Doubleday, 2001), pp. 444–45.

where the addressees are exhorted to destroy 'Amalek'[16]. The name of Amalek is not attested in extra-biblical contemporaneous sources; according to the Bible Amalek is linked to the descendants of Esau and appears as Israel's enemy in the book of Judges as well as in the Saul stories. In the Persian edition Deut. 25.17–19 can be understood as a midrash of a sort of Exod. 17, sharpening the negative image of the 'Arabs' and preparing for the later utilization of the term as an expression for all adversaries of the true Israel.

In the book of Joshua the segregationist reworking is particularly evident in the additions which were made to Joshua's original farewell speech in 23.4–8, 10, 12, 16b (especially vv. 7 and 12: no shared worship and no marriages with the nations). The same redactor has also expanded the exilic introduction to the time of the Judges by adding Judg. 2.13, 17, 20–23; 3.1–6[17] (v. 6 states that the warnings of Josh. 23.7 and 12 had been pronounced in vain).

The segregationist reworking of the Deuteronomistic History is, some few passages excepted, much less perceptible in the following chapters and books.[18] This means that these redactors were mostly interested in introducing this theme into the law book and the conquest story, which they considered as programmatic for the minority group of the Golah community.

2.2. From Monolatry to Monotheism

One may describe with Juha Pakkala the Deuteronomistic ideology during the Assyrian and Neo-Babylonian domination as 'intolerant

---

16.   It is also possible that this text already belongs to the exilic tradition and prepared for 1 Sam. 15; see above pp. 132 and 146.

17.   One may even distinguish two different redactional layers in these verses. According to 3.2 the other nations remain in the land to allow Yahweh to teach Israel the art of warfare, whereas following 2.22 and 3.4 their presence is a test for Israel.

18.   A notable exception is the reworking of the appraisal of Solomon in 1 Kgs 11.1*, 2, 3b, 6–8 (see above V/.3.5.1). 2 Kgs 21* may perhaps also reflect a negative attitude to foreign women. The two appendices in 2 Kgs 17.24–33 and 34–41 also reflect positions which come close to the ideology of the books of Ezra–Nehemiah on one hand and Chronicles on the other. But it is difficult to decide if these chapters, which are written in a quite different Hebrew, were inserted by the Deuteronomists or later redactors (see Macchi, J.-D., 'Les controverses théologiques dans le judaïsme de l'époque postexilique: l'exemple de 2 Rois 17, 24–41', *Transeuphratène* 5 [1992], pp. 85–93).

Monolatry':[19] Yahweh is the only god whom Israel should worship, but the existence of other deities is not contested at all; on the contrary: the book of Deuteronomy is full of exhortation not to 'follow the other gods', which probably alludes to processions of cultic statues. At the beginning of the Persian period there was apparently a switch among the elite to a more radical monotheism as is especially shown in the polemic against cultic statues and the deities of the nations in the so-called Second Isaiah (Isa. 40–55). Some late texts in the Deuteronomistic History reflect this change from monolatry to monotheism. This is especially the case for Deut. 4, which is commonly considered as belonging to the latest additions to the book of Deuteronomy.[20] This chapter provides, after an introduction (vv. 1–9), a new interpretation of the events at Horeb presented in ch. 5 (vv. 10–24). The author of Deut. 4 emphasizes the second commandment of the Decalogue, the interdiction of cult statues, and puts forth the idea that no form of Yhwh was seen at Horeb (this might reflect a polemic against a statue of Yahweh that probably stood in the Jerusalem temple during the monarchy). He amplifies the interdiction of the representation of Yahweh into a general denial of any cultic representation. Verses 21–31 allude to the coming exile, the worship of idols and the possibility of return (these verses are close to Deut. 30, also a Persian-time addition), which has become reality at the time this passage was written. The chapter concludes with a poem (vv. 32–40), which insists on the fact that Yahweh who brought Israel out of Egypt is also the creator of all mankind. The idea of Yahweh as a creator god does not appear in the Assyrian and exilic layers of the Deuteronomistic History. Rather, this idea is clearly related to the switch to monotheistic ideology. But if Yahweh is not only Israel's tutelary deity but also the only 'real god' of the universe (see the refrain in vv. 35 and 39), how does one explain his special relationship to Israel? The answer is given by the idea of election: Yahweh has

---

19.   Pakkala, J., *Intolerant Monolatry in the Deuteronomistic History* (Publications of the Finnish Exegetical Society 76; Helsinki and Göttingen: Finnish Exegetical Society: Vandenhoeck & Ruprecht, 1999).

20.   Most commentators consider vv. 16b–18 as an interpolation, since they allude to the Priestly creation story of Gen. 1. If one locates Deut. 4 in the first half of the Persian period, which is also the time when the Priestly document was written, there is no need however to extract these verses. The priests and the Deuteronomists certainly shared offices in or next to the temple.

chosen Israel as his special people. In the late monotheistic texts of Deuteronomy, creation is often linked to election (v. 37);[21] this is the case in Deut. 10.14–22, which has also been written during the Persian era.[22] Deut. 10.16, as well as 30.6, emphasizes the idea of a 'circumcision of the heart'; this might be understood as polemical against the Priestly attempt to transform the ritual of circumcision into a distinctive sign of rising Judaism.[23] Deut 30.1–14 addresses the returned elite from Babylon, underlining their distinctiveness from other people because of their 'direct access' to the divine word and will.

A clear monotheistic perspective further appears in Deut. 26.12–15: v. 15 underlines that Yahweh does not dwell in the temple, but in heaven, his 'holy habitation'.

Most of the Deuteronomistic texts that reveal a clear monotheistic conception are limited to the book of Deuteronomy. Does this mean that this 'monotheistic redaction' restricted its activity to this book?

In the following books one may mention the renaming of the ark in Josh. 3–4, which becomes in 3.11–12 'the ark of the treaty of (Yahweh), the lord of all the earth' (see for the same title Zech. 4.14; 6.5 and Isa. 54.5). A monotheistic ideology, comparable to the one found in Second Isaiah, may also underlie the so-called ark narrative in 1 Sam. 4–6.[24] Finally, the idea that Yahweh's power is not limited to Israel and Judah also appears in the latest additions to Solomon's temple inauguration, which emphasize the worship of Yahweh by strangers coming from far away (1 Kgs 8.41–45) as well as the assertion that Yahweh is the only God and that he should be venerated by all the people of the earth (8.56–61, especially v. 60). Since the monotheistic redaction appears much clearer in the book of Deuteronomy than in the following books, one may ask why this redaction focused on Moses' speech. Was there already an intention to separate Deuteronomy from the following books in order to link it with the Priestly texts? In any case the monotheistic ideology was no

21.   This was demonstrated by Rendtorff, R., 'Die Erwählung Israels als Thema der deuteronomischen Theologie', in J. Jeremias and L. Perlitt (eds), *Die Botschaft und die Boten: Festschrift für Hans Walter Wolff zum 70. Geburtstag* (Neukirchen–Vluyn: Neukirchener Verlag, 1981), pp. 75–86.

22.   Like Deut. 4.16b–18, 10.22 also presupposes the Priestly history (Gen. 46.27; Exod. 1.5).

23.   I owe this suggestion to Diana Edelman. Gen. 17 suggests a transfer of this *rite de passage* from puberty to new-born children.

24.   See for more details above V/.3.3.3.

problem for the Deuteronomists of the Persian period. In a way it was even a possibility to reflect the Persian worldview according to which all nations of the world had become or were about to become parts of the universal empire. Monotheistic ideology was a way to take into account this universalistic ideology.

2.3. Golah and Diaspora

During the first part of the Persian period, the economic and religious power in Yehud was concentrated in the hands of the Priestly and scribal elite whose members descended from the former Babylonian Golah. Since not all of the Babylonian Jewish elite was eager to return to Yehud, the Deuteronomists had to deal with a double bind of a sort. On the one hand they emphasize the fact that all the members of the 'true Israel' should live in the land that Yahweh has already promised to the forefathers in Egypt and given to his people by the conquest of Joshua. The return from exile is therefore understood as a 'new conquest'; on the other hand there is the reality that members of the same 'true Israel' prefer to stay in Babylon. The Golah redaction of the Deuteronomistic History tries to handle this dilemma, which still exists in contemporaneous Judaism, in legitimating, together with the ideology of return into the land, the possibility to live outside the land (the province of Yehud). This is effectuated in several ways. One strategy is to include in texts dealing with the conquest a description of the borders of the promised land which extends as far as the Euphrates, but interestingly not as far as the Egyptian delta: Deut. 1.7b; 11.22–25;[25] Josh. 1.3–4.[26] This description apparently wants to present the region where the Babylonian Jews were living as a part of 'Israel's land' and to declare the whole Persian province of Transeuphratene as a land where Jews could live. A quite similar topic appears in Deut.

---

25.   The major part of Deut. 11 belongs to a late stage of editing. This chapter is like a patchwork combining themes from other chapters of Deuteronomy (compare 11.10–17 and Deut. 8; 11.18–21 and Deut. 6.4–10; 11.26–30 and Deut. 27–28). The beginning of the chapter (vv. 2–9), which presupposes the account of Num. 16, could hardly have been composed before the Persian period.

26.   One may easily recognize these verses as an interpolation since they interrupt the speech addressed to Joshua in the singular (vv. 2 and 5) by a plural address.

12.20–28: the idea of a widening of the territory also reflects a Diaspora situation, which does not allow for frequent travels to the central sanctuary (see above III/.3). The integration of Jews dwelling outside Yehud is also operated by the addition of Josh. 22.9–34*. The first version of this addition accepts the fact that 'Israelites' live elsewhere than in Judah, but strengthens the idea that there cannot be a sacrificial cult outside Jerusalem. The altar that the Transjordanian tribes have built is therefore transformed into a monument that witnesses Yahweh's deeds for his people (22.28). Even if the idea of sacrificial centralization remained an ideological and economic concern for the Deuteronomists of the Persian time, this idea was not accepted everywhere. This is obvious for the Jewish Diaspora of Elephantine, an island in the centre of the Nile, near Aswan. In Elephantine, at the beginning of the Persian period, there was a temple of Yahweh (Yaho) who was venerated as the supreme god of a triad, and there may also have been another temple in the region occupied by the Edomites.[27] The Jerusalemite establishment was not very happy with those temples; therefore it seems that the Deuteronomists elaborated a compromise of a sort, preparing the way for the first synagogues. There is no clear evidence for the origins of the first synagogues, but it seems quite likely that they came into existence because of the Diaspora situation of the Persian time. The addition in Deut. 6.6–9 makes sense in this context.[28] The passage ends with the exhortation to inscribe the words of the Law on the doorposts of every house. This means that every house can become a temple of a sort since divine instructions are normally written on the walls of sanctuaries. The same ideology can be detected in the rewriting of the account of Josiah's reform during the Persian period. As we have seen (above in III/.2), the last reworking of this account (especially 2 Kgs 22.8, 10–13*; 23.2, 16–19; the latter verses were inserted together with 1 Kgs 13), which included the motive of the book-finding, insists on the fact that the whole temple was cleansed

---

27.   Bolin, T.M., 'The temple of *yhw* in Elephantine and Persian Religious Policy', in D.V. Edelman (ed.), *The Triumph of Elohim: >From Yahwisms to Judaisms* (Grand Rapids, MI: Eerdmans, 1996), pp. 127–42; Lemaire, A., 'Nouveau temple de Yahou (IVe s. av. J.-C.)', in M. Augustin and H.M. Niemann (eds), '*Basel und Bibel*': *Collected Communications to the XVIIth Congress of the International Organization for the Study of the Old Testament, Basel 2001* (BATAJ 51; Frankfurt am Main: Peter Lang, 2004), pp. 265–73.

28.   A literal understanding of this passage has given rise to phylacteries and mezuzoth.

from all cultic symbols and became above all a place where the Law book was read to the people. The replacement of the sacrificial cult by the reading of the Torah in 2 Kgs 22–23 (besides the reading of the book, Josiah only celebrates the festival of Passover) can be understood as a strategy to emphasize the importance of the written scroll. In doing so, the Deuteronomists prepared the transformation of Judaism into a 'religion of the book'.

The Persian redactors of the Deuteronomistic History also added a new ending to the story, which clearly indicates the acceptance of a Diaspora situation. 2 Kgs 25.27–30 tells of a rehabilitation of the exiled king Jehoiachin who becomes a privileged host of the Babylonian king 'all the days of his life'. This short text shares literary conventions with the so-called 'Diaspora novels': the stories of Esther and Mordecai, Joseph (Gen. 37–45), and the narratives in the first part of the book of Daniel (Dan. 2–6). In all cases an exiled person leaves prison and becomes in a way second to the king (2 Kgs 25.28; Est. 10.3; Gen. 41.40; Dan. 2.48) and the accession to this new status is symbolized by changing clothes (2 Kgs 25.29; Est. 6.10–11; 8.15; Gen. 41.42; Dan. 5.29). All these stories insist on the fact that the land of deportation has become a land where Jews can live and even manage interesting careers. Exile is transformed into Diaspora. This was necessary because of the very strong ideological and economic links between the Babylonian Golah and the Deuteronomists who had returned to Jerusalem. The last edition of the Deuteronomistic History was therefore acceptable for the (Babylonian) Diaspora,[29] as well as for the elite gathered around the rebuilt temple of Jerusalem.

Summing up, we may say that the editors of the Deuteronomistic History during the first part of the Persian period were driven by three major preoccupations: segregation, monotheism and integration of Golah concerns. Of course, there certainly were further additions which are not concerned with these topics, for instance the enlargement of the so-called 'Succession Narrative' in 2 Sam. 11–12; 15–17*; 19*, where the Davidic line appears in quite a negative way. These additions aimed perhaps to counter messianic expectations linked to the arrival of Zerubbabel. The reinforcement of Manasseh's negative portrait in

---

29. The Egyptian Diaspora was apparently much less 'Deuteronomistic' than the Babylonian one. If the Joseph story was originally composed in the Egyptian Diaspora, as it would now be argued by several scholars, it shows that the Jews living in Egypt had a much more open position.

2 Kgs 21.4, 10–15 and 24.4 may reflect similar concerns, by showing that the Davidic dynasty could also produce an archetype of an evil king, so that one should not hope for the reintroduction of a Judean monarchy. At that time, the Deuteronomists had made their arrangements with the Persian authority, which probably conceded some autonomy to the Priestly and scribal elites. Interestingly, there is no direct allusion to the Persian period in the whole Deuteronomistic History, in contrast to the book of Chronicles that ends with the edict of the Persian king Cyrus, allowing the deportees to return to their homeland. Since the Deuteronomists agreed to the existence of a Diaspora, they could hardly include in their history the fact that there was (theoretically) no more need to stay in Babylonia. In addition, the omission of any reference to Persian domination was probably motivated by the fear of displeasing the imperial administration.

The books (scrolls) of Joshua, Judges, Samuel and Kings continued to be edited after the work of the Deuteronomistic school in the Persian period. But at this time, they were no longer part of a 'Deuteronomistic History'; this literary work had ceased to exist with the constitution of the Torah, and the inclusion of Deuteronomy with the books of Genesis to Numbers.

3. The Death of the Deuteronomistic History and the Birth of the Torah

Select Bibliography

Albertz, R., *A History of Israelite Religion in the Old Testament Period*. II. *From the Exile to the Maccabees* (trans. J. Bowden; London: SCM Press, 1992).

Otto, E., 'The Pentateuch in Synchronical and Diachronical Perspectives: Protorabbinical Scribal Erudition Mediating Between Deuteronomy and the Priestly Code', in E. Otto and R. Achenbach (eds), *Das Deuteronomium zwischen Pentateuch und Deuteronomistischem Geschichtswerk* (FRLANT 206; Göttingen: Vandenhoeck & Ruprecht, 2004), pp. 14–35.

Römer, T.C., and M.Z. Brettler, 'Deuteronomy 34 and the Case for a Persian Hexateuch', *JBL* 119 (2000), pp. 401–19.

Watts, J.W. (ed.), *Persia and Torah: The Theory of the Imperial Authorization of the Pentateuch* (SBL Symposium Series 17; Atlanta, GA: Society of Biblical Literature, 2001).

At the end of the first half of the Persian period, around 400 BCE, started the edition of the Torah, which was to become the ideological basis for the rising Judaism. The books of Ezra and Nehemiah relate the arrival of Ezra, sent by the Persian king from Babylon to Jerusalem. His mission is linked to the public reading of a 'Law', which is then accepted by the people. This Law-book has often been identified with a Proto-Pentateuch of a sort and this might well be the case. Whether the tradition of Ezra as the promulgator of the Law has any historical basis or not, it is quite likely that the gathering of different law codes and narratives into one 'book' with five parts, the Pentateuch, goes back indeed to the time of Ezra's mission in Jerusalem. Interestingly, Ezra is presented in Ezra 7.1–6 simultaneously as a priest and a scribe; in this way, he symbolizes the fact that the publication of the Pentateuch resulted mainly from a compromise between the Priestly school and the Deuteronomistic school. Some have even assumed that the edition of the Torah would have been compelled by the Persian local adminis-tration, which would have been willing to recognize it as official Law for the province of Yehud. But this theory of the so-called 'imperial authorization' is difficult to maintain, since the parallels which are generally invoked for this theory cannot be compared with the Pentateuch; in particular, they always concern one specific cultic problem and are considerably shorter than the Torah. The latter's publication should therefore be explained by internal reasons. There was certainly a need for the Priestly and scribal elite to produce one document, which could give a common identity to the rising Judaism. This document was intended to be acceptable for the Priestly and Deuteronomistic elite, for the Jews in the land and for those of the Diaspora as well. The priestly school produced during the Babylonian and early Persian period a document which started with the creation of the world (Gen. 1) and ended with the installation of the sacrificial cult (Lev. 9). This document was then enlarged by adding the ritual, purity and other laws in the book of Leviticus. The Deuteronomists had produced their history (Deuteronomy to Kings), and both works had to be combined. There was probably soon an agreement that this new document should be restricted to the pre-monarchic origins, since monarchy was not an option for the Jewish elites under Persian domination. But there was obviously a debate about whether the 'Torah' should comprise the books of Genesis to Joshua (a Hexateuch), or if the document should be a Pentateuch and end with the book of Deuteronomy. Apparently a Deuteronomistic–Priestly minority coalesced to promote the publication of a Hexateuch. This group composed Josh. 24, which interrupts the Deuteronomistic sequence of Josh. 23 followed by Judg. 2.6–19*. Josh. 24 parallels in a way the foregoing chapter since it contains a new speech of Joshua; but this speech contains a recapitulation of the people's history, which starts, contrary to the Deuteronomistic summaries (Deut. 26.5–9), with the Patriarchs (or even before) and ends with the conquest of the land. Josh. 24 looks like a Hexateuch *en miniature*; its aim is to cut the book of Joshua from the following books and to connect it instead closely with the foregoing ones. At the end of this chapter Joshua is depicted like a second Moses: like Moses, Joshua concludes a covenant; like Moses he enacts laws and decrees (24.25); and like Moses he is concerned with a book. Josh. 24.26 states: 'and Joshua wrote all the words in the Book of the Law of God.' The expression *seper tôrat hā'elōhîm* has only one parallel in the Hebrew Bible, Neh. 8.18: 'day after day ... Ezra read from the book of the Law of God'.[30] It is possible that this expression was coined as the title for the Hexateuch, in contrast to 'the torah of Moses' (and its variants), which refers to the shorter Pentateuch, understood to be given through the mediation of Moses. The existence of a Deuteronomistic–Priestly Hexateuch coalition also explains why the Deuteromistic book of Josh incorporates a number of 'Priestly' texts.[31] In addition, several texts, such as Josh. 3–4 and Josh. 6, are so blended with Deuteronomistic and Priestly elements that no scholar has convincingly succeeded in making out the different strata composing these chapters. Although Priestly influence is later seen in 1 Kgs 8.1–11 (Masoretic text) and 62–66, in no other place in the Former Prophets after Joshua is there so much Priestly material. For the advocates of the Hexateuch, the land appears as the central topic of Jewish identity. This was certainly considered as somewhat dangerous by the Priestly and Deuteronomistic majority, especially because of the violent conquest account, which in a Persian context was certainly not the best way to express goodwill towards the Achemenide authorities. Therefore the Torah ended outside the land with the death of Moses (Deut. 34). The

---

30.   Neh. 8.16–18 clearly presupposes a combination of Priestly (cf. v. 18 and Lev. 23.36) and Deuteronomistic legal texts (cf. the 'joy' of v. 17 in reference to Deut. 16.14). Interestingly, v. 17 says that such a commemoration had not been celebrated *since the time of Joshua*.

31.   Most of the list material in Josh. 13–19 is often considererd as 'Priestly'. In the narrative sections, Josh. 5 is also sometimes considered 'Priestly'.

centre of the Torah, the Pentateuch, was not the land but Moses' law given for a life in the land but also outside the land. Therefore this Torah was a 'portable fatherland' as the poet Heinrich Heine put it. The separation of Deuteronomy from the following books was underlined by the conclusion, which the redactors of the Pentateuch inserted at the end of Deut. 34: 'never since has there arisen a prophet in Israel like Moses, whom Yahweh knew face to face. He was unequalled for all the signs and wonders that Yahweh sent him to perform in the land of Egypt ... in the sight of all Israel' (vv. 10–12). These verses modify the Deuteronomistic conception of Moses as the first of an ongoing series of prophets (18.15–20), in arguing that no one compares to Moses. Moses himself becomes the only mediator for the Torah, understood as the main, if not the exclusive mediation of God's will. The same redactors also inserted the land promise to the Patriarchs in Deut. 34.4 underlining the fact that Deuteronomy is no more the introduction to a Deuteronomistic History but the end of the Torah (all the identifications of the 'fathers' in Deuteronomy with Abraham, Isaac and Jacob are due to the editors of the Pentateuch). When Deuteronomy was cut off from the following books, new chapters were added: the blessings of Moses in Deut. 33, which parallel him with Jacob (Gen. 49) and reinforce the structural and narrative coherence of the Pentateuch. Deut. 11.26–31 and Deut. 27 were probably added in order to facilitate the acceptance of the Torah by the religious elite of the province of Samaria (Josh. 24 is located at Shechem because of a similar intention).[32] The Torah never mentions the place where Yahweh will have his name dwell: for the Judeans this place was of course Jerusalem (see the allusion in Gen. 14 and 22); however, Deut. 27 offered an alternative interpretation for the Samarians. The editors of the Pentateuch inserted perhaps also Deut. 32, the 'song of Moses'. Since the Pentateuch ended with Moses' death, Deut. 32 offers a summary of the coming negative events in the land even if these are not part of the

---

32.   One could also imagine that these texts were added by the 'Hexateuch redactors', since one finds a similar text in Josh. 8.30–36. But since this passage stands at another place in the Greek translation it might be a very late insertion. See on all these texts Na'aman, N., 'The Law of the Altar in Deuteronomy and the Cultic Site near Shechem', in S.L. McKenzie and T. Römer (eds), *Rethinking the Foundations: Historiography in the Ancient World and in the Bible. Essays in Honour of John Van Seters* (BZAW 294; Berlin and New York: de Gruyter, 2000), pp. 141–61.

Torah. This transformation of the book of Deuteronomy was the end of the Deuteronomistic History. From now on Joshua, Judges, Samuel and Kings became what later will be called the 'Former Prophets'. There was still editing on these books but no more in a Deuteronomistic Perspective. In Joshua the Rahab story in ch. 2 (together with 6.17b, 22–25*) was interpolated between the Deuteronomistic sequel Josh. 1 and Josh. 3 in order to correct somewhat the segregationist ideology of the conquest account.[33] The addition of Josh. 24 interrupted the Deuteronomistic transition between the time of the conquest and the period of the Judges. The book of Judges also received a new introduction in 1.1–2.5. Finally, the post-Deuteronomistic editors separated Samuel from the time of the Judges (the Deuteronomists had presented him as the last Judge), and they added the Greek-like stories of the sacrifice of Jephthah's daughter (in Judg. 11.29–40*) and of the Hebrew Hercules Samson (Judg. 13–16). It is difficult to decide if the Samson stories were integrated earlier, later or at the same time as chs 17–21 which provide a very negative conclusion to the book of Judges with stories about sex and crime. Interestingly, the most scandalous story is located in a Benjaminite town, Gibeah (Judg. 19), and the first negative king of Israel, Saul, is also from the tribe of Benjamin. The stories in Judg. 17–21 contain the following refrain, 'In those days there was no king in Israel; everyone did what was right in his eyes', which appears also at the very end of the book. This refrain prepares of course the narratives about the rise of the Israelite monarchy in the books of Samuel. The post-Deuteronomistic editors also reorganized the Deuteronomistic presentation of kingship by interrupting the sequence in 2 Sam 20*; 1 Kgs 1 through the addition of 2 Sam. 21–24. David's psalm in 2 Sam. 22 refers back to Hannah's psalm in 1 Sam. 2,[34] which was interpolated by the same hands in order to frame the newly created book of Samuel by poetic texts. As to the books of Kings, one may argue that most of the prophetic stories about Elijah and Elisha were integrated in the books only after the Deuteronomistic History split off. The redactors who inserted them probably wanted to make the books

---

33.   Maybe the same holds true for the story of the integration of the Gibeonites in Josh 9.

34.   The late interpolation of these texts has been demonstrated by Mathys, H.-P., *Dichter und Beter: Theologen aus spätalttestamentlicher Zeit* (OBO 132; Freiburg (Switzerland): Göttingen: Universitätsverlag und Vandenhoeck & Ruprecht, 1994).

of Kings more 'prophetic', so that they fitted better with the new collection in which the scrolls of Joshua, Judges, Samuel and Kings were now arranged: the Prophets. The Deuteronomistic school disappeared together with the Deuteronomistic History, but numerous Deuteronomistic ideas, recycled, entered into the rabbinic milieu and also into the New Testament.

Index of Passages Cited

185

ANCIENT NEAR EAST

GREEK WRITINGS

RABBINIC LITERATURE

INDEX OF AUTHORS